Learn, Teach...

Succeed...

With **REA's TExES Mathematics (115) 4–8**
test prep, you'll be in a class all your own.

WE'D LIKE TO HEAR FROM YOU!
Visit **www.rea.com** to send us your comments

TExES™ 115 MATHEMATICS GRADES 4-8

TEXAS EXAMINATIONS OF EDUCATOR STANDARDS™

TestWare® Edition

Trena Wilkerson, Ph.D.
Associate Professor
Baylor University
Waco, Texas

Research & Education Association

Research & Education Association
61 Ethel Road West
Piscataway, New Jersey 08854
E-mail: info@rea.com

TExES Mathematics (115) 4-8
With TestWare® on CD

Published 2015

Printed in the United States of America

Library of Congress Control Number 2010931555

ISBN-13: 978-0-7386-0645-3
ISBN-10: 0-7386-0645-6

For all references in this book, Teacher Education Agency (TEA™) and TExES™ are trademarks, in the U.S. and/
or other countries, of the Teacher Education Agency and Educational Testing Service (ETS), Inc., or its affiliates.

Windows® is a registered trademark of Microsoft Corporation. All other trademarks cited in this publication are
the property of their respective owners.

The Mathematics Test Objectives presented in this book were created and implemented by the State Board of
Teacher Education/Teacher Education Agency (TEA™) and Educational Testing Service (ETS). For further
information visit TEA website at www.tea.state.tx.us/.

Cover image: Jose Luis Pelaez Inc./Blend Images/Getty Images

About the Author

Trena L. Wilkerson, Ph.D. is an Associate Professor with a focus in mathematics education in the Department of Curriculum and Instruction at Baylor University in Waco, Texas. She currently works with both preservice and inservice mathematics teachers across grades PK-12. She was a secondary school mathematics teacher for 18 years and has worked in higher education for the past 17 years.

She received her undergraduate degree from Mississippi College in 1976 with a major in mathematics. Her master's work was completed in 1980 at Southeastern Louisiana University in Hammond, Louisiana, with an emphasis in mathematics education. In 1992 she received her Ph.D. from the University of Southern Mississippi in Hattiesburg, Mississippi, in Curriculum & Instruction with a focus in mathematics.

Her professional interests include mathematics education, teacher education, teacher efficacy, teaching and learning of mathematics, professional development, and assessment. She is interested in effective teaching of mathematics and its effects on student learning.

Acknowledgments

We would like to thank REA's Larry B. Kling, Vice President, Editorial, for supervising development; Pam Weston, Publisher, for setting the quality standards for production integrity and managing the publication to completion; John Paul Cording, Vice President, Technology, for coordinating the design and development of REA's TestWare®; Charlie Heinle, Senior Editor, for revisions and preflight editorial review; Alice Leonard, Senior Editor, for post-production quality assurance; Heena Patel, software project manager, for her software testing efforts; and Christine Saul, Senior Graphic Artist, for cover design.

We gratefully acknowledge Mel Friedman, Senior Math Editor, for ensuring the integrity of the mathematics in this publication.

We also gratefully acknowledge Transcend Creative Services for typesetting; Laura Hoffman and June Rohrbach for technical editing; Laura Meiselman for copyediting; and Stephanie Reymann for creating the index.

About Research & Education Association

Founded in 1959, Research & Education Association is dedicated to publishing the finest and most effective educational materials—including study guides and test preps—for students in middle school, high school, college, graduate school, and beyond.

Today, REA's wide-ranging catalog is a leading resource for teachers, students, and professionals. Visit *www.rea.com* to see a complete listing of all our titles.

Contents

TExES

Mathematics 4-8 Test (115)

Review

Introduction

About This Book and TestWare®

REA's *TExES Mathematics 4–8 (115)* test prep is a comprehensive guide designed to assist you in preparing to take this TExES test, the purpose of which is to ensure that you have the prerequisite content and professional knowledge necessary for an entry-level position in Texas public schools. To help you to succeed in this important step toward your teaching career, this book features:

- An accurate and complete overview of the competencies for the test

- The information you need to know about how the exam works

- A targeted review of each section of the exam

- Tips and strategies for successfully completing standardized tests

- Diagnostic tools to identify areas of strength and weakness

- Two full-length practice tests that replicate the question format and level of difficulty. The practice tests are provided in two formats: in printed form in this book and on the enclosed TestWare® CD-ROM.

- Detailed explanations for each answer on the practice tests. Designed specifically to clarify the material, the explanations not only provide the correct answers, but also explain why the other answer choices are incorrect.

When creating this test prep, the authors and editors considered the most recent test administrations and professional standards. They also researched information from the

Texas Education Agency, professional journals, textbooks, and educators. The result is the best TExES test preparation materials based on the latest information available.

We strongly recommend that you begin you preparation with the TestWare® tests, which provide timed conditions and instantaneous, accurate scoring. To get the most out of your studying time, follow the Study Schedule that appears on page 9 of this book. It details how you can best budget your time.

About the TExES Mathematics 4–8 Test

The purpose of the TExES Mathematics 4–8 test is to assess the knowledge and skills of prospective Texas teachers in the areas of mathematics. The Mathematics 4-8 test will contain 80 scorable multiple-choice items and approximately 10 nonscorable items. Your final scaled score will be based only on scorable items. The nonscorable multiple-choice items are included for the purpose of pilot-testing of proposed new questions. These pilot questions do not count toward your score. However, they are not identified on the test either.

There will be four answer choices for each multiple-choice question. Answers will be marked on a separate answer sheet.

Examinees are provided with both a definitions/formula page and a scientific calculator.

What Does the Test Cover?

The following table lists the domains and competencies used as the basis for the TExES Mathematics 4-8 Test and the approximate percentage of questions in each domain. A thorough review of all the specific germane skills is the focus of this book.

Test Framework

Domain No	Domain Title	Approx. Percent of Test	Typical Number of Scorable Multiple-Choice Items
I.	**Number Concepts**	16%	13
II.	**Patterns and Algebra**	21%	17

Domain No	Domain Title	Approx. Percent of Test	Typical Number of Scorable Multiple-Choice Items
III.	Geometry and Measurement	21%	16
IV.	Probability and Statistics	16%	13
V.	Mathematical Processes and Perspectives	10%	8
IV.	Mathematical Learning, Instruction, and Assessment	16%	13

Who Administers the Test?

The Texas Education Agency has contracted with Educational Testing Service (ETS) to assist in the development and administration of the TExES.

For additional information you can contact:

ETS-Texas Educator Certification Program
PO Box 6051
Princeton, NJ 08541-6051
Telephone: 1-800-205-2626 (U.S., U.S. Territories, and Canada)
1-609-771-7393 (all other locations)
Hours: Monday-Friday 8:00 a.m.-5:00 p.m. Central time
Fax: 1-973-735-0156 or 1-866-484-5860
E-mail: texes-excet_inquiries@ets.org

Test Administration

The TExES tests are administered six times during the testing year. Each test date has morning and afternoon test sessions. Each session is five hours long.

Do I Pay a Registration Fee?

To take the TExES, you must pay a registration fee. For information about the fees, log on to http://www.texes.ets.org/texes/AboutTheTest/.

How Is the TExES Mathematics 4–8 Test Scored?

Test results are reported as scaled scores in a range from 100 to 300. Your total scaled score shows how you performed on the test as a whole and whether you passed the test. Your report will include Domain and Competency performance on each domain and each competency.

The scale score allows comparison among any version of the same test. The raw scores cannot be compared from one version of a test to another. You receive one point for each correct response and no points for each incorrect response. Most tests will also include nonscorable questions. Therefore the total number of questions reported on your score report is usually less than the total number of questions that you saw on the test. The nonscorable questions will not be used in the calculation of your score.

A total test scaled score that is reported on a scale of 100-300. The minimum passing score is a scaled score of 240. This score represents the minimum level of competency required to be an entry-level educator in this field in Texas public schools.

To gauge how well you do on the practice tests in this book and TestWare®, calculate your percentage right; a score of a 75% correct will assure that you will pass the TExES 115 exam.

When Will I Receive My Score Report, and What Will It Look Like?

Approximately four weeks after the test, you will receive a score report in the mail. The report will say if you have passed the test and will include your performance in the major content domains of the test and in the specific content competencies of the test. Be aware that this information may be less reliable because it may be based on fewer test questions.

Unofficial test scores will be posted on the Internet on the score report mailing date of each test administration. You can find information about receiving your unofficial scores, your score scale, and other score report topics on the SBEC Web site at www.sbec.state.tx.us.

Can I Retake the Test?

Retaking a Test. If you wish to retake the paper-based test, you may do so at any subsequent paper-based test administration. You must wait 60 days to retake the test online. Please consult the TExES website at http://texes.ets.org/texes/ for information about test registration. The TExES website also includes information regarding test retakes and score reports.

When Should I Start Studying?

It is never too early to start studying for the TExES Mathematics 4-8 test. The earlier you begin, the more time you will have to sharpen your skills. Do not procrastinate! Cramming is not an effective way to study because it does not allow you the time you need to think about the content, review the domains, and take the practice tests.

What Do the Review Sections Cover?

The targeted review in this book is designed to help you sharpen the mathematical skills you need to approach the TExES Mathematics 4-8 Test, as well as provide strategies for attacking the questions.

Each competency area included in the TExES Mathematics 4-8 test is examined in a separate chapter. The skills required for all domains are extensively discussed to optimize your understanding of what the examination covers.

Your schooling has taught you most of the information you need to answer the questions on the test. The review sections in this book are designed to help you fit the information you have acquired into the domains and competencies specified on the TExES. Going over your class notes and textbooks together with the reviews provided here will give you an excellent springboard for passing the examination.

Studying for the TExES Mathematics 4–8 Test

Choose the time and place for studying that works best for you. Some people set aside a certain number of hours every morning to study, while others prefer to study at night before going to sleep. Other people study off and on during the day for instance, while waiting for a bus or during a lunch break. Only you can determine when and where your study time will be most effective.

Be consistent and use your time efficiently. Work out a study routine and stick to it.

When you take the practice tests, simulate the conditions of the actual test as closely as possible. Turn off your television and radio, and sit down at a table in a quiet room, free from distraction. On completing a practice test, score it and thoroughly review the explanations to the questions you answered incorrectly; however, do not review too much at any one time. Concentrate on one problem area at a time by reviewing the question and explanation, and by studying the review in this guide until you are confident that you have mastered the material. Keep track of your scores so you can gauge your progress and discover general weaknesses in particular sections. Give extra attention to the reviews that cover your areas of difficulty, so you can build your skills in those areas. Many have found the use of study or note cards very helpful for this review.

But you can condense or expand the time-line to suit your personal schedule. It is vital that you adhere to a structured plan and set aside ample time each day to study. The more time you devote to studying, the more prepared and confident you will be on the day of the test. Don't wait until the last minute to begin your studying!

How Can I Use My Study Time Efficiently?

Test-Taking Tips

Although you may not be familiar with tests like the TExES, this book will acquaint you with this type of exam and help alleviate your test-taking anxieties. By following the seven suggestions listed here, you can become more relaxed about taking the TExES, as well as other tests.

Tip 1. Become comfortable with the format of the TExES. When you are practicing, stay calm and pace yourself. After simulating the test only once, you will boost your chances of doing well, and you will be able to sit down for the actual TExES with much more confidence.

Study Schedule

The following study schedule allows for thorough preparation to pass the TExES Mathematics 4-8 (115) exam. This is a suggested seven-week course of study. However, you can condense this schedule if you are in a time crunch or expand it if you have more time to study. You may decide to use your weekends for study and preparation and go about your business during the week. Or, you may decide to study two hours each night. However you decide to study, be sure to adhere to the structured schedule you devise.

Week 1	After reading this first chapter to understand the format and content of this exam, take the first practice test on CD-ROM. The scores will indicate your strengths and weaknesses. Make sure you simulate real exam conditions when you take the test. After your test is scored, review the explanations, especially for questions you answered incorrectly and begin to review the appropriate chapter sections.
Week 2	Continue your review of the explanations for the questions you missed, and review the appropriate chapter sections. Useful study techniques include highlighting key terms and information, taking notes as you review each section, and putting new terms and information on note cards to help retain the information.
Weeks 3 and 4	Reread all your note cards, refresh your understanding of the competencies and skills included in the exam, review your college textbooks, review the appropriate chapters in this book, and read over notes you took in your college classes. This is also the time to consider any other supplementary materials that your counselor or the TExES Department of Education suggests. Visit the department's Website at **www.texes.ets.org.**
Week 5	Begin to condense your notes and findings. A structured list of important skills and concepts, based on your note cards and the TExES 115 Mathematics 4-8 domains and competencies, will help you thoroughly review for the test. Again, review the answers and explanations for any questions you missed.
Week 6	Have someone quiz you using the note cards you created. Take the second practice test, adhering to the time limits and simulated test day conditions. Again review the explanations for any questions that you missed along with the related material in the book that is related to them.
Week 7	Using all your study materials, continue to review areas of weakness revealed by your score on the second practice test. If time allows, retake the practice tests printed in this book.

Tip 2. Read all the possible answers. Just because you think you have found the correct response, do not automatically assume that it is the best answer. Read through each choice to be sure that you are not making a mistake by jumping to conclusions.

Tip 3. Use the process of elimination. Go through each answer to a question and eliminate as many of the answer choices as possible. If you can eliminate two answer choices, you have given yourself a better chance of getting the item correct, because only two choices are left from which to make your guess. Do not leave an answer blank; it is better to guess than not to answer a question on the TExES test because you will not be penalized for incorrect answers.

Tip 4. Place a question mark in your answer booklet next to the answers you guessed, and then recheck them later if you have time.

Tip 5. Work quickly and steadily. You will have a total of five hours to complete the test. Taking the practice tests in this book will help you learn to budget your time.

Tip 6. Learn the directions and format of the test. This will not only save time but also will help you avoid anxiety (and the mistakes caused by being anxious).

Tip 7. When taking the multiple-choice portion of the test, be sure that the answer oval you fill in corresponds to the number of the question in the test booklet. The multiple-choice test is graded by machine, and marking one wrong answer can throw off your answer key and your score. Be extremely careful.

The Day of the Test

Before the Test

On the morning of the test, be sure to dress comfortably so you are not distracted by being too hot or too cold while taking the test. Plan to arrive at the test center early. This will allow you to collect your thoughts and relax before the test and will also spare you the anguish that comes with rushing. You should check your TExES Registration Bulletin to find out what time to arrive at the center.

What to Bring

Before you leave for the test center, make sure that you have your admission ticket. Your admission ticket lists your test selection, test site, test date, and reporting time. See the test selection at www.texes.ets.org/faq. You must also bring personal identification that includes one piece of current, government-issued identification, in the name in which you registered, bearing a recent photograph and signature and one additional piece of identification (with or without a photograph). If the name on your identification differs from the name in which you are registered, you must bring official verification of the change (e.g., marriage certificate, court order). Be sure to check the TExES website for any updates or changes in the identification policy.

You must bring several sharpened No. 2 pencils with erasers, because none will be provided at the test center. No mechanical pencils or mechanical erasers may be used. If you like, you can wear a watch to the test center. However, you cannot wear one that makes noise, because it might disturb the other test takers. Dictionaries, textbooks, notebooks, cell phones, beepers, PDAs, scratch paper, listening and recording devices, briefcases, or packages are not permitted. Drinking, smoking, and eating during the test are prohibited. Very especially, remember that cell phones are not allowed in the test center. Using or having a cell phone in your possession in the test center may be grounds for dismissal.

Security Measures

As part of the identity verification process, your thumbprint, or your photograph or videotape may be taken at the test site. A refusal to participate would lead to dismissal with no refund of test fees. This is in addition to the requirement that you must present acceptable and valid identification. It is important that you visit the testing website for the latest updates and security requirements and updates at http://texes.ets.org/texes/DayOfTheTest/.

Late Arrival Policy

You must report to the test site by the time stipulated. If you are late for a test session you will not be admitted.

During the Test

Any time that you take for restroom breaks is considered part of the available testing time, and additional testing time will not be granted. Procedures will be followed to maintain test security. Once you enter the test center, follow all the rules and instructions given by the test supervisor. If you do not, you risk being dismissed from the test and having your score canceled.

Once the test begins, mark only one answer per question, completely erase unwanted answers and marks, and fill in answers darkly and neatly.

After the Test

When you finish your test, hand in your materials and you will be dismissed. Then, go home and relax you deserve it!

2

Number Concepts

Real Numbers

Most of the numbers that are used in K-12 school mathematics are real numbers. While the real numbers are a subset of the complex number system, we will deal with the complex number system later in the chapter. Subsets of the real number system include integers, natural numbers, whole numbers, irrational numbers, and rational numbers (including fractions and decimal fractions). Figure 2.1 is a tree diagram that shows the relationship among the different types of the numbers that are subsets of the real numbers.

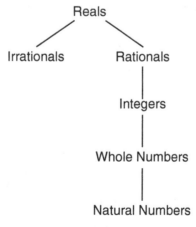

Figure 2.1

Real numbers are the union (symbolized as $\cup$) of rational and irrational numbers denoted typically as Q and S, respectively. That is $Q \cup S = R$. Formal definitions follow with examples:

Natural Numbers: $N = \{1, 2, 3, 4, 5, ...\}$
Whole Numbers: $W = \{0, 1, 2, 3, 4, 5, ...\}$
Integers: $I = \{...-5, -4, -3, -2, -1, 0, 1, 2, 3, 4, 5, ...\}$
Rational Numbers: $Q = \{\frac{a}{b}$ where $a, b \in I$ and $b \neq 0\}$.

Irrational Numbers: Denoted as S, are real numbers that cannot be written as a quotient of two integers.

With respect to the tree diagram in Figure 2.1, note that each category of numbers is a **proper subset** of any category above it. The symbol for proper subset is $\subset$. Set A is a proper subset of B if each element of A is also found in B. As examples, $N \subset I$ and $W \subset Q$.

Typically, children begin learning about natural numbers and whole numbers and then move to negative whole numbers which, then gives them access to working with integers. At some point they are introduced to fractions, which are rational numbers. Later they are introduced to irrational numbers, which provides them with the entire real number system.

The real numbers can be represented graphically on a real number line where 0 is positioned as a point on the number line and labeled as 0. Similarly, the other real numbers are positioned on the number line relative to zero with positives to the right and negatives to the left with values increasing from left to right. *Zero is neither positive nor negative.* There is a one-to-one correspondence between the numbers on a number line and the real number system. Figure 2.2 illustrates this relationship.

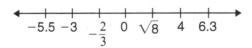

Figure 2.2

All rational numbers can be written as either terminating decimals (which means there is a remainder of 0 when a is divided by b) or repeating decimals (which means that there is a repeating pattern of integers when a is divided by b).

Here are several examples of rational numbers:

$$\frac{1}{2}, -\frac{2}{3}, -0.34, \sqrt{25}, -\sqrt[3]{8}, 11, \frac{17}{1}, 4.\overline{2}, \text{ and } \sqrt{\frac{4}{49}}.$$

A number that <u>cannot</u> be written as a simple fraction is irrational, that is, it cannot be written as a quotient of two integers and thus is a non-repeating, non-ending decimal when divided.

Here are examples of irrational numbers:

$$\sqrt{2}, -\sqrt{5}, \sqrt[3]{12}, \pi, e, \text{ and } 1.04004000400004\ldots.$$

Example 1   Identify each number as an integer, a non-integer rational number, or an irrational number.

$$18, -1.4, 0, 0.05, \sqrt{4}, -\sqrt{6}, \frac{5}{6}, \sqrt[4]{3}, e, 5.\overline{24}, \frac{14}{3}, -5, \frac{21}{7},$$

$$3.121121112111112111112\ldots\ldots, \text{ and } \sqrt[3]{\frac{1}{27}}$$

Solution: The integers are $18, 0, \sqrt{4}, -5,$ and $\frac{21}{7}$. $(\sqrt{4} = 2)$.

The non-integer rational numbers are $-1.4, 0.05, \frac{5}{6}, 5.\overline{24}, \frac{14}{3},$ and $\sqrt[3]{\frac{1}{27}}$. (Note that $\sqrt[3]{\frac{1}{27}} = \frac{1}{3}$).

The irrational numbers are $-\sqrt{6}, \sqrt[4]{3}, e,$ and $3.121121112111112111112\ldots\ldots.$

None of these numbers can be written as a quotient of two integers.

Also, the number e represents the infinite sum

$$1 + \frac{1}{1} + \frac{1}{1 \times 2} + \frac{1}{1 \times 2 \times 3} + \frac{1}{1 \times 2 \times 3 \times 4} + \ldots$$

Properties and Relationships of Numbers

It is important to understand the properties of numbers in the various numbers systems and to apply those properties to simplify expressions, make calculations, and solve problems.

Properties of real numbers provide guidance in operations on them. The operations of addition and multiplication are the foundational operations, but subtraction and division are also defined for real numbers. In fact, in most instances, it is possible to perform subtraction by using the following definition:

For real numbers a and b, $a - b = a + (-b)$. Similarly with division, for real numbers a and b where $b \neq 0$, there exists a number $\frac{1}{b}$, also written as b^{-1}, such that $a \div b = \frac{a}{b} = a \cdot b^{-1}$

Here is a listing of various properties of real numbers.

Reflexive: $a = a$

Symmetric: If $a = b$, then $b = a$

Transitive: If $a = b$ and $b = c$, then $a = c$

Closure: $a + b$ is a real number, and $a \times b$ is a real number.

Commutative Property of Addition: $a + b = b + a$

Commutative Property of Multiplication: $a \times b = b \times a$

Associative Property of Addition: $(a + b) + c = a + (b + c)$

Associative Property of Multiplication: $(a \times b) \times c = a \times (b \times c)$

Distributive Property of Multiplication over Addition: $(a) \times (b + c) = (a \times b) + (a \times c)$

Identity Element of Addition: There exists a number 0 such that $a + 0 = 0 + a = a$.

Identity Element of Multiplication: There exists a number 1 such that $a \cdot 1 = 1 \cdot a = a$.

Additive Inverse: There exists a number $-a$ such that $a + (-a) = 0$.

Multiplicative Inverse: There exists a number $a^{-1} = \frac{1}{a}$, such that $a \times a^{-1} = a \times \frac{1}{a} = 1$.

Order of Operations

Operations with real numbers have an accepted order used by the mathematical community. Many recall using the mnemonic "Please Excuse My Dear Aunt Sally" (PEMDAS) to remember the order of operations where P stands for parentheses, E for exponents, M for multiplication, D for division, A for addition, and S for subtraction. *While this is an accepted order, one must take care in applying it correctly and understanding numerical properties in relation to this order.* When parentheses are present, operations within the parentheses must be done first using the same order of operations related to exponents, multiplication, division, addition, and subtraction. Exponents are computed first. Then multiplication and division (whichever comes first) are completed from left to right, followed by addition and subtraction computations (whichever comes first) from left to right. While these general rules give our number system an order to operations, ultimately what is applied and essential is an understanding of the various number properties that will be discussed in a later section. These properties provide the underlying rationale and structure for operations.

Example 2   What is the value of $70 - 20 \div 4 + 1 - 18 + 2 \times 8$?

Solution: The first step is $20 \div 4 = 5$. Then, perform the operation $2 \times 8 = 16$. Thus, $70 - 5 + 1 - 18 + 16 = 64$.

Example 3   What is the value of $-(-3)^2 + 15 \div (3 - 8) + 2 \div 2^3$?

Solution: $(-3)^2 = (-3)(-3) = 9$, so $-(-3)^2 = -9$. Also, $3 - 8 = -5$, $2^3 = 8$, $15 \div (-5) = -3$, and $2 \div 8 = \frac{1}{4}$. Thus, $-9 + (-3) + \frac{1}{4} = -11\frac{3}{4}$.

Absolute Value

The **absolute value** of a number a, denoted as $|a|$, can be understood with respect to a real number line as the distance that a point lies from 0. Thus, $|4|$ is 4 because it is 4 units to the right of 0. Similarly, $|-4| = 4$, since it is 4 units to the left of 0. Note that $|4| = |-4| = 4$.

Formally defined, the absolute value of a real number a is defined as $|a| = a$ if $a \geq 0$ and $|a| = -a$ if $a < 0$. Related properties include the following, where a and b are real numbers.

(1) $|-a| = |a|$

(2) $|a| \geq 0$ with $|a| = 0$ if $a = 0$

(3) $|ab| = |a| \cdot |b|$

(4) $|a|^2 = a^2$

(5) $\left|\dfrac{a}{b}\right| = \dfrac{|a|}{|b|}, b \neq 0$

(6) $|a - b| = |b - a|$

Note that $|a + b|$ <u>need not</u> be equal to $|a| + |b|$. For example, if $a = 2$ and $b = -5$, $|a + b| = 3$, whereas $|a| + |b| = 7$.

Fractions

A **fraction** is expressed as $\dfrac{a}{b}$, where the numerator a and the denominator b are real numbers and $b \neq 0$ since division by zero is undefined. Improper fractions occur when the numerator is the same or greater than the denominator, such as $\dfrac{5}{4}$.

An improper fraction can be written as a mixed number such that it is the sum of a whole number and a fraction. Thus $\dfrac{5}{4} = \dfrac{4}{4} + \dfrac{1}{4} = 1 + \dfrac{1}{4} = 1\dfrac{1}{4}$.

Teachers need to work with students to ensure they have a deep conceptual understanding of fractions using a variety of types of models including both discrete and continuous models. There are many materials available to model fractions. Further, it is essential that this lead to an understanding of operations with fractions including addition, subtraction, multiplication, and division. Working with operations with fractions leads to the understanding and application of least common denominators (LCD), factoring, greatest common factors or GCF (also known as the greatest common divisor or GCD), and prime factorization.

Models for Fractions

Many teacher-made and commercial materials can be used to model fractions and their operations. These include, but are not limited to, pattern blocks, Tangrams (which consist of five triangles, one square, and one parallelogram), fraction circles, fraction squares, number lines, shaded regions of shapes, and color tiles (or other discrete objects). Space does not permit the exploration of every model, but one key thing to keep in mind is to always know what represents the whole, and a second thing is to give students multiple experiences in varying the model and in varying what piece is the whole.

For example, with pattern blocks, as shown in Figure 2.3.

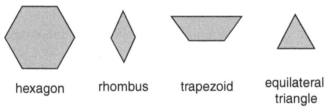

hexagon   rhombus   trapezoid   equilateral
                                                     triangle

Figure 2.3

If the hexagon is the whole, then the equilateral triangle is $\frac{1}{6}$, the trapezoid is $\frac{1}{2}$, and the rhombus is $\frac{1}{3}$. However, if the trapezoid is the whole, then the triangle becomes $\frac{1}{3}$, the rhombus becomes $\frac{2}{3}$, and the hexagon becomes 2.

Now suppose that two hexagons are put together to represent the whole, as shown in Figure 2.4.

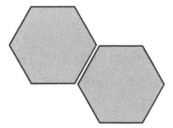

Figure 2.4

Then the trapezoid becomes $\left(\dfrac{1}{2}\right)\left(\dfrac{1}{2}\right)=\dfrac{1}{4}$, the triangle becomes $\left(\dfrac{1}{2}\right)\left(\dfrac{1}{6}\right)=\dfrac{1}{12}$, and the rhombus becomes $\left(\dfrac{1}{2}\right)\left(\dfrac{1}{3}\right)=\dfrac{1}{6}$. Following this idea, one can also represent addition and subtraction with fractions as well.

You may find it beneficial to explore other models to be sure you understand the representation in relation to fractions and their operations.

Operations with Fractions

To find the sum of two fractions that have a common denominator, simply add the numerators and use the common denominator. Follow a similar procedure for subtraction. Thus, for any real numbers a, b, and c, where $c \neq 0$, $\dfrac{a}{c} \pm \dfrac{b}{c} = \dfrac{a \pm b}{c}$. As an example, $\dfrac{5}{7}+\dfrac{6}{7}=\dfrac{5+6}{7}=\dfrac{11}{7}$ or $1\dfrac{4}{7}$.

If the dominators are different, then the most common way of adding or subtracting the fractions is to rewrite the fractions so that they have the same denominators. Then complete the operation as described previously for addition or subtraction with common denominators. Generally the common denominator is found by finding the least common denominator (LCD) of the two different denominators. The LCD is the smallest whole number that is a multiple of the denominators. That is, it is the smallest number that is divisible by each of the denominators. Actually any common multiple of the denominator will work, but may require additional simplification once the sum or difference is computed.

Example 4 What is the value of $\dfrac{5}{18}+\dfrac{5}{24}$?

Solution: We can write 18 and 24 in prime factorization form. We find that $18 = 2 \times 3^2$ and $24 = 2^2 \times 3$. The LCD is found by using each different prime base (which are 2 and 3) and selecting the highest exponent found for each base.

Thus, the LCD $=2^3 \times 3^2 = 72$. Now change $\dfrac{5}{18}$ to $\dfrac{20}{72}$ and change $\dfrac{5}{24}$ to $\dfrac{15}{72}$. Finally, $\dfrac{20}{72}+\dfrac{15}{72}=\dfrac{35}{72}$.

NOTE:

> Another method (which is sometimes longer) for finding the LCD is to list the multiples of each number in the denominator until you find the lowest common multiple. Thus for 18 we would have 18, 36, 54, 72, 90, … and for 24 we would have 24, 48, 72, 96, 120, …

The LCD is 72. This is also referred to as the lowest common multiple or LCM.

In general for a, b, c, and d where c and $d \neq 0$ then $\dfrac{a}{c} \pm \dfrac{b}{d} = \dfrac{ad \pm bc}{cd}$

As an example, $\dfrac{3}{2} - \dfrac{4}{7} = \dfrac{(3)(7)-(2)(4)}{(2)(7)} = \dfrac{21-8}{14} = \dfrac{13}{14}$.

Decimals

When working with decimals, it is important to emphasize the meaning of place value. Remember that middle school students have had experiences with various models to develop place value concepts as well as operations with whole numbers. Middle grade teachers should build on these experiences to continue the development of decimal understanding. As a reminder, when we divide the denominator of a fraction into its numerator, the result is a decimal or decimal fraction. The decimal fraction is based upon the denominator being a power of 10, that is, 10, 100, 1,000, ….. and is written with a decimal point. Let's illustrate this concept with the fraction $\dfrac{3}{4}$. By dividing the denominator into the numerator (see computation below) we get .75 (or 0.75), which is read 75 hundredths.

$$
\begin{array}{r}
.75 \\
4\overline{)3.00} \\
\underline{28} \\
020 \\
\underline{020} \\
000
\end{array}
$$

Another example would be $3\dfrac{9}{100}$, which would be 3.09. This decimal number is read as three and nine hundredths.

Addition and Subtraction with Decimals

When you add numbers containing decimals, you must "line up the decimals" one beneath the other. Why? The reason is that you must add the correct place values to one another. Just as when you add a three-digit number to a two-digit number vertically, you line up the ones, tens, and so on, the same is true with decimals. You want to add the same place values together.

Example 5 $3.719 + 4.29 = \underline{\hspace{1cm}}$

Solution:

$$\begin{array}{r} 3.719 \\ + \ 4.290 \\ \hline 8.009 \end{array}$$

Multiplication and Division with Decimals

Typically students are taught to multiply decimals as you would whole numbers. Then you determine where the decimal is placed by counting the total number of decimal places in the numbers being multiplied.

Example 6   What is the value of 3.221×4.2?

Solution:

$$\begin{array}{r} 3.221 \\ \times 4.2 \\ \hline 6442 \\ 12884 \quad\ \\ \hline 13.5282 \end{array}$$

Note that there are three decimal places in 3.221 and one decimal place in 4.2. Thus, the answer will contain four decimal places. That said, teachers should remember to teach operations with decimals using place value. It is especially beneficial if teachers continue with place value models, such as base ten blocks, to develop the procedures for operations with decimals, rather than having students memorize a specific procedure without any understanding of the process. Students should also consider reasonableness. For example, in the problem above, it would be reasonable for the solution to be just over 12 since we are multiplying decimals that are approximately 3 and 4, respectively.

For division, the understanding of place value is critical and should be carefully developed with the use of place value concepts and models. Essentially the typical procedure used requires that the divisor be made a whole number by moving the decimal point the appropriate number of places to the right, and then the decimal point of the dividend should also be moved the same number of places. The decimal point in the quotient should be placed directly in line with the decimal point of the dividend.

Example 7   What is the value of 14.828 ÷ 2.2?

Solution:

$$
\begin{array}{r}
6.74 \\
22\overline{)148.28} \\
\underline{132} \\
162 \\
\underline{154} \\
88 \\
\underline{88} \\
0
\end{array}
$$

While the number 2.2 is not a whole number, but it can be made a whole number by moving the decimal point one place to the right. Then, the decimal point in the dividend must also be moved one place to the right. The problem 14.828 ÷ 2.2 is equivalent to 148.38 ÷ 22. You can check both answers with a calculator to confirm this solution.

Percents

A percent represents a way of expressing the relationship between a part and the whole, where the whole is defined to be 100%. Since the symbol refers to per hundred, a percent can always be written (and is defined) as a fraction with denominator of 100. Since decimals can be written as fractions (or decimal fractions as they are often called), both decimals and fractions can be represented as percents. As examples, $0.36 = \dfrac{36}{100} = 36\%$ and $\dfrac{5}{4} = \dfrac{125}{100} = 125\%$.

The rules for conversion from one form to another are as follows:

(a) To convert a decimal to a percent, move the decimal point two places to the right and add a percent sign. (Add zeros if necessary.) Thus, 0.7 = 70%.

(b) To convert a percent to a decimal, move the decimal point two places to the left and remove the percent sign. (Add zeros if necessary.) Thus, 325% = 3.25.

(c) To convert a fraction to a percent, multiply by 100 and add the percent sign. Thus, $\frac{3}{8} = (\frac{3}{8} \times 100)\% = 37.5\%$.

(d) To convert a percent to a fraction, remove the percent sign, place the number over 100, and reduce the answer to its simplest form. Thus, $1.5\% = \frac{1.5}{100} = \frac{15}{1000} = \frac{3}{200}$.

One should be able to find the percent of a given number, determine what percent one number is of another, convert a decimal to a percent, and convert a percent to a decimal. These computations are shown in a variety of different contexts.

Example 8   What number is 80% of 200?

Solution: First convert 80% to 0.80. Then since "of" means "times," the answer is (0.80) (200) = 160.

Example 9   45.5 is what percent of 50?

Solution: We need to change $\frac{45.5}{50}$ to a percent. The answer is $\left(\frac{45.5}{50}\right)(100)\% = 91\%$.

Example 10   28 is 1.6% of what number?

Solution: Let x represent the unknown number. Then $\frac{28}{x} = \frac{1.6}{100}$. Cross-multiply to get $1.6x = 2800$. Then $x = \frac{2800}{1.6} = 1750$.

Example 11   Arrange the following numbers in order, from least to greatest.

$$\frac{2}{3}, 60\%, 0.04, 2, 0.8\%, \frac{7}{11}, 0.0005$$

Solution: We can change each number to its decimal equivalent, rounded off (if required) to the nearest ten-thousandth. Here is how the original list would appear in the decimal form: 0.6667, 0.6000, 0.0400, 2.0000, 0.0080, 0.6364, 0.0005. By mentally removing the decimal point and removing zeros to the left of the first nonzero digit, the numbers would appear as 6667, 6000, 400, 20000, 80, 6364, and 5.

So $5 < 80 < 400 < 6000 < 6364 < 6667 < 20000$. Thus, the correct order of the original numbers is $0.0005, 0.8\%, 0.04, 60\%, \frac{7}{11}, \frac{2}{3}, 2$.

Exponents

Another commonly used operation is **exponentiation**, which represents repeated multiplication. Thus, $5 \times 5 \times 5$ can be written as 5^3, and $\frac{1}{2} \times \frac{1}{2}$ can be written as $\left(\frac{1}{2}\right)^2$. When a number is multiplied by itself multiple times we say that the number is raised to a power. So that for a^n, a is multiplied by itself n times. The letter a is called the **base** and the letter n represents the **exponent** or **power**. Exponentiation also applies to negative numbers, so that $\left(\frac{2}{3}\right)^{-2} = \frac{1}{(2/3)^2}$ (that is, $a^{-n} = \frac{1}{a^n}$, $a \neq 0$) and $(-3)^5 = (-3)(-3)$ $(-3)(-3)(-3)$. When the exponent is zero, the result is 1. In general, $a^0 = 1$, $a \neq 0$. As an example, $5^0 = 1$. This is a special curiosity for middle grade students, thus the teacher should have multiple means of having students explore this concept and examines why this is true. One possibility is to present the following argument, after the student learns the laws of exponents.

We know that $4^1 \times 4^0 = 4^{0+1} = 4^1$, by the addition rule of exponents when multiplying like bases. Since $4^1 = 4$, this means that $4 \times 4^0 = 4$. However, $4 \times 1 = 4$, so 4^0 must be equivalent to 1.

Following are the basic laws that govern exponents.

(1) $a^m a^n = a^{m+n}$

(2) $(a^m)^n = a^{mn}$

(3) $\dfrac{a^m}{a^n} = a^{m-n}$

(4) $(ab)^m = a^m b^m$

(5) $\left(\dfrac{a}{b}\right)^m = \dfrac{a^m}{b^m}, b \neq 0$

(6) $a^{\frac{m}{n}} = \sqrt[n]{a^m}$

Example 12   What is the value of $(-2)^3 \times (-2)^4 \div \left(\dfrac{2}{3}\right)^2$?

Solution: $(-2)^3 \times (-2)^4 = (-2)^7 = -128$ and $\left(\dfrac{2}{3}\right)^2 = \dfrac{4}{9}$.
Thus, $-128 \div \dfrac{4}{9} = \left(-\dfrac{128}{1}\right)\left(\dfrac{9}{4}\right) = -288$.

Example 13   What is the value of $\left(\dfrac{1}{3}\right)^{-3} - (2^3)^3 \div 16^{\frac{3}{2}}$?

Solution: $\left(\dfrac{1}{3}\right)^{-3} = \dfrac{1}{(1/3)^3} = \dfrac{1}{1/27} = 27; (2^3)^3 = 2^9 = 512;$

$16^{\frac{3}{2}} = (\sqrt{16})^3 = 4^3 = 64$. Thus, $27 - 512 \div 64 = 27 - 8 = 19$.

Scientific Notation

Scientific notation is a way to write numbers using exponents. It is commonly used to write very small or very large numbers, but may be used for any integer or decimal number. This notation uses a number between 1 and 10 multiplied by an integer power of 10.

Here is a summary of several numbers with integer exponents and with 10 as a base.
$10^{-3} = \frac{1}{1000}, 10^{-2} = \frac{1}{100}, 10^{-1} = \frac{1}{10}, 10^0 = 1, 10^1 = 10, 10^2 = 100$, and $10^3 = 1000$.

For example, $720,000,000 = 7.2 \times 100,000,000$. In scientific notation, it is written as 7.2×10^8. As a second example, $0.00364 = \frac{3.64}{1000} = (3.64)\left(\frac{1}{1000}\right)$. In scientific notation, it is written as 3.64×10^{-3}.

Example 14   What is the scientific notation for $-125,000$?

   Solution: Insert the decimal point between the digits 1 and 2. Since $-125,000 = (-1.25)(100,000)$, the answer becomes -1.25×10^5.

Example 15   What is the scientific notation for 0.0329?

   Solution: Since $0.0329 = (3.29)\left(\frac{1}{100}\right)$, the answer becomes (3.29×10^{-2}).

Example 16   What is the scientific notation for $\frac{4}{3}$?

   Solution: $\frac{4}{3} = 1\frac{1}{3} = 1.\bar{3}$. We can write $1.\bar{3}$ as $(1.\bar{3})(1)$, so the answer becomes $1.\bar{3} \times 10^0$.

Complex Numbers

A complex number is a number that can be written in the form $a + bi$, where a and b are real numbers and $i = \sqrt{-1}$. The real part of the complex number is a and the imaginary part is the number bi. You may recall in the discussion of real numbers and exponents that the square of a real number is always positive with the exception of zero, and the square of zero is zero. So i is defined to be a number such that $i^2 = -1$. Many properties of real numbers also apply to complex numbers. Here are three basic properties:

(A) $(a + bi) + (c + di) = (a + c) + (b + d)i$.

As an example, $(5 + 2i) + (3 + 4i) = (5 + 3) + (2 + 4)i = 8 + 6i$.

(B) $(a + bi) - (c + di) = (a - c) + (b - d)i$

As an example, $(5 + 2i) - (3 + 4i) = (5 - 3) + (2 - 4)i = 2 + -2i = 2 - 2i$.

(C) $(a + bi) \times (c + di) = ac + adi + bci + bdi^2 = (ac - bd) + (ad + bc)i$

Example 17   What is the simplified form for $(5 + 2i) \times (3 + 4i)$?

Solution: $(5 + 2i) \times (3 + 4i) = (5)(3) + (5)(4i) + (2i)(3) + (2i)(4i) =$ $15 + 20i + 6i + 8i^2 = 15 + 26i + (-8) = 7 + 26i$.

When simplifying these operations, remember to combine all real components with real components and all imaginary components with imaginary components.

When dividing complex numbers, one usually uses the conjugate of a complex number. The **conjugate** of $a + bi$, is defined as the quantity $a - bi$. Note that $(a + bi)(a - bi) = a^2 + b^2$. When complex expressions or solutions are given in simplified form, they contain no complex numbers in the denominator; thus using the conjugate in division is useful. This procedure is illustrated in Example 18.

Example 18   What is the simplified form for $(2 + 3i) \div (1 + 2i)$?

Solution: $\dfrac{2 + 3i}{1 + 2i} = \dfrac{2 + 3i}{1 + 2i} \times \dfrac{1 - 2i}{1 - 2i} = \dfrac{(2 + 6) + (-4 + 3)i}{1 + 4} = \dfrac{8 + -i}{5} =$ $\dfrac{8 - i}{5}$.

In general, $\dfrac{a + bi}{c + di} = \dfrac{a + bi}{c + di} \times \dfrac{c - di}{c - di} = \dfrac{(ac + bd) + (bc - ad)i}{c^2 + d^2}$.

One particular place where using complex numbers arises is when solving quadratic equations. This topic will appear later in this book, so remember to review these operations as needed.

Our last topic involves the properties of powers of the imaginary number i.

We know that $i^2 = -1$. Note that $i^3 = (i^2)(i) = -1i = -i$ and that $i^4 = (i^2)(i^2)$ $= (-1)(-1) = 1$. Subsequent powers of i show that the pattern i, -1, $-i$, 1 repeats for each cycle of 4. Thus, $i = i^5 = i^9 = i^{13} = ...,$ $i^2 = i^6 = i^{10} = i^{14} = ...,$ $i^3 = i^7 = i^{11}$ $= i^{15} = ...,$ and $i^4 = i^8 = i^{11} = i^{16} = ...$

Example 19 What is the simplified form for $5i^3 - 4i + i^{20} + 7i^{26}$?

Solution: $5i^3 - 4i + i^{20} + 7i^{26} = (5)(-i) - 4i + 1 + (7)(-1) = -9i - 6$

Quiz for Chapter 2

1. What is the scientific notation for $\dfrac{3}{20}$?

    (A) 0.15×10^0

    (B) 1.5×10^{-1}

    (C) 15×10^{-2}

    (D) 0.015×10^1

2. Which one of the following is an irrational number?

    (A) $\sqrt[3]{125}$

    (B) 0

    (C) $\sqrt{10}$

    (D) $8.\overline{12}$

3. What is the sum of the multiplicative inverse and additive inverse of 4?

    (A) -3.75

    (B) -1

    (C) 1

    (D) 3.75

4. For any two real numbers a and b, which one of the following is <u>not necessarily</u> true?

    (A) $|-a| = |a|$

    (B) $\left|\dfrac{a}{b}\right| = \dfrac{a}{b}$ *could also be* $-\dfrac{a}{b}$

    (C) $|a| \times |b| = |ab|$

    (D) If $a > b$, then $|a - b| = a - b$

5. What is the least common denominator for the fractions $\dfrac{7}{18}$ and $\dfrac{2}{27}$?

    (A) 9

    (B) 14

    (C) 54

    (D) 486

6. Given the numbers 0.9, $\dfrac{11}{12}$, $0.9\bar{1}$, and 91%, which of the following shows these numbers in order from least to greatest?

    (A) $0.9, 91\%, \dfrac{11}{12}, 0.9\bar{1}$

    (B) $0.9, 91\%, 0.9\bar{1}, \dfrac{11}{12}$

    (C) $0.9, \dfrac{11}{12}, 91\%, 0.9\bar{1}$

    (D) $0.9, 0.9\bar{1}, 91\%, \dfrac{11}{12}$

7. The expression $(-3)(2 + 7)$ can be evaluated by the Distributive Property of Multiplication over Addition. Which one of the following illustrates this approach?

    (A) $(2 + 7)(-3)$

    (B) $(-3)(9)$

    (C) $(-3)(2) + 7$

    (D) $(-3)(2) + (-3)(7)$

8. What is the simplified form for $\dfrac{2-i}{1+4i}$?

    (A) $\dfrac{6+7i}{15}$

    (B) $\dfrac{6+7i}{17}$

    (C) $\dfrac{-2-9i}{15}$

    (D) $\dfrac{-2-9i}{17}$

9. What is the simplified form for $i^3 + 2i^5 - 3i^8 - 4i^{10}$?

    (A) $i+1$

    (B) $i-1$

    (C) $3i-1$

    (D) $3i+1$

10. 35% of 80 is equivalent to ___% of 22.4?

    (A) 151.2

    (B) 125

    (C) 51.2

    (D) 25

Quiz for Chapter 2 Solutions

1. **(B)**

    Divide 20 into 3 to get 0.15. Then $0.15 = (1.5)\left(\dfrac{1}{10}\right) = 1.5 \times 10^{-1}$.

2. (C)

$\sqrt{10}$ cannot be written as a quotient of two integers. Thus, it is irrational. (Note that answer choice (D) can be written as $\dfrac{268}{33}$, which means that it is rational.)

3. (A)

For the number 4, its multiplicative inverse is $\dfrac{1}{4}$ and its additive inverse is -4. Then $\dfrac{1}{4} - 4 = -3\dfrac{3}{4} = -3.75.$

4. (B)

As an example, if $a = -10$ and $b = 5$, $\left|\dfrac{-10}{5}\right| = |-2| = 2$. However, $\dfrac{a}{b} = \dfrac{-10}{5} = -2$.

5. (C)

$18 = 2 \times 3^2$ and $27 = 3^3$. Thus, the least common denominator is $2 \times 3^3 = 54$.

6. (B)

Change each number to a decimal with three decimal places. Round off if necessary. Then the original numbers appear as 0.900, 0.917, 0.911, and 0.910. Then $0.900 < 0.910 < 0.911 < 0.917$. Thus, the correct order is

$0.9, 91\%, 0.9\overline{1}, \dfrac{11}{12}.$

7. (D)

By using the Distributive Property of Multiplication over Addition, $(-3)(2 + 7) = (-3)(2) + (-3)(7)$.

8. (D)

Multiply the numerator and denominator of the original fraction by the conjugate of $1 + 4i$, which is $1 - 4i$. Then $\dfrac{2-i}{1+4i} \times \dfrac{1-4i}{1-4i} = \dfrac{2 - 8i - i + 4i^2}{1 - 16i^2} = \dfrac{-2 - 9i}{17}.$

9. (A)

$$i^3 + 2i^5 - 3i^8 - 4i^{10} = -i + 2i - 3 + 4 = i + 1$$

10. (B)

35% of 80 means $(0.35)(80) = 28$. So, we must solve the question "28 is what percent of 22.4?" Let x represent the missing percent. Then $\dfrac{28}{22.4} = \dfrac{x}{100}$. Cross-multiply to get $22.4x = 2800$. Thus, $x = \dfrac{2800}{22.4} = 125$.

3

Patterns and Algebra

Introduction

This chapter explores the Domain II Competencies 004 − 007 related to patterns and algebra. This domain addresses the role of patterns and connection to the development of algebraic thinking, symbolism, and structure. The domain requires the teacher to understand the relationship between variables, linear and non-linear functions, apply equations and inequalities, and be able to use a variety of representations within this area to model and solve problems. This aids in laying the foundation for understanding concepts of calculus related to rate of change, limits, and measurement as related to grades 4 − 8 mathematics.

Inductive Reasoning Applied to Patterns

Identifying, predicting, and extending patterns is a key concept that middle school students have encountered in elementary school. These skills will aid them in building conceptual understandings that will assist them in working with algebra. Middle school teachers should build on this foundation and support students as they begin to encounter the more abstract portions of algebraic concepts. Supporting these seemingly abstract ideas with concrete materials, models, and appropriate applications will facilitate middle school students in developing a deep understanding of functions and other algebraic ideas. Algebraic thinking is central to the success of middle school students as they prepare for high school mathematics.

Both inductive and deductive reasoning are essential to reach conclusions based on given information. In the middle school, students need multiple experiences in using inductive reasoning to extend patterns and formulate conjectures through a variety of representations, such as graphically, verbally (in words), numerically, symbolically, and pictorially.

Example 1   Given the sequence of numbers $1, \dfrac{1}{2}, \dfrac{1}{4}, \dfrac{1}{8}, \dfrac{1}{16}, \dfrac{1}{32}$, predict the next term in the sequence.

Solution: It appears that the numerators remain constant, with 1 in each term of the sequence. The denominator doubles for each term. Thus the next term would be $\dfrac{1}{2 \times 32} = \dfrac{1}{64}$. In fact, the nth term can be expressed as $\dfrac{1}{2^{n-1}}$, for $n \geq 0$, where n is an integer.

Example 2   Suppose you have a sequence of tiles, as illustrated in the Figure below.

If the pattern continued, what would the next (5th) drawing look like? Predict the number of tiles in the 10th drawing. Write a rule that would determine the nth term of the sequence.

Solution: The next drawing would be as shown below.

The number of tiles in the sequence is 2, 4, 6, and 8. The number of tiles increases by 2 each time. Since the 4th term has 8 tiles, then by adding 2, the 5th term will have 10 tiles. Since the number of tiles is double the number of the term, we can express the general rule as $a_n = 2n$. Thus, the 10th drawing will have 20 tiles.

NOTE:

> For each of Examples 1 and 2, a **recursive** rule for a sequence gives the beginning term or terms of the sequence and then relates the next term to the previous term or terms. In Example 1, we observe that $a_1 = 1$, $a_2 = \frac{1}{2}$, $a_3 = \frac{1}{4}$, and $a_4 = \frac{1}{8}$. In general, for $n > 1$, $a_n = \frac{1}{2}a_{n-1}$.

In Example 2, we see that $a_1 = 2$, $a_2 = 4$, $a_3 = 6$, and $a_4 = 8$. Thus, $a_5 = 8 + 2$. In general, for $n > 1$, $a_n = a_{n-1} + 2$. So to find the 10th term in this sequence, one could complete the sequence for 9 terms (drawing the picture, writing out the sequence, graphing, or constructing a table of values) and then use that to find the 10th term.

Variables, Algebraic Expressions & Properties

In algebra, letters are often used to represent variables. It is incumbent upon the middle school teacher to understand the various ways that variables are used in mathematics. Typically, a variable is represented by a letter that has a single value. However, in some cases the variable may have several values. Historically, x and y are commonly used to represent variables, but other letters can be used as well. It is often helpful for the letter that is used to be appropriate for the application, such as using c for cost or t for time.

Algebraic expressions are made up of parts referred to as **terms**. These terms can be a constant number, a variable, or a combination of numbers and variables. If a term has both a number and variable(s), then the number is called a **coefficient** of the term. For example, in the expression $-2x^2 + 3x + 6$, -2 and 3 are coefficients of the terms $-2x^2$ and $3x$, respectively. The number 6 is a constant term, since it is not multiplied by a variable.

If a variable is written without a coefficient, the coefficient is understood to be 1. This is important for middle school students to understand, as often they will say that the coefficient of a term such as x^3 is zero rather than one! It is helpful to use some type of manipulative representation to illustrate variables and related algebraic expressions. One such model is algebra tiles. While space does not allow for a full explanation of using the tiles, some examples using algebra tiles will be provided. The reader is encouraged to seek other resources to aid in understanding the use of these tiles as well as other models. Algebra tiles can be used to represent expressions, operations with expressions, understanding properties of expressions, solving equations, factoring polynomials, and more!

NOTE:

> Algebra tiles can be used to visualize or model this relationship.

Let ☐ represent a 1 by 1 unit square with a value of 1.

Let ▨ represent -1.

Let ▭ represent 1 unit by x units with a value of x.

Let ▬ represent $-x$.

Let ☐ represent x^2 since its dimensions are x by x.

Let ▨ represent $-x^2$.

Therefore, $4x^2 - x + 9$ would be represented using algebra tiles as

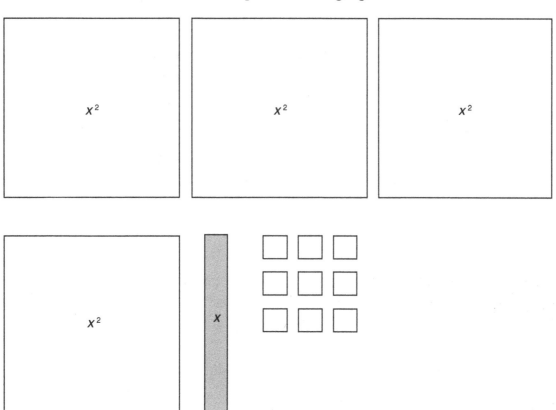

Algebraic expressions are classified according to the number of terms they contain. A monomial has one term, a binomial has two terms, and a trinomial has three terms. In general, an algebraic expression with two or more terms is called a polynomial.

Example 3   For the polynomial $4x^2 - x + 9$, how many terms are there, how would you classify the polynomial by the number of its terms, and what is the coefficient of x?

Solution: $4x^2 - x + 9$ is a polynomial with three terms, which is called a trinomial. The coefficient of x is -1.

Operations with Polynomials

One can add, subtract, multiply, and divide polynomials following the properties previously discussed in Chapter 2. However, only like terms may be added or subtracted.

Like terms are terms in an expression that have the same variable to the same exponent. For example, x^2 and $-2x^2$ are like terms. In contrast, x and x^3 are not like terms. Again, students often need a concrete representation to understand this idea. Modeling with algebra tiles reinforces the idea of like terms as they represent like area models. Constant terms are also like terms.

Addition of Polynomials

Adding polynomials is accomplished by combining like terms. This means adding the coefficients of the like terms (in the case of variables) and adding any constant terms.

Example 4   Write as a single polynomial: $(2n^2 + 3n - 5) + (-n^2 + 2n + 1)$.

>   **Solution:**   The two polynomials are separated with parentheses. By using the properties of Commutativity and Associativity, we can combine these two polynomials by rewriting the sum as $(2n^2 - n^2) + (3n + 2n) + (-5 + 1)$.

Using the Distributive Property of addition over multiplication, we have

$$(2 - 1)n^2 + (3 + 2)n + (-5 + 1) = n^2 + 5n - 4$$

NOTE:

> We are actually adding the coefficients of the like terms. Students should notice this pattern but be mindful of signed numbers and attend to the order of operations and properties.

Subtraction of Polynomials

The operation of subtraction is accomplished by first changing the signs of all the terms in the expression, which are being subtracted, and then adding the results. This is actually using the definition of subtraction noted in Chapter 2. The most common error is to fail to distribute the subtraction operation to all terms of the polynomial being subtracted.

Example 5   Write $(3x^2 + 2x - 4) - (x^3 + 2x^2 - 5x + 8)$ as a single polynomial.

Solution: By distributing the subtraction symbol and removing the parentheses, we get $3x^2 + 2x - 4 - x^3 - 2x^2 + 5x - 8$. We can regroup the terms so that the polynomial appears as $-x^3 + (3x^2 - 2x^2) + (2x + 5x) + (-4-8)$. The answer is $-x^3 + x^2 + 7x - 12$.

(Note that Associative, Commutative, and Distributive properties were used.)

Multiplication of Polynomials

For multiplication, there are several cases to consider. In general, multiplication of polynomials is accomplished by using the laws of exponents, order of operations, Commutative, Associative, and Distributive properties, and rules of signed numbers.

Multiplication of a monomial by a monomial

First multiply the coefficients and any constants, then multiply the variables by applying the laws of exponents.

Example 6   Write $(x^2)(xy)(3)(4x^2)(-3xy^2)$ as a simplified monomial.

Solution: Rewrite this expression as $(3)(4)(-3)(x^2)(x)(x^2)(x)(y)(y^2)$. Then use the rules of signed numbers and exponents to arrive at the answer $-36x^6y^3$.

Example 7   Write $(4a^2b)(3a + 2b^2)$ as a simplified polynomial.

Solution: Using the Distributive Property, we can write the original expression as $(4a^2b)(3a) + (4a^2b)(2b^2)$. Then applying the rules of exponents, we get the answer $12a^3b + 8a^2b^3$.

Multiplication of a polynomial by a polynomial

Multiply each of the terms of one polynomial by each of the terms of the other polynomial (essentially using the Distributive Property) and combining the results.

Example 8 Write $(3n^2 + 2mn - 1)(n + m)$ as a simplified polynomial.

> **Solution:** The individual products become $[(3n^2)(n) + (3n^2)(m)] + [(2mn)(n) + (2mn)(m)] + [(-1)(n)+(-1)(m)] = 3n^3 + 3mn^2 + 2mn^2 + 2m^2n - n - m$. We can combine the second and third terms, because they are like terms. Thus, the final answer is $3n^3 + 5mn^2 + 2m^2n - n - m$.

Division of Polynomials

There are three cases to consider when dividing polynomials: (a) dividing two monomials, (b) dividing a polynomial by a monomial, and (c) dividing two polynomials. Dividing a monomial by a monomial is accomplished by dividing the coefficients according to number properties and then using exponent properties to divide each similar variable.

Example 9 Write $8x^4y^2 \div 2x^2y$ as a simplified monomial.

> **Solution:** The original division problem can be expressed in fraction form as $\dfrac{8x^4y^2}{2x^2y}$. The answer is found by $(\dfrac{8}{2})(\dfrac{x^4}{x^2})(\dfrac{y^2}{y}) = 4x^2y$.

Dividing a polynomial by a monomial is accomplished by writing it as a fraction and dividing each term in the numerator by the term in the denominator. Then apply appropriate properties such as those related to operations with exponents.

Example 10 Write $(10m^3 + 5m^2 - 25m) \div 5m$ as a simplified polynomial.

> **Solution:** We begin with $\dfrac{10m^3 + 5m^2 - 25m}{5m}$. Then we write this expression as three separate fractions: $\dfrac{10m^3}{5m} + \dfrac{5m^2}{5m} - \dfrac{25m}{5m}$. Finally, by following the rules for dividing monomials, the answer is $2m^2 + m - 5$.

Dividing a polynomial by a polynomial can be accomplished using the long division procedure. Students should be familiar with this from dividing whole numbers. First, all terms in each polynomial must be arranged in either ascending or descending order according to the powers of one variable. (This is similar to place value concepts). Basically, the division problem will be solved as Dividend ÷ Divisor = Quotient + Remainder/Divisor.

Example 11   What is the quotient of $4x^2 + 6x + 3 \div 2x + 1$?

Solution: We are actually simplifying the fraction $\dfrac{4x^2 + 6x + 3}{2x + 1}$ so that it becomes a polynomial, with the remainder written as a reduced fraction. The steps are shown below.

$$
\begin{array}{r}
2x + 2 \\
2x + 1 \overline{\smash{)}\ 4x^2 + 6x + 3} \\
\underline{4x^2 + 2x} \\
4x + 3 \\
\underline{4x + 2} \\
1
\end{array}
$$

The answer is $2x + 2 + \dfrac{1}{2x + 1}$.

There are cases for which a term may be "missing," which can occur if there is a "gap" between consecutive terms in the dividend. The best remedy for this situation is to provide a zero coefficient for the missing term(s).

Example 12   What is the quotient of $3x^3 - 5x + 4 \div x - 1$?

Solution: We recognize that there is a "gap" between the first and third terms, since there is no x^2 term. In order to remedy this situation, we insert the term $0x^2$. The steps for solving appear below.

$$\begin{array}{r} 3x^2 + 3x - 2 \\ x-1\overline{\smash{\big)}\ 3x^3 + 0x^2 - 5x + 4} \\ \underline{3x^3 - 3x^2} \\ 3x^2 - 5x \\ \underline{3x^2 - 3x} \\ -2x + 4 \\ \underline{-2x + 2} \\ 2 \end{array}$$

The answer is $3x^2 + 3x - 2 + \dfrac{2}{x-1}$.

Cartesian Coordinate System

In the Cartesian Coordinate system, named after the French mathematician Rene Descartes, there are two lines drawn in a plane such that they are perpendicular to each other. The horizontal line is the x-axis and the vertical line is the y-axis. The two lines divide the plane into four sections called **quadrants**. These quadrants are assigned the roman numerals I, II, III, and IV, beginning on the upper right hand side and continuing in a counterclockwise direction. The intersection of the two axes is called the **origin** and has the coordinates $(0, 0)$. Figure 3.3 illustrates this system.

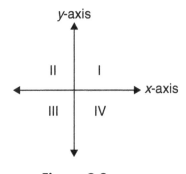

Figure 3.3

To locate a point on the coordinate plane, one measures the distance of x units along the x-axis horizontally and then measures the distance of y units vertically along the y-axis, Figure 3.4 illustrates the origin and several points.

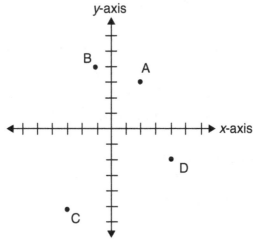

Figure 3.4

The labeling of each point is as follows: A is located at $(2, 3)$, B is located at $(-1, 4)$, C is located at $(-3, -5)$, and D is located at $(4, -2)$.

Points that have either an x-coordinate of zero or a y-coordinate of zero do not fall in any of the quadrants. Instead, they fall on one of the axes. Figure 3.5 illustrates several points that lie on one of the axes.

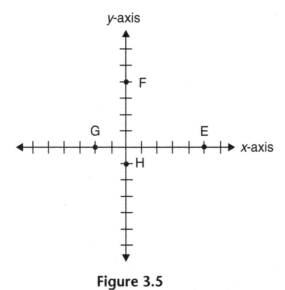

Figure 3.5

The coordinates of each point is as follows: E is at $(5, 0)$, F is at $(0, 4)$, G is at $(-2, 0)$, and H is at $(0, -1)$.

Relations and Functions

A **relation** is a set of ordered pairs in which each ordered pair is called an **element**. An example of a relation with three elements is $S = \{(-1, 2), (3, 5), (7, 11)\}$. As with any set, no element may be repeated. For example, a relation may have the elements $(2, 3)$ and $(3, 2)$, but it would <u>not</u> contain two elements that are each identified as $(3, 2)$.

The set of all first parts of the ordered pairs in the relation is called the **domain** (also referred to as the independent variable). The set of the second parts is called the **range** (also referred to as the dependent variable).

Example 13   What are the domain and range of the relation
$T = \{(-3, 2),(2, 1),(-3, 4),(0, -3)\}$?

   Solution: Let D represent the domain and let R represent the range. Then $D = \{-3, 2, 0\}$ and $R = \{2, 1, 4, -3\}$.

A **function** is a special type of relation for which each element in the domain is assigned exactly one element in the range. In Example 13, T is <u>not</u> a function because the number -3 in the domain is assigned to both 2 and 4 in the range.

However, it is permissible for a function to have more than one element in the domain assigned to the same element in the range. As an example, let $V = \{(4, 1),(-7, 3),(9, 1)\}$ The domain is $\{4, -7, 9\}$ and the range is $\{1, 3\}$. V is a function since each element in its domain is assigned to exactly one element in its range. Notice that both 4 and 9 in the domain are paired with the same number (1) in the range.

Example 14   Given the relation $W = \{(2, 5), (8, 2), \text{ and } (6, \underline{\quad})\}$, what number(s) can be assigned to blank so that W is <u>not</u> a function?

   Solution: Hopefully, you were not fooled by this question. The answer is that W is a function regardless of the value assigned to the blank. The domain consists of three numbers, and each will be assigned to exactly one number in the range.

Graphs of Functions and Relations

In order to determine whether a given graph represents a function, we can use the **vertical line** test. If the graph does represent a function, then any vertical line will intersect the graph at most only once.

Example 15   Using the graph of $y = x^2$, determine whether this relation is a function.

Solution: Choose the following values of x: $-2, -1, 0, 1$, and 2. By substituting these values into the equation $y = x^2$, the corresponding y values are $4, 1, 0, 1$, and 4. Now graph the points $(-2, 4)$, $(-1, 1)$, $(0, 0)$, $(1, 1)$, and $(2, 4)$, as shown in Figure 3.6.

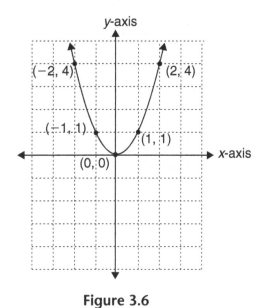

Figure 3.6

If we draw any vertical line, it will not intersect this graph more than once. Therefore, $y = x^2$ is a function.

Now consider the relation defined by $x = y^2$. We'll choose the x values of 0, 1, and 4. If $x = 0$, the only value of y is zero. If $x = 1$, both 1 and -1 are valid y values. Similarly, if $x = 4$, both 2 and -2 are valid y values. The five points we have are $(0, 0)$, $(1, -1)$, $(1, 1)$, $(4, -2)$, and $(4, 2)$. Figure 3.7 shows the graph of this relation.

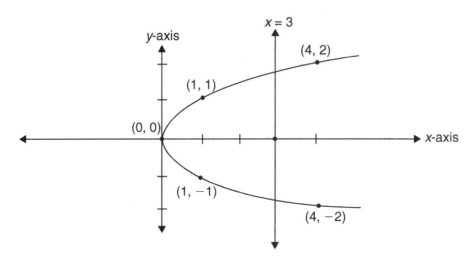

Figure 3.7

There are many vertical lines that can be drawn which will intersect this graph in two points. The line whose equation is $x = 3$ is shown as one example. Therefore, $x = y^2$ is not a function.

Linear Functions

Middle School mathematics begins the formal study of linear functions. A thorough understanding of linear functions can support students in their future understanding of non-linear functions. Thus, it is important for teachers to provide middle school students with multiple experiences with linear functions. Teachers should include real-world applications so students can appropriately interpret linear functions. The concepts in linear functions include slope, domain, range, and intercepts.

The **slope** of a line refers to the rate in which the y-coordinate changes for each unit change in the x-coordinate. Given a line that contains two points labeled as (x_1, y_1) and (x_2, y_2), the slope is represented by m and is found by $\dfrac{y_2 - y_1}{x_2 - x_1}$.

Horizontal lines have a slope of zero and vertical lines have undefined slope. Equivalently, we can state that vertical lines have no slope. Parallel lines have equal slopes, and perpendicular lines have slopes that are negative reciprocals of each other.

While there are several forms of an equation of a line, one of the most useful forms is slope-intercept form, $y = mx + b$ where m represents the slope and b is the y-intercept. The exception is a vertical line, whose equation is $x = k$ where k is a constant (Recall that a vertical line has undefined slope.)

Example 16   What is the slope of a line that passes through the points $(2, -1)$ and $(10, 3)$?

> **Solution:** $m = \dfrac{3 - (-1)}{10 - 2} = \dfrac{4}{8} = \dfrac{1}{2}$

Example 17   Write the slope-intercept form for the equation of the line that passes through the points in Example 16.

> **Solution:**   Since $m = \dfrac{1}{2}$, we can write the equation as $y = \dfrac{1}{2}x + b$.

We can now select either given point and substitute the x and y values into this equation. Using $(2, -1)$, we get $-1 = \dfrac{1}{2}(2) + b$. Then $b = -2$. Thus, the required equation is $y = \dfrac{1}{2}x - 2$.

Example 18   Write the slope intercept form of the equation of the line that passes through $(3, -4)$ and is perpendicular to the line that has a slope of -3.

> **Solution:**   The negative reciprocal of a number c is expressed as $-\dfrac{1}{c}$. The slope of the required line would be $\dfrac{1}{3}$ since it is the negative reciprocal of -3. Then substituting the given point with the slope in the slope-intercept form, we get $-4 = \dfrac{1}{3}(3) + b$. Then $b = -5$. Thus, the required equation is $y = \dfrac{1}{3}x - 5$.

Example 19   Find the slope, x-intercept, and y-intercept of the line with equation $2x - 3y - 18 = 0$.

Solution: To find the slope we can solve the given equation for y, thus writing it in slope-intercept form. Adding 18 to both sides of the equation we get $2x - 3y = 18$. Subtracting $2x$ from both sides of the equation we get $-3y = -2x + 18$. Dividing both sides by -3 we get $y = \frac{2}{3}x - 6$, so the slope is $\frac{2}{3}$.

To find the x-intercept, we need to recall what that means in terms of the graph. The x-intercept has a y-coordinate of 0 since it lies on the x-axis. Thus we substitute 0 in for y in the equation of the line. That is, we need to solve $0 = \frac{2}{3}x - 6$. The next step is $\frac{2}{3}x = 6$, so $x = \frac{6}{2/3} = 9$. From the equation $y = \frac{2}{3}x - 6$, we observe that the y-intercept is -6. (This answer can also be determined by the substitution of 0 for x in the equation $y = \frac{2}{3}x - 6$.)

Note, in some textbooks, the x- and y-intercepts are referenced by their coordinates. Thus, we can state that the x-intercept is $(9, 0)$ and the y-intercept is $(0, -6)$.

There are other forms of a linear equation such as Standard Form, $ax + by + c = 0$, two-point form, $\frac{y - y_1}{x - x_1} = \frac{y_2 - y_1}{x_2 - x_1}$, and point-slope form, $y - y_1 = m(x - x_1)$. Each can be useful at times, but the important thing to understand is what the slope and intercepts are, how they are calculated, and how they are related to the graph of the line.

Example 20 Write the slope-intercept form of the equation $4x + 5y = 10$ and graph the associated line.

Solution: Subtract $4x$ from each side to get $5y = -4x + 10$. Then, dividing both sides by 5, we get $y = -\frac{4}{5}x + 2$.

Thus the graph will be a line with slope of $\frac{-4}{5}$ and a y-intercept of 2 (passing through the point $(0, 2)$). To graph the line, plot the point $(0, 2)$, and then use the slope to determine another point through which the line passes. If the slope is $\frac{-4}{5}$, then it means that as the y decreases by 4 units the x increases by 5 units. We are using the idea of slope as $\frac{rise}{run}$, indicating the change in y related to the change in x. Beginning at (0, 2), we find the next point by adding 5 units to the x value and subtracting 4 units from the y value. This instruction would lead us to the point (5, −2). (Note that other points on the line, such as (10, −6), can be found by substituting values for x and solving for y). The graph of $y = -\dfrac{4}{5} x + 2$ is shown below in Figure 3.8.

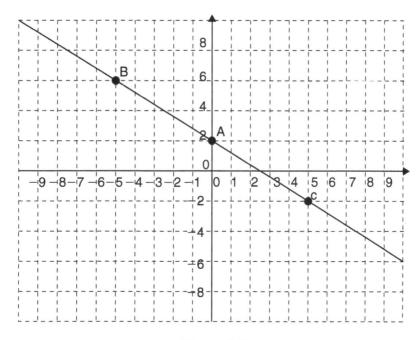

Figure 3.8

Function Transformations

Before discussing non-linear functions in detail, we should review some basic transformations. While there are many types of transformations, there are a few basic ones that result from linear movements of a given function $f(x)$, which is referred to as the *parent* function. These related functions, along with the parent function, comprise a *family* of functions. In particular, we will look at functions that result from (a) vertical shifts, (b) horizontal shifts, (c) reflections over the x-axis, and (d) reflections over the y-axis.

Vertical and Horizontal Shifts

These two shifts relate to adding or subtracting a constant with respect to the parent function, *f(x)*. Graphing tools such as graphing calculators or software are helpful to use when exploring the shifts. Let k be a positive real number. Here is the summary of the equation of the function $g(x)$ under the basic vertical and horizontal shifts.

(a) Vertical shift upwards k units $\qquad$ $g(x) = f(x) + k$

(b) Vertical shift downwards k units $\qquad$ $g(x) = f(x) - k$

(c) Horizontal shift to the left k units $\qquad$ $g(x) = f(x + k)$

(d) Horizontal shift to the right k units $\qquad$ $g(x) = f(x - k)$

For Examples 21, 22, and 23, let $f(x) = x^3$ represent the parent function, and let $g(x)$ represent the function that results from the shift(s).

Example 21 What is the equation of $g(x)$ if the graph of $f(x)$ is shifted downwards two units?

          Solution: Since $k = -2$, $g(x) = x^3 - 2$.

Figure 3.9 shows the comparison of the graphs of $f(x) = x^3$ and $g(x) = x^3 - 2$.

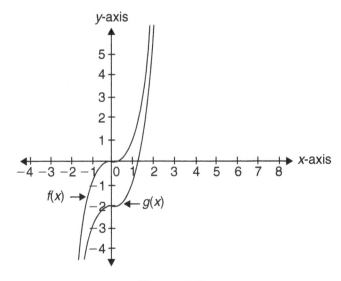

Figure 3.9

Example 22 What is the equation of $g(x)$ if the graph of $f(x)$ is shifted four units to the right?

Solution: Replace x by $x - 4$. Then $g(x) = (x - 4)^3 = (x - 4)(x - 4)$
$(x - 4) = (x^2 - 8x + 16)(x - 4) = x^3 - 12x^2 + 48x - 64$.

Example 23   What is the equation of $g(x)$ if the graph of $f(x)$ is shifted upwards one unit and three units to the left?

Solution: In order to shift one unit upward, we replace x^3 by $x^3 + 1$. Next, we need to shift the graph three units to the left. So, $x^3 + 1$ must change to $(x + 3)^3 + 1$. Thus, $g(x) = (x + 3)^3 + 1 = (x + 3)(x + 3)$ $(x + 3) + 1 = (x^2 + 6x + 9)(x + 3) + 1 = x^3 + 9x^2 + 27x + 28$.

NOTE:

We can verify the accuracy of these shifts by substituting points. Let's check the equation for $g(x)$ in Example 23. If $x = 2$, then $f(x) = 2^3 = 8$, which means that $(2, 8)$ lies on the graph of $f(x)$. By shifting one unit upward and three units to the left, the point $(2, 8)$ changes to $(-1, 9)$. This point should lie on the graph of $g(x)$. Sure enough, we observe that $g(-1) = (-1)^3 + (9)(-1)^2 + (27)(-1) + 28 = -1 + 9 - 27 + 28 = 9$.

Reflections

Reflections about the x-axis or y-axis are another common type of transformation and are represented as follows:

(a) If $g(x) = -f(x)$, then the graph of $g(x)$ is a reflection of the graph of $f(x)$ about the x-axis. In terms of coordinates, if the point (x, y) lies on the graph of $f(x)$, then the point $(x, -y)$ must lie on the graph of $g(x)$.

(b) If $g(x) = f(-x)$, then the graph of $g(x)$ is a reflection of the graph of $f(x)$ about the y-axis. In terms of coordinates, if the point (x, y) lies on the graph of $f(x)$, then the point $(-x, y)$ must lie on the graph of $g(x)$.

Example 24   Given the graph of $f(x) = x^3$, let $g(x)$ represent the graph of the reflection of $f(x)$ about the x-axis. What is the equation of $g(x)$?

Solution: $g(x) = -f(x) = -(x^3) = -x^3$.

Figures 3.10 and 3.11 illustrate the graphs of $f(x) = x^3$ and $g(x) = -x^3$.

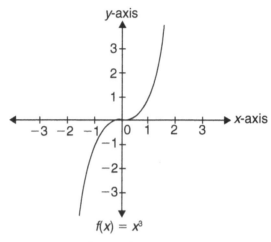

$$f(x) = x^3$$

Figure 3.10

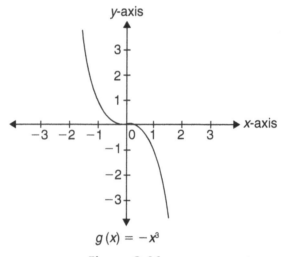

$$g(x) = -x^3$$

Figure 3.11

Example 25   Given the graph of $f(x) = x^2 + x + 1$, let $h(x)$ represent the graph of the reflection of $f(x)$ about the x-axis. What is the equation of $h(x)$?

Solution: $h(x) = -f(x) = -(x^2 + x + 1) = -x^2 - x - 1$.

Example 26   Given the graph of $f(x) = x^3$, let $k(x)$ represent the graph of the reflection of $f(x)$ about the y-axis. What is the equation of $k(x)$?

Solution: $k(x) = f(-x) = (-x)^3 = -x^3$.

NOTE:

> You may think that there must be a mistake in the solution to Example 26, since it matches the solution to Example 24. But, do not change the solution! Whenever a function is in the form $f(x) = x^k$, where k is an odd integer, the equation of the function that represents the reflection about either axis is the same.

Example 27 Given the graph of $f(x) = x^2 + x + 1$, let $m(x)$ represent the graph of the reflection of $f(x)$ about the y-axis. What is the equation of $m(x)$?

Solution: $m(x) = f(-x) = (-x)^2 + (-x) + 1 = x^2 - x + 1$.

Nonlinear Functions

While a major focus of functions in middle grade mathematics is related to linear functions, it is important to introduce nonlinear function so students understand that not all relationships are linear. It is even more important that middle grade teachers have a thorough understanding of nonlinear functions to aid them in selecting appropriate tasks for their students. In the previous discussion of transformations, the reader has been introduced to several nonlinear functions.

Quadratics are the most common nonlinear functions. In this section we will examine quadratic functions through equations, graphs, and tables, along with methods for solving quadratic equations. A **quadratic equation** is a second-degree equation in the form $ax^2 + bx + c = 0$, where a, b, and c are real numbers. A solution involves finding values of x (also referred to as roots of the equation) that satisfy the equation. This can be done by taking the square root through directly solving, factoring, completing the square, graphing and/or using the quadratic formula. Graphically, the solutions to $ax^2 + bx + c = 0$ are the x values of the points where the graph of $y = ax^2 + bx + c$ crosses the x-axis. Here are some examples:

Example 28 Solve for x: $x^2 - 25 = 0$

Solution: By isolating x we have $x^2 = 25$. By taking the square root of both sides we have $x = \pm 5$. Examining the graph, shown in Figure 3.12, we see that the quadratic function $y = x^2$ crosses the x-axis at $+5$ and -5. Therefore $+5$ and -5 are the solutions to the equation.

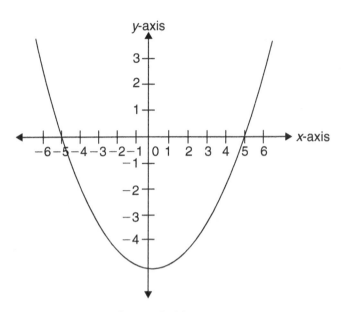

Figure 3.12

Example 29   Solve for x: $2x^2 + 5x - 3 = 0$

Solution: We'll use the factoring method. By expressing $2x^2 + 5x - 3$ as a product of two binomials, we get $(2x - 1)(x + 3) = 0$. This means that $2x - 1 = 0$ and $x + 3 = 0$. Thus, the two solutions are $x = \dfrac{1}{2}$ and $x = -3$. Figure 3.13 shows that the function $y = 2x^2 + 5x - 3$ crosses the x-axis at $\dfrac{1}{2}$ and -3, which are the two solutions to the equation.

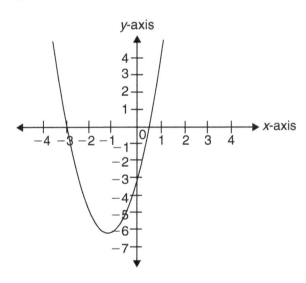

Figure 3.13

Example 30 Solve for x: $x^2 - 10x + 4 = 0$

Solution: Since this equation cannot be factored, we can use a method called "completing the square." This method is shown in the following steps.

1. $x^2 - 10x = -4$ Subtract 4 from each side.

2. $x^2 - 10x + 25 = -4 + 25$ Create a perfect trinomial square by taking half the coefficient of the x term and squaring it. Add this amount (25) to both sides of the equation.

3. $(x - 5)^2 = 21$ Simplify the equation in step 2 and factor the left side.

4. $x - 5 = \pm\sqrt{21}$ Take the square root of each side.

5. $x = 5 \pm \sqrt{21}$ Add 5 to each side.

This means that $5 - \sqrt{21}$ and $5 + \sqrt{21}$ are the solutions. These values are approximately 0.42 and 9.58, respectively, and they represent the x-intercepts of $y = x^2 - 10x + 4$. The graph of this function is shown in Figure 3.14.

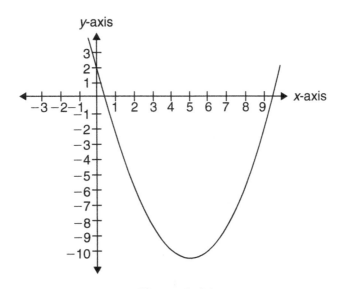

Figure 3.14

Example 31 Solve for x: $2x^2 + 3x - 6 = 0$

Solution: Similar to Example 30, this equation cannot be factored. Using the completing the square method would be rather lengthy, so we will use the Quadratic formula. This formula can be used to solve any quadratic equation, even if factoring is possible.

The Quadratic formula states that for any equation in the form $ax^2 + bx + c = 0$ the solutions are given by $x = \dfrac{-b \pm \sqrt{b^2 - 4ac}}{2a}$. (This formula can be derived by using the completing the square method.) By substituting $a = 2$, $b = 3$ and $c = -6$, we get $x = \dfrac{-3 \pm \sqrt{3^2 - (4)(3)(-6)}}{(2)(2)} = \dfrac{-3 \pm \sqrt{57}}{4}$. Thus, the solutions are $\dfrac{-3 - \sqrt{57}}{4}$ or $\dfrac{-3 + \sqrt{57}}{4}$. These values are approximately -2.64 and 1.14, respectively.

Figure 3.15 shows the graph of the function $y = 2x^2 + 3x - 6$. As expected, the x-intercepts are -2.64 and 1.14.

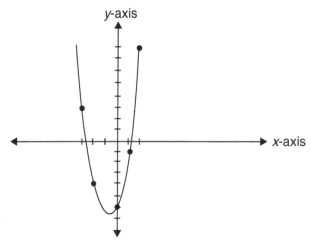

Figure 3.15

Example 32   Solve for x: $2x^2 - 4x + 3 = 0$

Solution: Using the Quadratic formula with $a = 2$, $b = -4$, and $c = 3$, we have $x = \dfrac{-(-4) \pm \sqrt{(-4)^2 - (4)(2)(3)}}{(2)(2)} = \dfrac{4 \pm \sqrt{-8}}{4}$. Since $\sqrt{-8} = i\sqrt{8} = 2i\sqrt{2}$, we can simplify the solutions to $\dfrac{4 \pm 2i\sqrt{2}}{4} = 1 \pm \dfrac{i\sqrt{2}}{2}$.

Figure 3.16 shows the graph of $y = 2x^2 - 4x + 3$.

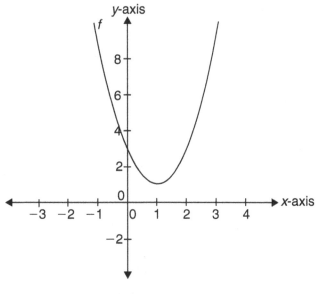

Figure 3.16

NOTE:

The graph of $y = 2x^2 - 4x + 3$ has no x-intercepts. This is expected, since the two solutions are complex numbers. Only real values can correspond to x-intercepts.

The Discriminant of a Quadratic Function

In addition to finding solutions to quadratic equations, part of the Quadratic formula can be used to examine the nature of the roots of the equation. The **discriminant** of the quadratic equation is $b^2 - 4ac$.

(a) If $b^2 - 4ac < 0$, then the roots (solutions) are two complex numbers.

(b) If $b^2 - 4ac = 0$, then there is one real root.

(c) $b^2 - 4ac > 0$, then there are two real roots.

Example 33 If the equation $3x^2 - 5x + c = 0$ has two complex roots, what are the restrictions for c?

Solution: In order for the roots to be complex, we must have $(-5)^2 - (4)(3)(c) < 0$. This inequality simplifies to $25 - 12c < 0$, so the solution is $c > \dfrac{25}{12}$.

Example 34   If the equation $ax^2 + 6x + 2 = 0$ has exactly one real root, what are the restrictions for a?

Solution: In order for there to exist only one real root, we must have $6^2 - (4)(a)(2) = 0$. Then $36 = 8a$, so the solution is $a = 4.5$.

Example 35   Write a quadratic equation for which the two real roots are -2 and 6.

Solution: One possible answer is to create factors of $(x + 2)$ and $(x - 6)$. Then $(x + 2)(x - 6) = 0$, which becomes $x^2 - 4x - 12 = 0$.

Graphical Properties of a Quadratic Function

The graph of a quadratic function, which can be expressed as $f(x) = ax^2 + bx + c$ Creates a curve called a **parabola**. This curve appeared in each of Examples 28 through 32. Another useful form of a quadratic function is $f(x) = a(x - h)^2 + k$ where a, h, and k are constants and $a \neq 0$. In this form, the vertex of the parabola is given by the point (h, k). If $a > 0$, the vertex is the lowest point of the curve. If $a < 0$, the vertex is the highest point of the curve. If the curve has a lowest point, then it is said to open upward; in a similar manner, if the curve has a highest point, then it is said to open downward. Each parabola has an **axis of symmetry**, which is a line that contains the vertex and divides the parabola into two equivalent parts. The equation of the axis of symmetry is $x = h$.

Example 36   What is the vertex and the equation of the axis of symmetry of $f(x) = 2(x + 4)^2$?

Solution: This function can be written as $f(x) = 2(x + 4)^2 + 0$. Thus, the vertex is located at $(-4, 0)$ and the equation of the axis of symmetry is $x = -4$.

NOTE:

> Since $a > 0$, this parabola has its lowest point at the vertex.

Example 37 Identify the vertex and axis of symmetry of $f(x) = -3(x-1)^2 - 2$. Then graph the function.

Solution: The vertex is located at $(1, -2)$ and the equation of the axis of symmetry is $x = 1$. Additionally, since the value of a (-3) is less than zero, the graph must open downward. Figure 3.17 shows the graph and the axis of symmetry.

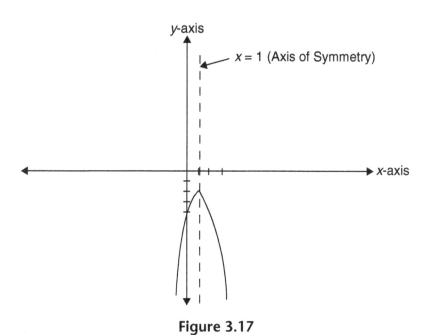

Figure 3.17

Solving Systems of Linear Equations

There are several methods for solving systems of linear equations including elimination (also referred to as the addition/subtraction method), substitution, and graphing).

Matrices can also be used, but will not be addressed in this chapter. A linear system can have one solution, infinitely many solutions, or no solution. An example of each method will be provided.

If the equations represent the same line (i.e. the same slope and same y-intercept) then they are referred to as **dependent** equations and thus every point on the line is a solution of the system. For such a system, there are an infinite number of solutions. An example would be

$$\begin{cases} x + 3y = 5 \\ 2x + 6y = 10 \end{cases}$$

A system is termed **consistent** if there is only one solution and **inconsistent** if it does not have a solution.

Example 38   Find the solution to the following system of equations.

$$\begin{cases} 2x - y = 8 \\ x + y = 7 \end{cases}$$

Solution: By using the **elimination method**, we can add the two equations.

$$\begin{array}{l} 2x - y = 8 \\ \underline{x + y = 7} \\ 3x = 15 \\ x = 5 \end{array}$$

Substituting 5 in for x in either of the given equations, we can find y. By substituting in $x + y = 7$, we get $5 + y = 7$; so $y = 2$. The solution is the point $(5, 2)$.

NOTE:

We could have solved Example 38 by the **substitution** method. Using one equation, we express one variable in terms of the other variable. Then we substitute this expression in the other equation. For example, solving $x + y = 7$ for y, we get $y = 7 - x$. Then substituting $7 - x$ for y in the equation $2x - y = 8$ leads to $2x - (7 - x) = 8$. This equation simplifies to $2x - 7 + x = 8$. Further simplification leads to $3x = 15$, so $x = 5$. Using this value we then substitute it into $y = 7 - x$ to get $y = 2$. The solution to the system is the point $(5, 2)$.

We can also use the **graphing method**. Below is the graph of each equation showing the point of intersection. If you have a graphing tool such as a graphing calculator, put both equations in slope-intercept form and enter them into your calculator.

The equations is example 38 in slope-intercept form are $y = 2x - 8$ and $y = -x + 7$. Figure 3.18 shows the graph of the two lines and their intersection point of (5, 2).

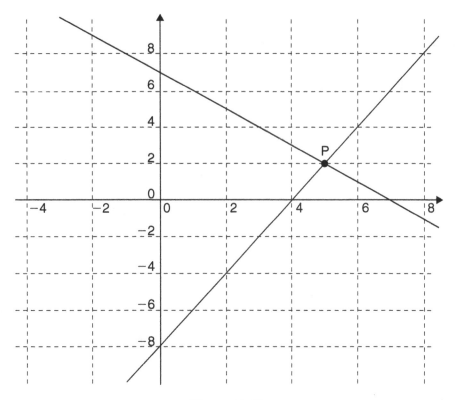

Figure 3.18

Example 39   Solve the following system of equations by the elimination method.

$$\begin{cases} 2x - 3y = 7 \\ 3x + y = 5 \end{cases}$$

Solution: In order to use the elimination method, our goal will be to multiply one (or both) of the equations by a constant such that one of the variables is eliminated when these resulting equations are added or subtracted. In this case if we multiply the second equation by 3, then y will be replaced by $3y$. Then we add the equations together to eliminate y and solve for x. Once we solve for x, we can substitute that value into either of the two given equations to find y.

$$2x - 3y = 7$$
$$\underline{9x + 3y = 15}$$
$$11x = 22$$
$$x = 2$$

Now by substituting $x = 2$ into the first equation, we get $2(2) - 3y = 7$ and then $y = -1$. Thus the solution to the system is $(2, -1)$. You may also want to graph these equations to confirm you results.

Example 40   Solve the following system of equations by the elimination method.

$$\begin{cases} 5x + 3y = 9 \\ 2x - 4y = 14 \end{cases}$$

Solution: We can multiply the top equation by 4 and multiply the bottom equation by 3. In this way, each of the equations will contain the term $12y$. The original two equations become

$$20x + 12y = 36$$

$$6x - 12y = 42.$$

By adding these new equations, we get $26x = 78$. Thus, $x = 3$. We can substitute $x = 3$ into either of the original equations. By choosing $5x + 3y = 9$, we have $(5)(3) + 3y = 9$. Then $3y = 9 - 15 = -6$. Thus, $y = -2$. The solution to the system is $(3, -2)$.

Example 41   Solve the following system of equations.

$$\begin{cases} 2x - y = 3 \\ 8x - 4y = 1 \end{cases}$$

Solution: A quick way to solve this system is to write each equation in the form $y = mx + b$. Then the top equation becomes $y = 2x - 3$ and the bottom equation becomes $y = 2x - \dfrac{1}{4}$. Since these equations have the same slope, they represent parallel lines. Parallel lines do not intersect, so there is no solution.

NOTE:

> Another approach would be to multiply the top equation by 4, so that it becomes $8x - 4y = 12$. Now subtract the bottom equation from $8x - 4y = 12$ to get $0 = 11$. Since $0 = 11$ is always false, there is no solution.

Applications of Equations, Relations, and Functions

While this chapter has focused on procedures and processes related to algebraic thinking along with connections between mathematical concepts, another area that is essential is the application of these concepts, processes, and procedures to real world situations. Here are several examples that apply the concepts related to both linear and nonlinear functions within real world contexts.

Use the following information for Examples 42 − 45.

Water was released at a constant rate into a vat such that when measured at time intervals 2 minutes apart for 10 minutes, the following heights in inches were recorded. Assume that the trend in the table continues.

Time (in minutes)	Height (in inches)
0	0
2	12
4	24
6	36
8	48
10	60

Example 42 Graph the data, using h to represent the height in inches as the dependent variable and using t to represent the time in minutes as the independent variable.

Solution: Figure 3.19 shows the graph of a line, with the points (0, 0), (2, 12), (4, 24), (6, 36), (8, 48), and (10, 60).

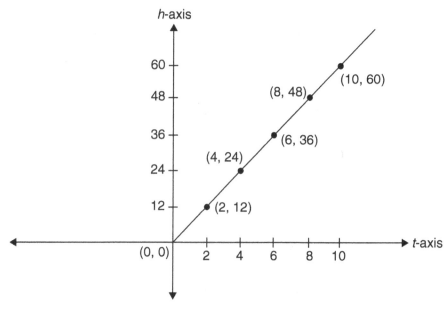

Figure 3.19

Example 43 Write an equation that would give the height in inches at any given time.

Solution: Note that the height is increasing at a constant rate of 12 inches for every 2 minutes, which reduces to 6 inches per minute. Therefore, the slope is 6. Then $h = 6t + b$, where b is the h-intercept. Since (0, 0) belongs to this equation, we can see that $b = 0$. Thus, the equation is $h = 6t$.

Example 44 What would be the height of the water after 25 minutes?

Solution: $h = (6)(25) = 150$ inches.

Example 45 How long will the water have been running when the height reaches 10 feet?

Solution: Change 10 feet to 120 inches. Then $120 = 6t$, so $t = 20$ minutes.

Example 46 Fencing is needed to enclose a rectangular region adjacent to a barn. How much fencing is needed for this region of 60 square yards if one side (width) is the barn and the length is 3 yards greater than the width?

Solution: Figure 3.20 shows the rectangular region.

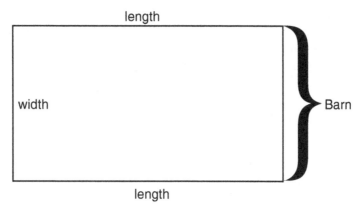

Figure 3.20

Let w represent the width and l represent the length. Since the length is 3 yards greater than the width, we can write $l = 3+w$. Using the area formula for a rectangle, we know that $w(3+w)=60$, which is equivalent to $w^2 + 3w - 60 = 0$. Using the quadratic formula, and eliminating any negative solutions, we find that $w = \dfrac{-3+\sqrt{3^2 - (4)(1)(-60)}}{2} = \dfrac{-3+\sqrt{249}}{2} \approx 6.39$ yards, which means that the length is approximately 9.39 yards. The total fencing consists of two lengths and one width, which becomes $(2)(9.39) + 6.39 = 25.17$ yards.

Example 47 Determine the amount of money, to the nearest dollar, that Marty should invest in a money market account that provides an annual rate of 5% compounded quarterly if he wants to have $8000 in the account at the end of 10 years.

Solution: Use the compound interest equation, $A = P\left(1+\dfrac{r}{n}\right)^{nt}$ where A is the final amount, P is the principal or initial investment, r is the annual interest rate, t is the number of years or the term, and n is the number of times interest is paid or the divisions within the term. Then $8000 = (P)(1 + \frac{0.05}{4})^{(4)(10)}$, which simplifies to $8000 = (P)(1.0125)^{40}$. Since $(1.0125)^{40} \approx 1.6436$, $P = \frac{\$8000}{1.6436} \approx \$4867$.

Use the following information for Examples 48–51.

The cost of mailing a letter is $0.44 for the first ounce and $0.24 for each additional ounce or portion thereof up to a maximum of one pound (16 ounces). For any letter that weighs more than one pound, there is a flat rate of $5.00.

Example 48   Describe this piecewise function algebraically.

Solution: Let $p(x)$ represent the cost function. This piecewise function can be split into three portions, as shown below.

$$p(x) = \begin{cases} \$0.44, \textit{if } 0 < x \leq 1 \\ \$0.44, + (\$0.24)(x-1), \textit{if } 1 < x \leq 16 \\ \$5.00, \textit{if } x > 16 \end{cases}$$

Example 49   Represent this function graphically.

Solution: Figure 3.21 illustrates this function.

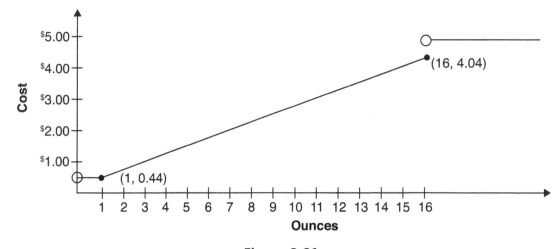

Figure 3.21

Example 50   What is the cost of mailing a letter that weighs 12 ounces?

Solution: Using the second part of the function, the cost is $0.44 + ($0.24)(12 − 1)= $0.44 + $2.64 = $3.08.

Example 51   If a letter costs $2.12, what is the domain of values that can represent the weight (in ounces) of this letter?

Solution: We use the equation $2.12 = $0.44 + ($0.24)(x − 1). This equation simplifies to $2.12 = $0.44 + $0.24x − $0.24, which becomes $1.92 = $0.24x. Then x = 8. But eight ounces is not the only answer. We need to be aware that if the letter weighs any amount over 7 ounces and less than 8 ounces, its price is computed as if it were exactly 8 ounces. Thus, the weight of the letter, in ounces, can be expressed as $7 < x \le 8$.

Example 52   A local middle school sold 896 tickets to their championship football game. The price of a ticket for a student was $5.50 and a ticket for adults was $7.00. The total receipt of ticket sales for the game was $6038. How many of each type of ticket were sold?

Solution: Let s represent the number of student tickets sold and a represent the number of adult tickets sold. We can set up two equations with one representing the total number of tickets sold and the other the total amount in sales.

$s + a = 896$

$5.50s + 7a = 6038$

Multiply the top equation by 7 to get $7s + 7a = 6272$. Now, subtracting the second equation from this new equation yields $1.5s = 234$, so $s = 156$. Substituting this value of s into the first equation, we get $156 + a = 896$. Then, $a = 740$. Thus, there were 156 student tickets and 740 adult tickets.

Direct Variation

We can state that **y varies directly as** *x* if both variables either increase or decrease proportionally. This means that if the *x* value doubled, then the *y* value must also double. Similarly, if the *x* value were reduced to one-third of its value, the *y* value must also be reduced to one-third of its value. It should be mentioned that if *y* varies directly as *x*, then it is also true that *x* varies directly as *y*. Let's introduce some notation. We will use x_1 to represent the first *x* value and x_2 to represent the second *x* value.

Likewise, let y_1 and y_2 represent the first and second *y* values, respectively. Then the proportion we can use to show direct variation is $\dfrac{x_1}{x_2} = \dfrac{y_1}{y_2}$.

Note that this equation can also be written as $\dfrac{x_1}{y_1} = \dfrac{x_2}{y_2}$. Also, we can write $y = kx$, where *k* is called the **constant of proportionality**.

The table that was used for Examples 42 − 45 represents an example of a direct variation between the variables *h* and *t*. In Example 43, we found that $h = 6t$. This implies that we could write the proportion $\dfrac{t_1}{t_2} = \dfrac{h_1}{h_2}$.

Example 53   The cost for cleaning a carpet varies directly as the carpet's area. Suppose that the cost for cleaning an area of 30 square feet is $75. What is the cost for cleaning an area of 50 square feet?

Solution: Let the *x*'s represent the areas, and let the *y*'s represent the cost. We know each of the areas, but we don't know the second cost (y_2).

Then, dropping the units of square feet and dollars, we can write $\dfrac{30}{50} = \dfrac{75}{y_2}$.

Cross-multiplying, $30y_2 = 3750$. So, $y_2 = \$125$.

Example 54   The number of miles a car can travel varies directly as the number of gallons of gas that it uses. When the car travels 35 miles, it uses 1.8 gallons of gas. To the nearest hundredth of a gallon, how many miles could this car travel using 3.2 gallons of gas?

Solution: Let the x's represent the gallons of gas and let the y's represent the number of miles traveled. Then we can write $\dfrac{1.8}{3.2} = \dfrac{35}{y_2}$. Then, $1.8y_2 = (3.2)(35) = 112$. So, $y_2 = 62.22$ miles.

Example 55 Suzanne is hosting a huge party. From previous experience, she knows that 200 pounds of potato salad can feed 300 people. If Suzanne orders 125 pounds of potato salad, how many people will that amount feed, if each person gets an equal portion?

Solution: Let the x's represent the number of people, and let the y's represent the number of pounds of potato salad. Then, since x_2 is unknown, we can write $\dfrac{300}{x_2} = \dfrac{200}{125}$.

This means $200x_2 = 37{,}500$. Solving, $x_2 = 187.5$. In this case, we must round <u>down</u>, so the answer is 187 people. We cannot feed 0.5 of a person!

SPECIAL NOTE:

In Example 55, the answer <u>must</u> be a whole number, and even though 187.5 usually rounds off to 188, the 125 pounds of potato salad will <u>not</u> suffice for 188 people. We are given the fact that each person will get the same portion, so that there certainly could be some potato salad left over after serving 187 people. (In fact, there would be $\dfrac{1}{3}$ pound of potato salad left over.)

Inverse Variation

We can state that **y varies inversely as x** if when one variable increases, the other variable decreases proportionally. This means that if the x value is doubled, then the y value must be divided by 2. Similarly, if the x value were reduced to one-third of its value, the y value must be tripled. It should be mentioned that if y varies inversely as x, then it is also true that x varies inversely as y. We will use the same notation as we used in the section on direct variation: x_1 represents the first x value, and x_2 represents the second x value. Likewise, let y_1 and y_2 represent the first and second y values, respectively. Then the proportion we can use to show inverse variation is $\frac{x_1}{x_2} = \frac{y_2}{y_1}$. Use extra care when applying this proportion; the first y value belongs on the <u>bottom</u> of the right-hand fraction. As in direct variation problems, it is not important which quantity is assigned to the x's and which quantity is assigned to the y's. However, you must be consistent within the problem.

Example 56   In going from City A to City B, a car traveling at an average speed of 45 miles per hour can cover this distance in 33 minutes. If speed varies inversely as time, to the nearest tenth of a minute, how many minutes would this trip take if the car were traveling at 40 miles per hour?

Solution: Let the x's represent the speeds in miles per hour, and let the y's represent the time in minutes. We know each of the speeds, but we don't know the second time (y_2). Then, dropping the units of miles per hour and minutes, we can write $\frac{45}{40} = \frac{y_2}{33}$. (Remember that the first y value belongs on the <u>bottom</u> of the right-hand fraction.) Cross-multiplying, we get $40y_2 \doteq (45)(33) = 1485$. Then $y_2 = 37.1$ minutes.

Example 57   In order to hold a large picnic, each person has agreed to pay the same amount of money. If 60 people attend, each person will pay $15. The number of people attending varies inversely as the cost per person. What will be the cost per person if only 50 people attend?

Solution: For this example, let the x's represent the number of people, and let the y's represent the cost in dollars. The proportion is $\frac{60}{50} = \frac{y_2}{15}$. Then $50y_2 = 900$, so $y_2 = \$18$.

Example 58   At Learning Tree University, the tuition charged per student varies inversely as the number of students. This year, the student enrollment is 5200 and the tuition is $800 per student. The university forecasts that the student enrollment for next year will be 5500. To the nearest dollar, what will the tuition per student next year be?

Solution: Let the x's represent the student enrollment, and let the y's represent the tuition per student. The proportion is $\dfrac{5200}{5500} = \dfrac{y_2}{800}$. Then $5500y_2 = 4{,}160{,}000$, so $y_2 \approx \$756$.

Graphing Inequalities on the Number Line

Using the number line, we can look at the order of real numbers m and n such that $m < n$, This relationship describes the set of real numbers where m is less than n. Another way to express this relationship is $n > m$, which means the set of real numbers where n is greater than m. If we write $m \leq n$, we are referring to the real numbers where m is less than or equal to n. Geometrically, $m < n$ if and only if m lies to the left of n on the real number line. Endpoints are not included if the relationship includes the "less than" symbol or the "greater than" symbol, and an open circle is used for the endpoints.

In examples that use the "less than or equal" or "greater than or equal" symbols, the endpoints are included, and a darkened black dot is used for the endpoints.

Example 59 Describe the subset of real numbers represented by each inequality by graphing it.

a. $a < 5$ b. $a \geq -4$ c. $-3 < a \leq 2$

Solutions:

a.

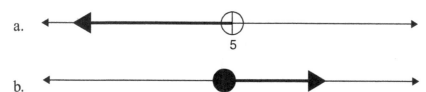

b.

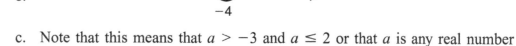

c. Note that this means that $a > -3$ and $a \leq 2$ or that a is any real number between -3 and 2.

Graphing Linear Inequalities

These inequalities involve x and y in the traditional coordinate plane. They are often used to model real-life problems such as those related to product consumerism, nutrition, and investments.

We begin with two definitions. The **right half-plane** is represented by the region that lies to the right of the y-axis. Similarly, the **left half-plane** is represented by the region that lies to the left of the y-axis. Note that the y-axis does not lie in either half-plane. Figure 3.22 illustrates these two half-planes.

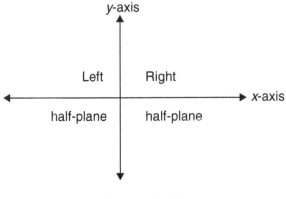

Figure 3.22

An example of a graph that lies entirely in the right-half plane would be $x > 3$. In the xy-coordinate plane, the set of points that satisfy this inequality would be any ordered pair in which the x value is greater than 3. Note that there is no restriction on the y value.

Figure 3.23 shows the graph of $x > 3$.

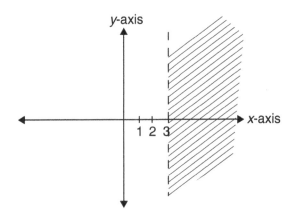

Figure 3.23

Note that the graph of $x > 3$ is represented by a dotted line. This means that any point on this dotted line is <u>not</u> part of the solution to $x > 3$.

As a second example, the graph of $x \leq -2$ lies entirely in the left half-plane. Since the inequality includes the equal sign, a solid line is used in graphing. This is shown in Figure 3.24.

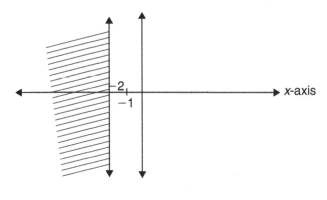

Figure 3.24

Note that the solid line represents points that do belong to the solution of $x \leq -2$.

Example 60   Graph the solution for the inequality $3x + y \leq 7$.

Solution: First, solve this inequality for y, yielding $y \leq -3x + 7$. The second step is to graph the equation $y = -3x + 7$. A quick way to graph this line would be to select two values of x, then find the corresponding y values. By selecting $x = 0$ and 1, we determine the two points to be (0, 7) and (1, 4). Finally, since we want all y values less than or equal to $-3x + 7$, we shade the section of the plane that lies below this solid line. (The line is solid because the inequality includes the equal sign.) Figure 3.25 shows the solution.

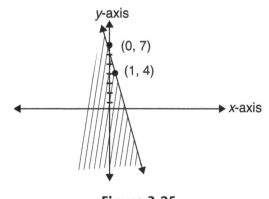

Figure 3.25

Example 61   Graph the system of inequalities $\begin{cases} 2x + y \le 4 \\ x - 3y < 2 \end{cases}$

Solution: Solving the first inequality for y leads to y $\le -2x + 4$. To graph the corresponding equation $y = -2x + 4$, let's use the x values of 1 and 2. The two selected points are $(1, 2)$ and $(2, 0)$. If we call the graph of $y = -2x + 4$ line l_1, we will shade the region below the solid line for l_1. Figure 3.26 shows the solution thus far.

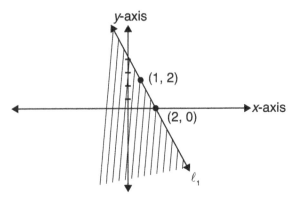

Figure 3.26

Now, in solving the second inequality for y, we first subtract x to get $-3y < -x + 2$. Next, divide by -3 and remember to reverse the inequality sign. This yields $y > \dfrac{1}{3}x - \dfrac{2}{3}$, so the associated equation is $y = \dfrac{1}{3}x - \dfrac{2}{3}$. We'll use x values of 5 and -1. The points to be graphed are $(5, 1)$ and $(-1, -1)$. Since the inequality is a "greater than" symbol, we will shade the region above the dotted line, which we will call l_2. The graph is shown in Figure 3.27.

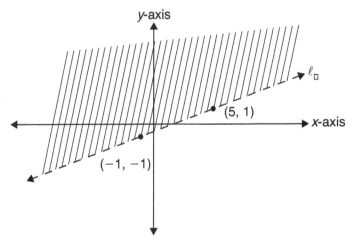

Figure 3.27

The last step is to place these two lines on the same coordinate axes and graph the intersection of the two regions obtained in Figures 3.26 and 3.27. Thus, the solution appears as shown in Figure 3.28.

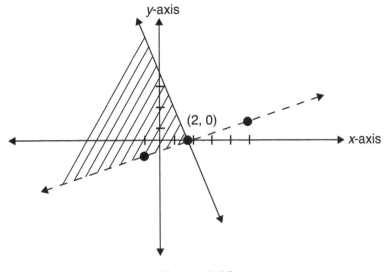

Figure 3.28

Notice that the point (2, 0) represents the intersection of the lines $y = -2x + 4$ and $y = \dfrac{1}{3}x - \dfrac{2}{3}$.

Graphing Quadratic Inequalities

The principles for graphing quadratic inequalities are very similar to those for graphing linear inequalities. We solve the corresponding equation for y. Use a solid curve for $\leq$ or $\geq$ or a dotted curve for $<$ or $>$. Finally, the inequality reveals whether we shade the region above or below the curve. You recall that the graph of a quadratic equation is a parabola.

Example 62 Graph the inequality $2x^2 - y < 8$.

Solution: Rewrite this inequality as $y > 2x^2 - 8$. The next step is to graph the parabola $y = 2x^2 - 8$ as a dotted curve. Since the inequality states "greater than," shading the region above the dotted curve will represent our solution. To get a general sketch for the equation, we can use the x

values of $-2, -1, 0, 1$, and 2. Then the five points of the graph are $(-2, 0)$, $(-1, -6)$, $(0, -8)$, $(1, -6)$, and $(2, 0)$. Figure 3.29 shows the solution.

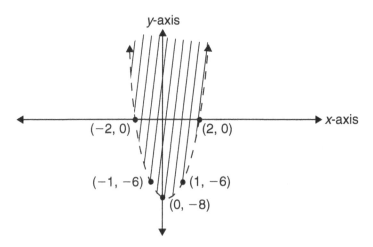

Figure 3.29

Example 63   Graph the following system: $\begin{cases} x^2 + y^2 \leq 9 \\ y \leq \dfrac{1}{2}x + 1 \end{cases}$

Solution: This system contains both a linear inequality and a quadratic inequality.

We recall that the graph of $x^2 + y^2 = 9$ is a circle with center at $(0, 0)$ and a radius of 3.

A few convenient points we can use for graphing are $(0, 3)$, $(0, -3)$, $(3, 0)$, and $(-3, 0)$. Since the inequality is $\leq$, we need to make a solid circle and shade the region inside the circle as shown in Figure 3.30.

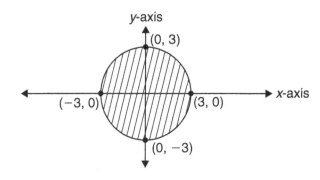

Figure 3.30

For the inequality $y \le \frac{1}{2}x + 1$, we graph the solid line $y = \frac{1}{2}x + 1$, and then shade the region below it. Let's use the points (0, 1) and (2, 2), so that the shaded region appears as shown in Figure 3.31.

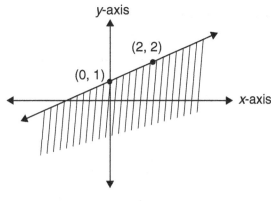

Figure 3.31

As in Example 61, the last step is to merge these graphs together. Figure 3.32 illustrates the solution region.

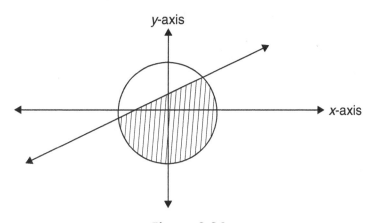

Figure 3.32

Example 64   Graph the following system: $\begin{cases} 2x^2 + y \le 2 \\ x \le 1 \\ y \ge 0 \end{cases}$

Solution: The required shaded region is the intersection of three graphs. Let's attempt to develop the solution with a single set of coordinate axes. The line $x = 1$ is a vertical line that lies 1 unit to the right of the y-axis.

The line $y = 0$ is the x-axis. Thus far, the solution region is confined to the section of the coordinate plane that lies above the x-axis and to the left of the line $x = 1$. For the inequality $2x^2 + y \leq 2$, we first change it to $y \leq -2x^2 + 2$. Next, we graph the parabola $y = -2x^2 + 2$ by choosing x values of $-2, -1, 0, 1,$ and 2. The five reference points of the parabola are $(-2, -6), (-1, 0), (0, 2), (1, 0),$ and $(2, -6)$. Finally, our solution region must lie below the parabola, above the x-axis, and to the left of the line $x = 1$. Figure 3.33 illustrates the required region.

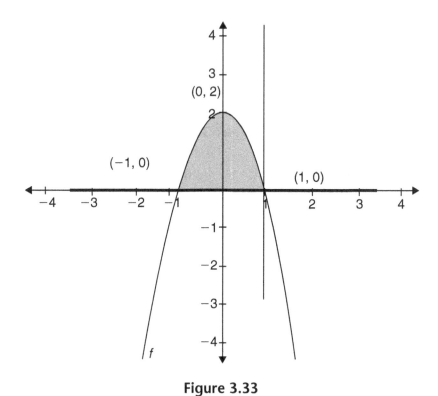

Figure 3.33

Example 65   Given the following system of inequalities $\begin{cases} -2x + y \geq 4 \\ y < 0 \\ -x + 2y \leq -4 \end{cases}$, determine which one(s) of the points $(-2, 1), (-1, -2),$ and $(-5, -6)$ belong to the solution region.

Solution: The point $(-2, 1)$ automatically does not satisfy the second inequality, since $1 < 0$ is false.

Substituting the point $(-1, -2)$ into the first inequality, we get $(-2)(-1) + (-2) = 0 \geq 4$, which is false. Thus, $(-1, -2)$ does not satisfy this system of inequalities.

Lastly, we substitute $(-5, -6)$ into each inequality. In the first inequality, $(-2)(-5) + (-6) = 4 \geq 4$, which is true. Since $-6 < 0$, the second inequality is also true. For the third inequality, $-(-5) + (2)(-6) = -7 \leq -4$, which is true. Our conclusion is that of the three given points, only the point $(-5, -6)$ satisfies all three inequalities.

NOTE:

By graphing the system in Example 65, we can easily spot other points that belong to the solution region, such as $(-7, -9)$ and $(-10, -15)$.

Foundations of Calculus

While middle school mathematics does not usually address formal calculus that includes work with derivatives, integrals, and limits, there are several concepts that are addressed in middle school that provide the foundation for some of these concepts. Among these are ideas concerning limits, rate of change, area, and volume.

Activities that make use of paper folding and other hands-on approaches aid in formulating ideas about limits. For example, one could explore the box problem where you are given a square grid of paper and asked to design an open box by cutting out the corner square grids. First take one square from each corner and then fold up to make a box, then take two, then take three, etc. By determining the volume of each box, looking at a table of values and perhaps graphing the collected data, one can begin to get a sense of maximums, minimums, and limits from this informal approach.

Limits

There are several terms related to calculus concepts that may be helpful to define and illustrate. A **limit** refers to a value that something (such as a function) approaches and either reaches or comes infinitely close to reaching. In everyday life speed limit signs are a good example. When the sign reads, "Speed Limit 70 mph," one knows that you can drive up to, but are not to exceed, 70 mph. You are not supposed to exceed the limit!

Consider folding a piece of paper in half, recording the number of sections made, folding in half again and recording sections made, and continue folding in half. Theoretically, one can continue to fold the paper in half indefinitely, although in reality there is a physical limit to how many times an individual can fold a sheet of paper! Interesting patterns evolve such as $f(x) = 2^n$ would represent the total number of rectangles formed on the sheet on a particular fold, n. Each section would be the fraction $\frac{1}{2^n}$. Using limit notation we could say that $\lim_{x \to \infty} \frac{1}{2^n} = 0$ where n is a positive integer greater than 0. This would be an example of the limit of a function, which approaches zero but never actually equals zero. In general, functions can (a) have limits, (b) not have a limit, or (c) have limits only at certain points. Even when middle school students graph a function such as $f(x) = \frac{1}{x}$, they can visualize a limit since the graph shows that the graph of the function gets infinitely close to both axes but never reaches either. The graph of $f(x) = \frac{1}{x}$ is shown below in Figure 3.34.

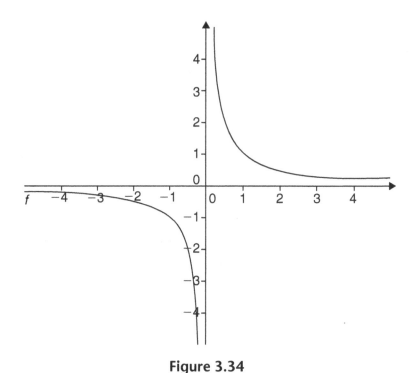

Figure 3.34

Average rate of change

An **average rate of change** is similar to slope and can be positive, negative, or zero. It is actually the slope of the secant line at a point on a nonlinear graph. For a nonlinear graph whose slope changes at each point, the average rate of change between any two given points $(x, f(x))$ and $(y, f(y))$, is the slope of the line through those two points and is calculated as $\dfrac{f(y) - f(x)}{y - x}$.

Example 66   The function $R = 25.71t^3 - 99.65t^2 + 405.2t - 190$ where $5 \le t \le 10$, represents a model for the estimated revenue R (in billions of dollars) from sales of digital videos from 2005 to 2010. What is the average rate of change of the model from 2005 to 2010?

Solution: This quantity can be found by calculating the slope of the secant line through the points $(5, f(5))$ and $(10, f(10))$, which by substitution become $(5, 2558.5)$ and $(10, 19{,}607)$. Thus, the average rate of change is $\dfrac{19{,}607 - 2558.5}{10 - 5} = 3409.7$.

Derivatives

A **derivative** is the *instantaneous* rate of change of a function $f(x)$ and can be written as $\dfrac{dy}{dx}$ or as $\dfrac{\Delta y}{\Delta x}$ (read "delta y over delta x"). It can be viewed as the slope of the tangent line to the curve $y = f(x)$ at a point $(x, f(x))$. Often $f'(x)$ is used to denote the first derivative and is read "f prime of x." A **second derivative** would be written as $f''(x)$, and it would represent the instantaneous change of the first derivative. The process of finding a derivative is called **differentiation**. One real-world application would be using the first derivative to represent velocity and the second derivative to represent acceleration. The actual techniques for differentiation of functions are beyond the scope of this book.

Integration

The reverse of differentiation is **integration**, which is basically finding the sum of the rectangular regions that are subdivided under a given curve. This is equivalent to finding the area under a curve, bound by the x-axis and two vertical lines. The symbol $\displaystyle\int_a^b$ is used to indicate the integral over the interval with endpoints of $x = a$ and $x = b$. Thus, $\displaystyle\int_a^b f(x)\,dx$ represents the integral of a function $f(x)$ between the limits a and b. As with the discussion on derivatives, the actual integration techniques are beyond the scope of this book.

With respect to middle school mathematics, if a student wanted to estimate the area under the curve $f(x) = -2x^4 + 3x^3 + 2x^2 - 1$ and bound by the x-axis then the student might consider dividing the section into shapes for which they do know the area (such as a rectangle or trapezoid) to get a good approximation. Of course, the smaller the divisions, the better the approximation is to the actual area. Figure 3.35 represents the graph of $f(x) = -2x^4 + 3x^3 + 2x^2 - 1$.

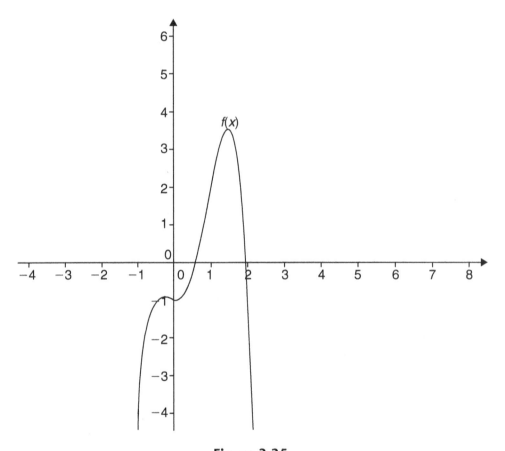

Figure 3.35

Differentiation and integration are inverses of each other. Together, they form the basis for the Fundamental Theorem of Calculus. That is, if a continuous function (one with no "holes") is integrated and then differentiated, the result is the original function.

Quiz for Chapter 3

1. What is the quotient of $24a^6b^3 \div 6a^2b$?

   (A) $4a^4b^2$

   (B) $4a^3b^3$

   (C) $8a^4b^2$

   (D) $4a^2b^2$

2. Solve for all values of x: $x^2 - 6x + 25 = 0$.

   (A) $4 \pm 3i$

   (B) $7i$

   (C) $12i$

   (D) $3 \pm 4i$

3. Which function represents a shift of 2 units to the right for the parent function $f(x) = |x|$?

   (A) $f(x) = |x| - 2$

   (B) $f(x) = |x - 2|$

   (C) $f(x) = |x| + 2$

   (D) $f(x) = |x + 2|$

4. The graph below shows the intersection of two lines l_1 and l_2 and a shaded region. For which system of inequalities would the shaded region represent the solution?

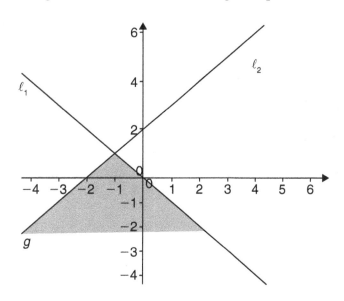

(A) $\begin{aligned} x+y &\geq 0 \\ x-y &\geq -2 \end{aligned}$

(B) $\begin{aligned} x+y &\leq 0 \\ x-y &\leq -2 \end{aligned}$

(C) $\begin{aligned} x+y &\geq 0 \\ x-y &\leq -2 \end{aligned}$

(D) $\begin{aligned} x+y &\leq 0 \\ x-y &\geq -2 \end{aligned}$

5. What is the y-intercept of the line that passes through the points $(-4, 12)$ and $(2, 0)$?

    (A) 4

    (B) 2

    (C) -2

    (D) -4

6. Determine which graph represents the following function with the indicated domain.

$$\begin{cases} f(x) = x, 0 \leq x \leq 2 \\ f(x) = 2, 2 < x < 6 \\ f(x) = 2x - 10, 6 \leq x \leq 10 \end{cases}$$

(A)

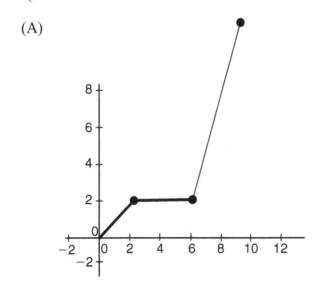

(B)

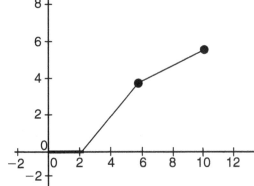

(C)

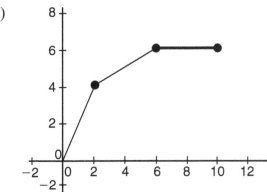

(D)

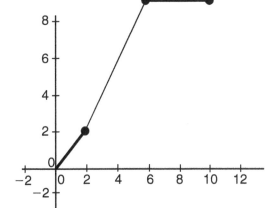

7. Which of the following equations represents a line that is perpendicular to the graph of $5x - 4y = 9$ and contains the point $(-3, 3)$?

(A) $y = \dfrac{-4}{5}x - \dfrac{3}{5}$

(B) $y = \dfrac{5}{4}x + \dfrac{3}{5}$

(C) $y = \dfrac{-4}{5}x + \dfrac{3}{5}$

(D) $y = \dfrac{5}{4}x - \dfrac{3}{5}$

8.   Determine how many solutions the given system of equations will have.
$$\begin{cases} x + 3y = 0 \\ 2x + 6y = 5 \end{cases}$$

(A)   1 unique solution

(B)   2 solutions

(C)   No solution

(D)   Infinitely many solutions

9.   Wally can process 16 invoice orders in 44 minutes. Assuming that the number of invoice orders that he can process varies directly with time, how many minutes would he need to process 36 invoice orders?

(A)   115

(B)   99

(C)   82

(D)   64

10.   Jolene is buying gasoline for her car. If the price of gasoline were $2.75 per gallon, she would have enough money in her wallet to buy 8 gallons of gas. However the price of gasoline is $2.95. To the nearest hundredth, how many gallons of gasoline can she buy?

(A)   7.22

(B)   7.46

(C)   7.94

(D)   8.58

Solutions

1. (A)

$$24a^6b^3 \div 6a^2b = \frac{24a^6b^3}{6a^2b^3}$$ By dividing 24 by 6 and then subtracting the exponents of the like variables we get $4a^4b^2$.

2 (D)

Using the quadratic formula with $a = 1$, $b = -6$, and $c = 25$ we get

$$x = \frac{-(-6) \pm \sqrt{(-6)^2 - 4(1)(25)}}{2(1)} = \frac{6 \pm \sqrt{-64}}{2} = 3 \pm 4i.$$

3. (B)

The graph of $f(x) = |x|$ is show below. Answer choice (B) moves the graph two units to the right and is shown on the graph as well. Answer choice (A) moves the parent function down 2 units. Answer choice (C) moves it up two units. Answer choice (D) moves the parent function two units to the left. You can check by using a graphing calculator!

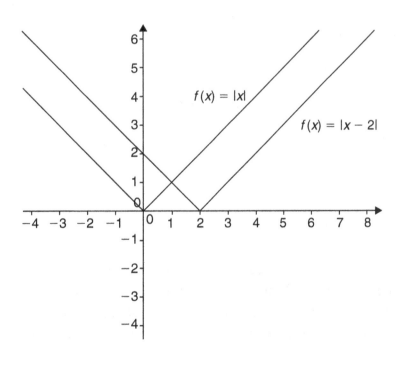

4. (D)

The equation $x + y = 0$ has a slope of -1 and a y-intercept of 0. So $x + y \leq 0$ must correspond to line l_1. Similarly, the equation $x - y = -2$ has a slope of 1 and a y-intercept of 2. So $x - y \geq -2$ must correspond to line l_2. Rewrite the two inequalities as $y \leq -x$ and $y \leq x + 2$. Therefore, the shaded region lies below each line.

5. (A)

The slope equals $\dfrac{0 - 12}{2 - (-4)} = \dfrac{-12}{6} = -2$. The equation of the line then is $y = -2x + 4$. For $x = 0$, $y = 4$. Thus 4 is the y-intercept.

6. (A)

When $0 \leq x \leq 2$, we find that $0 \leq y \leq 2$. Our answer choices are now narrowed down to either (A) or (D). When $2 < x < 6$, the y value is 2. This requirement eliminates answer choice (D). Furthermore, when $6 \leq x \leq 10$, we must have $2 \leq y \leq 10$, which is satisfied by answer choice (A).

7. (C)

Write the original equation as $y = \dfrac{5x}{4} - \dfrac{9}{4}$. Then the slope of a line perpendicular to the original line is $\dfrac{-4}{5}$, because it is the negative reciprocal of the slope of the given equation. The equation then becomes $y = \dfrac{-4}{5}x + b$. Substituting $(-3, 3)$, we get $3 = (-\dfrac{4}{5})(-3) + b$, which means that $b = \dfrac{3}{5}$, and the equation perpendicular to given line passing through $(-3, 3)$ is $y = \dfrac{-4}{5}x + \dfrac{3}{5}$.

8. (C)

Graphically, since the two equations have the same slope but different y-intercepts, there will be no intersection. They represent parallel lines. Another method would be to double the first equation so that it becomes $2x + 6y = 0$. By subtracting the second equation, the result is $0 = -5$. Since this statement is impossible, there is no solution.

9. (B)

Let x represent the number of minutes required. Then $\dfrac{16}{36} = \dfrac{44}{x}$. Cross-multiplying leads to $16x = 1584$. Thus, $x = 99$.

10. (B)

The cost of gasoline varies inversely as the number of gallons. Let x represent the number of gallons of gas she can buy. Then $\dfrac{2.75}{2.95} = \dfrac{x}{8}$. Cross-multiplying, we get $2.95x = 22$. Thus, $x \approx 7.46$.

CHAPTER

Geometry and Measurement

4

Introduction

This chapter focuses on Domain III Competencies 008–011 related to measurement ideas and geometric concepts. This domain analyzes the structure of Euclidean and transformational geometry through both two and three-dimensional shapes, their characteristics, and relationships. This includes the development of an axiomatic system of geometry, development of a variety of relationships and formulas in measurement, and an examination of the Cartesian coordinate system. The domain requires the teacher to understand the role of representations and proofs in developing geometric thinking.

Undefined Terms

The development of Euclidean geometry through its axiomatic structure gives learners a foundation for not only understanding plane and solid geometric concepts, but also for understanding Non-Euclidean geometry through the interesting developments in history related to the famous "fifth postulate." In this section, we will begin with what are often referred to as undefined terms, point, line, and plane. We will use those terms to develop postulates and theorems in order to understand properties, characteristics, and relationships among many geometric figures.

Point: A point has no dimension and is represented by a dot and named with a capital letter.

Line: A line has one-dimensional length and is represented as an infinite sequence of connected points with arrows on each end to indicate infinity; that is, it extends in both directions without ending. There are two commons ways to name a line. One way is using two points on the line and writing it with a line symbol above it (as two points determine a line). The second way is to use a lower case letter that labels the entire line. Figure 4.1 illustrates point A , a line with points B and C (written as $\overleftrightarrow{BC}$ or $\overleftrightarrow{CB}$), and a line l. A line contains an infinite number of points.

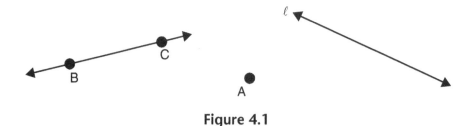

Figure 4.1

Plane: A plane has two dimensions, usually identified as length and width. A plane extends infinitely in both directions. When drawn on a two-dimensional surface, such as this page, it looks like a floor that is slanted (like a parallelogram) to give it the appearance of dimension. An axiom or postulate that serves as an accepted statement concerning a plane is that through any three points not on one line (that is three **non-collinear** points) there exists exactly one plane, named by a capital letter such as P, as shown in Figure 4.2. A plane contains an infinite numbers of lines. (Recall that **collinear** points are points on the same line and **coplanar** points are points in the same plane.)

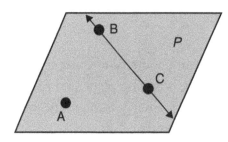

Figure 4.2

Defined Terms

Line segment: A line segment is a subset or part of a line that has two endpoints; it is finite in length. It is named using the two endpoints and a line segment symbol above these two points. In Figure 4.3, there is a line segment with endpoints R and S, which can be written as $\overline{RS}$ or $\overline{SR}$. When it is written as RS or as SR without the line segment symbol, it refers to the distance between the two points.

Figure 4.3

The **midpoint** of a segment is the point that is equidistant from each endpoint and thus forms two congruent segments. A segment bisector is any point, line, line segment, ray, or plane that intersects the segment at its midpoint. In Figure 4.4, M is the midpoint of $\overline{PQ}$ so that $\overline{PM} \cong \overline{MQ}$ (also expressed as $PM = MQ$), where $\cong$ is a symbol referring to **congruency**, and the use of the equal sign means the distance between the points is equivalent. Line s bisects $\overline{PQ}$.

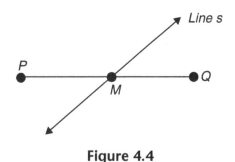

Figure 4.4

Ray: A ray is a subset or part of a line that has one endpoint and goes infinitely in one direction. It is named using its endpoint and one other point on the ray with a ray symbol over the two letters. Remember that in naming a ray, the first letter must be its endpoint. Figure 4.5 illustrates ray $\overrightarrow{MN}$ with endpoint M. Note that this ray cannot be named $\overrightarrow{NM}$, as this would indicate a ray with endpoint N going through M indefinitely in that direction.

Figure 4.5

Angle: An angle is the union of two different rays with the same endpoint. An angle can be named in several different ways, but all use the angle symbol $\angle$. One way is to use three letters where the middle letter is the common endpoint of the two rays (also know as the **vertex** of the angle) and a point from each **side** (ray) of the angle. The angle in Figure 4.6 can be named either $\angle XYZ$ or $\angle ZYX$ because point Y is the vertex. An angle can also be named by its vertex if there is only one angle in the diagram, and it is clear which angle is being named. In this case, the angle in Figure 4.6 can be named $\angle Y$. Sometimes an angle is named by a number that is written in the interior of the angle. In this case it could be named $\angle 1$.

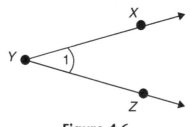

Figure 4.6

An angle is classified according to its measure. If its measure is less than 90°, it is an **acute** angle. If the angle is more than 90° but less than 180°, then it is an **obtuse** angle. If it is 90°, then it is a **right** angle. An angle whose measure is 180° forms a straight line and is classified as a **straight** angle. An angle that is greater than 180º but less than 360º is called a **reflex** angle. An angle can be measured with a protractor to find the measure of the angle.

An **angle bisector** is a ray that divides an angle into two angles that are congruent, which means they have the same measure. In Figure 4.7, $\overline{TV}$ bisects $\angle RTS$ such that $\angle RTV \cong \angle STV$; that is $m\angle RTV = m\angle STV$.

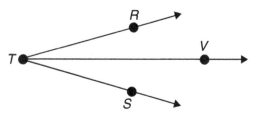

Figure 4.7

Other terms and relationships associated with angles are complementary, supplementary, and adjacent. **Complementary** angles are two angles whose measures add up to 90°. Two angles are **supplementary** if their measures add up to 180°. Two angles are **adjacent** if they share a common vertex and side but no interior points. When two lines intersect they form adjacent angles as well as **vertical angles**. Vertical angles (also called opposite angles) are congruent since they are supplementary to the same angle. In Figure 4.8, ∠1 and ∠2 are one of the four pairs of adjacent angles. Note that ∠1 and ∠3 are one of the two pairs of vertical angles. Vertical angles share a common vertex but have sides that form opposite rays.

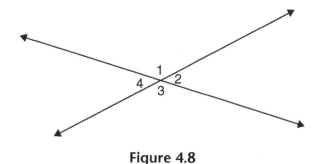

Figure 4.8

Example 1   Referring to Figure 4.7, if $m\angle RTS = 38°$ and $m\angle VTS = 2x - 1$, what is the value of x?

     Solution: Since $\overrightarrow{TV}$ bisects $\angle RTS$, $19 = 2x - 1$. Then $20 = 2x$, so $x = 10°$.

Example 2   Referring to Figure 4.8, if the measure of ∠1 is five times the measure of ∠2, what is the measure of ∠3?

Solution: Let x represent the measure of $\angle 2$ and let $5x$ represent the measure of $\angle 1$. Since these two angles are supplementary, $x + 5x = 180$. This equation simplifies to $6x = 180$, so $x = 30$. This means that $m\angle 1 = (5)(30) = 150°$. Finally, since $\angle 1$ and $\angle 3$ are vertical angles, $m\angle 3 = 150°$.

Example 3   Look at the following diagram.

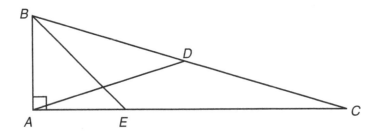

What is the measure of $\angle ADC$, if it is 15° less than twice the measure of $\angle BDA$?

Solution: Let x represent the measure of $\angle BDA$, so that $2x - 15$ represents the measure of $\angle ADC$. Since $\angle ADC$ and $\angle BDA$ are supplementary angles, we can write $x + (2x - 15) = 180$. This equation simplifies to $3x = 195$, so $x = 65$. Thus, $m\angle ADC = (2)(65) - 15 = 115°$.

Example 4   Refer to the diagram in Example 3. how many acute angles have vertices at either A or E?

Solution: Since $\angle A$ is a right angle, each of $\angle BAD$ and $\angle DAC$ must be acute. The only acute angle at E is $\angle BEA$. Thus, there are a total of three acute angles at either A or E.

Triangles

A **triangle** is defined to be the union of three non-collinear line segments joined at endpoints. Each triangle has three vertices, three sides, and three angles. A triangle is named with the triangle symbol followed by the three vertices in any order (note this is different from naming an angle!). See Figure 4.9.

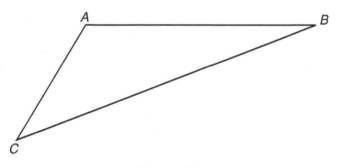

Figure 4.9

There are six ways to name the triangle in this figure, namely $\triangle ABC$, $\triangle ACB$, $\triangle BAC$, $\triangle BCA$, $\triangle CAB$, and $\triangle CBA$.

Based on the lengths of their sides, triangles can be classified as scalene, isosceles, or equilateral. By angle measure, they can be classified as acute, obtuse, or right. The definitions follow with some associated properties that can be proven using congruent triangle relationships (to be discussed later in this chapter).

Scalene Triangle: A triangle in which no two sides are congruent. An associated characteristic is that no two angles are congruent either!

Isosceles Triangle: A triangle with at least two congruent sides equal. An associated property is that the angles opposite the congruent sides are also congruent.

Equilateral Triangle: A triangle that has all three sides congruent. An associated characteristic is that all three angles are also congruent; thus, the triangle can also be referred to as an **equiangular triangle**.

Acute Triangle: A triangle in which each angle measures less than 90°.

Obtuse Triangle: A triangle where one angle measures more than 90°.

Right Triangle: A triangle with one right angle (90°).

Figure 4.10 illustrates these various classifications of triangles.

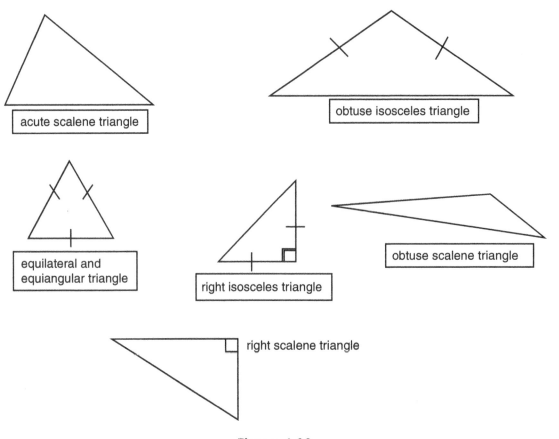

Figure 4.10

Other Segments Related to a Triangle

A **median** of a triangle is a segment that joins a vertex and the midpoint of the opposite side of the triangle. An **altitude** of a triangle is a segment that begins at a vertex and is perpendicular to the opposite side of the triangle. Note that **perpendicular** lines or segments are ones that intersect at a right angle. The symbol $\perp$ is used to indicate perpendicular. In Figure 4.11, $\overline{LP}$ is an altitude since $\overline{LP} \perp \overline{MN}$. $\overline{MT}$ is a median of $\triangle LMN$ since T is the midpoint of $\overline{LN}$.

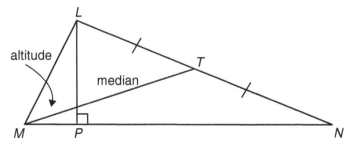

Figure 4.11

Additional important properties related to triangles include:

(a) The longest side of a triangle is opposite the largest angle.

(b) The sum of any two sides of a triangle must be greater than the length of the third side. (Triangle Inequality Theorem)

(c) A segment joining the midpoints of two sides of a triangle is parallel to and one-half the length of the third side of the triangle. (Midsegment Theorem)

Example 5   Two sides of a triangle are 9 and 7. What are the possible integer lengths of the third side?

Solution: Let x represent the length of the third side. Since the sum of the lengths of two sides must exceed the length of the third side, x must be less than $9 + 7 = 16$. So, the maximum integer value of x is 15. If x is the smallest value in the triangle, then $x + 7 > 9$, which means that $x > 2$. Thus, the minimum integer value of x is 3. Therefore, the possible integer lengths of the third side are 3, 4, 5, 6,..., 15. Note that we can also write the inequality $2 < x < 16$, where x is an integer.

Example 6   In $\triangle RST$, if $m\angle R = 72°$ and $m\angle S = 29°$. Which side is the longest and which side is the shortest?

Solution: $m\angle T = 180° - 72° - 29° = 79°$. Since $\angle T$ is the largest angle, $\overline{RS}$ is the longest side. Since $\angle S$ is the smallest angle, $\overline{RT}$ is the shortest side.

Example 7   A teacher provided the following figure:

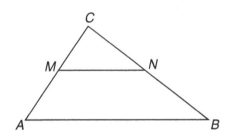

Given that $MN = 4$, $\overline{AB} = 8$, and $AM = MC$, the students were asked if there were any relationship between $\overline{MN}$ and $\overline{AB}$. One student claimed that $MN \parallel AB$. Explain why this conclusion is incorrect.

> **Solution:** There is no evidence that $\overline{MN}$ is a midsegment because we have no information concerning the lengths of $\overline{CN}$ and $\overline{NB}$. If we knew that $CN = NB$, then we could conclude that $\overline{MN}$ is a midsegment, which would imply that $\overline{MN} \parallel \overline{AB}$. Thus, there is no relationship between the lengths of MN and AB.

Polygons

A **polygon** is a figure in a plane that is closed, formed by three or more line segments in which consecutive sides intersect at the endpoints (called **vertices** or **vertex** for singular). A polygon is identified according to the number of its sides and named by listing the vertices in consecutive order starting with any vertex. A **regular polygon** is both equiangular and equilateral.

Polygons can be classified as **convex** or **concave**. A convex polygon is one in which given any two points X and Y that lie inside the polygon, the line segment $\overline{XY}$ must also lie completely inside the polygon. If a polygon is not convex, it is concave. Figure 4.12 shows both a convex and a concave polygon.

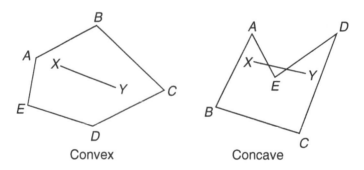

Convex   Concave

Figure 4.12

Below is a table that lists the names of the most common polygons.

Number of Sides	Name of Polygon
3	Triangle
4	Quadrilateral
5	Pentagon
6	Hexagon
7	Heptagon
8	Octagon
9	Nonagon
10	Decagon
11	Hendecagon
12	Dodecagon
n	n-gon

Parallel Lines

Two lines are considered **parallel** if they lie in the same plane but do not intersect. There are numerous angle and triangle relationships that result from this postulate. This is an important idea in Euclidean geometry. As Euclid developed his axiomatic approach, he provided his famous "Fifth Postulate" (so called because it was the 5th postulate he asserted in his famous book *Elements*). The fifth postulate is often stated in school texts as "Given a line and point not on the line, there is exactly one line that can be drawn through the point that is parallel to the given line." This is equivalent to the version usually associated with *Elements*: "If two lines are drawn and intersect a third line such that the sum of the interior angles on one side is less than two 180°, then the two lines must intersect each other on that side at some point."

Examples of non-Euclidean geometry would be those such as **spherical geometry** or hyperbolic geometry. In spherical geometry there are no such parallel lines since all "lines" (that is great circles) intersect one another. This is useful in navigation around the globe. **Hyperbolic geometry** has a curved surface similar to the bell of a trumpet. In this type of geometry, there can be two or more lines parallel to a given line through a point not on the line. It has applications in areas such as topology. Another major difference between Euclidean and non-Euclidean geometries deals with the sum of the interior angles of a triangle. All postulates, theorems, and figures in this book are based on Euclidean geometry.

Angles Formed by Parallel Lines

Given any two parallel lines, a line that intersects them is called a **transversal**.

Figure 4.13 shows the eight angles formed by parallel lines l_1 and l_2, with transversal l_3.

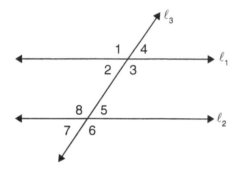

Figure 4.13

Corresponding angles have corresponding positions in relation to l_1 and l_2. The four pairs of corresponding angles are $\angle 1$ and $\angle 8$, $\angle 2$ and $\angle 7$, $\angle 4$ and $\angle 5$, and $\angle 3$ and $\angle 6$.

Alternate interior angles are angles that lie between the two lines and are on opposite sides of the transversal. The two pairs of alternate interior angles are $\angle 2$ and $\angle 5$ and $\angle 3$ and $\angle 8$.

Alternate exterior angles are angles that lie outside the two lines and are on opposite sides of the transversal. The two pairs of alternate exterior angles are $\angle 1$ and $\angle 6$ and $\angle 4$ and $\angle 7$.

Same-side interior angles are angles that lie between the two lines and on the same side of the transversal. The two pairs of same-side interior angles are $\angle 2$ and $\angle 8$ and $\angle 3$ and $\angle 5$.

Same-side exterior angles are angles that lie outside the two parallel lines and are on the same side of the transversal. The two pairs of same-side exterior angles are $\angle 1$ and $\angle 7$ and $\angle 4$ and $\angle 6$.

If the transversal cuts two parallel lines, then the angle pairs formed have special relationships. Usually in middle school and high school, one of the relationships is considered to be a postulate (that is accepted to be true) and the other relationships can be formally proven deductively. Many times students explore these relationships informally or in an inductive manner, then later learn to formally prove the relationships. **Inductive reasoning** is used to examine multiple cases and look for a pattern to determine a potential relationship, i.e., form a conjecture. Students may use measurement tools, drawings, or even dynamic geometry software to conduct explorations and to examine multiple cases. **Deductive reasoning** uses facts, definitions, postulates, and theorems to justify and support statements and steps used to prove a conjecture. For example, suppose we use the following postulate:

Two lines that are cut by a transversal are parallel if and only if corresponding angles are congruent.

We can then prove the following relationships:

(a) Two lines that are cut by a transversal are parallel, if and only if, their alternate interior angles are congruent.

(b) Two lines that are cut by a transversal are parallel, if and only if, their alternate exterior angles are congruent.

(c) Two lines that are cut by a transversal are parallel, if and only if, their same-side interior angles are supplementary.

(d) Two lines that are cut by a transversal are parallel, if and only if, their same-side exterior angles are supplementary.

Example 8   Given $a \parallel b$, prove that alternate interior angles are congruent, that is $\angle 1 \cong \angle 3$.

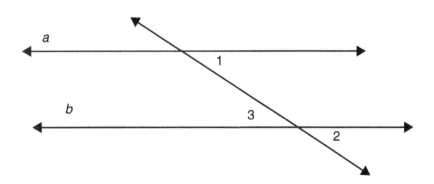

Solution: Using a two-column proof approach we have:

Statements	Reasons
1. a ∥ b	1. Given
2. ∠1 and ∠2 are corresponding angles	2. Definition of corresponding angles
3. ∠1 ≅ ∠2	3. If two lines are parallel the corresponding angles are congruent (Postulate)
4. ∠2 and ∠3 are vertical angles	4. Definition of vertical angles
5. ∠2 ≅ ∠3	5. Vertical Angles are congruent (discussed previously in this chapter)
6. ∠1 ≅ ∠3	6. Transitive Property of Congruency (Similar to transitive property of equality in Chapter 2)

Interior and Exterior Angle Sum Relationships in Polygons

Using the Parallel Postulate and related angle theorems described in this chapter, you can prove many related theorems and corollaries concerning angle sum relationships in polygons. Here are four such theorems.

(a) The sum of the measures of the three interior angles of any triangle is $180°$.

(b) The acute angles of a right triangle are complementary.

(c) The sum of the measures of the interior angles of any convex polygon can be found using the formula $S = (n - 2)(180°)$ where S is the sum of the measures of the interior angles and n is the number of sides of the polygon.

(d) The sum of the exterior angles of any n-gon is $360°$.

Example 9   What is the sum of the interior angles of an octagon?

Solution: Since an octagon has 8 sides, the sum of the angles is $(8 - 2)(180°) = 1080°$.

Let's take a closer look at why this formula works! Draw a convex octagon, as shown in Figure 4.14.

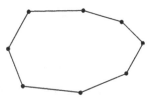

Figure 4.14

Since we know that the sum of the interior angles of a triangle is 180° we can draw the diagonals from one vertex to form the least number of triangles that divide the octagon. This is illustrated in Figure 4.15

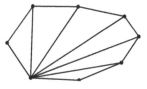

Figure 4.15

We see that we get 6 triangles; thus, we can multiply 6 times 180° to get 1080°. If you want, you can examine this for several different-sided polygons. You will notice that there are always 2 fewer triangles than there are number of sides!

Example 10   Given the diagram below, find the $m\angle LMN$ if $a \parallel b$.

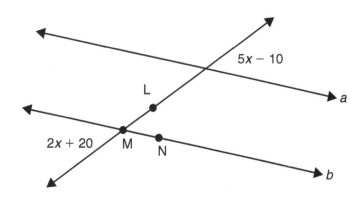

Solution: Since $a \parallel b$, alternate exterior angles are congruent, which means that $2x + 20 = 5x - 10$. Simplifying, we get $3x = 30$, so $x = 10$. Angle LMN and the angle identified with measure $2x + 20$ are vertical angles, so $m\angle LMN = 2x + 20$. Thus, $m\angle LMN = (2)(10) + 20 = 40°$.

Congruent Triangles

It is important to examine the properties, relationships, and theorems related to congruent triangles. **Congruent** triangles are exactly the same size and the same shape. Two triangles are said to be congruent if each of the three sides and angles of one triangle are congruent to the corresponding sides and angles of the other triangle. We use the symbol $\cong$ to represent congruency. For example if we state that $\triangle ABC \cong \triangle DEF$, then this means that $\overline{AB} \cong \overline{DE}, \overline{BC} \cong \overline{EF}, \overline{AC} \cong \overline{DF}, \angle A \cong \angle D, \angle B \cong \angle E, and \angle C \cong \angle F$. One key point is that the order in which the letters are written is important. The congruency must be written in the order of the corresponding vertices. It should also be noted that $\triangle ABC \cong \triangle DEF$ could be written in a different order as long as the correspondence indicated is kept in order. For example $\triangle BAC \cong \triangle EDF$ indicates the same correspondence of vertices, (which means the same correspondence of angles and sides). While it is true that all six congruency relationships are true if the two triangles are congruent, it only takes a minimum of three pairs of congruencies to prove that two triangles are congruent. There are only certain combinations that work to prove two triangles are congruent.

Here is a list of the possible congruency combinations that can be used to prove two triangles are congruent. In each case we are trying to prove that $\triangle ABC \cong \triangle DEF$.

1. <u>Side − Angle − Side (SAS):</u> Two sides of one triangle are congruent respectively to two sides of a second triangle. In addition, the included angles are congruent. In Figure 4.16, $\overline{AB} \cong \overline{DE}$, $\overline{AC} \cong \overline{DF}$, and $\angle A \cong \angle D$.

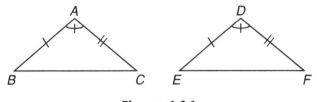

Figure 4.16

2. <u>Angle − Side − Angle (ASA):</u> Two angles of one triangle are congruent respectively to two angles of a second triangle. In addition, the included sides are congruent. In Figure 4.17, $\angle B \cong \angle E$, $\angle C \cong \angle F$, and $\overline{BC} \cong \overline{EF}$.

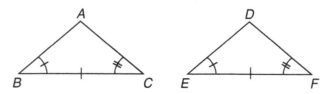

Figure 4.17

3. <u>Side − Angle − Angle (SAA):</u> Two angles of one triangle are congruent respectively to two angles of a second triangle. In addition, a pair of non-included sides are congruent. In Figure 4.18, $\angle B \cong \angle E$, $\angle C \cong \angle F$, and $\overline{AC} \cong \overline{DF}$. Note that SAA could also have been used with $\angle B \cong \angle E$, $\angle C \cong \angle F$, $= \overline{AB} \cong \overline{DE}$ (because $\overline{AB}$ and $\overline{DE}$ are also non-included sides of the congruent angles).

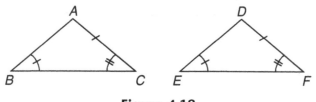

Figure 4.18

SPECIAL NOTE:

> When two pairs of corresponding angles are congruent for two given triangles, <u>any</u> pair of congruent sides will be sufficient to guarantee that the triangles are congruent.

4. <u>Side − Side − Side (SSS):</u> All three pairs of sides of one triangle are congruent respectively to all three pairs of a second triangle. In Figure 4.19, $\overline{AB} \cong \overline{DE}$, $\overline{AC} \cong \overline{DF}$, and $\overline{BC} \cong \overline{EF}$.

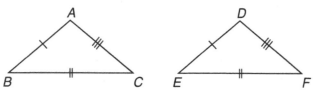

Figure 4.19

Caution: It is important to recognize that certain combinations of congruencies between the parts of two triangles do not imply that the triangles are congruent (although they may be). We'll label these as fallacies.

1. Side − Side − Angle Fallacy (SSA): Two sides of one triangle are congruent respectively to two sides of a second triangle. In addition, a pair of non-included angles are congruent. In Figure 4.20, $\overline{GH} \cong \overline{KL}$, $\overline{GJ} \cong \overline{KM}$, and $\angle H \cong \angle L$. However, these triangles are not congruent.

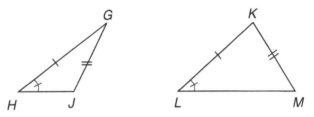

Figure 4.20

2. Angle − Angle − Angle Fallacy (AAA): All three angles of one triangle are congruent respectively to all three angles of a second triangle. In Figure 4.21, $\angle P \cong \angle S$, $\angle Q \cong \angle T$, and $\angle R \cong \angle U$. However, the triangles are not congruent.

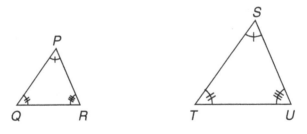

Figure 4.21

Caution: You must be certain that corresponding sides and angles match up when identifying a congruence between two triangles. Consider the two triangles in Figure 4.22.

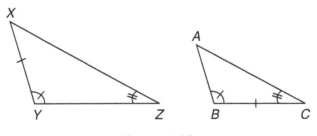

Figure 4.22

Even though $\angle Y \cong \angle B$ and $\angle Z \cong \angle C$, the corresponding sides of $\overline{YZ}$ and $\overline{BC}$ are not congruent. The fact that $\overline{XY} \cong \overline{BC}$, is not sufficient to establish a congruence between these two triangles.

In each of the cases, you may want to experiment with a drawing tool such as Geometer's Sketchpad, or a computer program or application for a graphing calculator to explore these congruent relationships. Another way to explore these theorems is to use tracing paper to examine the corresponding relationships.

Similar Triangles

Consider the second fallacy for congruence that was just discussed, namely Angle-Angle-Angle (AAA). When all three pairs of corresponding angles of two triangles are congruent, the triangles do have a special relationship. They are called **similar** triangles. Actually, we need to show only two pairs of corresponding congruent angles in order to identify similar triangles. The third pair would automatically be congruent because the sum of the interior angles of any triangle is 180°. The symbol ~ is use to indicate similarity between two geometric figures (not just triangles!). Referring back to Figure 4.21, we can write $\Delta PQR \sim \Delta STU$. Additionally, the corresponding sides are in proportion. This means that the ratio of any two corresponding sides must be constant. So, for Figure 4.21, we have $\dfrac{PQ}{ST} = \dfrac{QR}{TU} = \dfrac{PR}{SU}$.

Furthermore, the ratio of corresponding medians, altitudes, midsegments, and angle bisectors will be the same as the ratio of any two corresponding sides. Let's consider Figure 4.23, which is a re-creation of Figure 4.21, and also includes the altitudes $\overline{RB}$ and $\overline{UC}$.

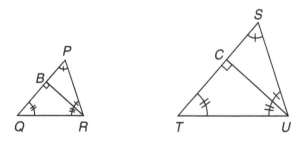

Figure 4.23

The ratio of these altitudes is equal to the ratio of any pair of corresponding sides. Choosing one pair of sides, we can write $\frac{RB}{UC} = \frac{PR}{SU}$. Likewise, the ratio of any pair of corresponding angle bisectors, medians, or midsegments would equal $\frac{PR}{SU}$. (Of course, we could have chosen a different pair of corresponding sides, but the ratio would have the same value.)

Example 11   Given that $\triangle LMN \sim \triangle TUV$ and that $\frac{LM}{TU} = \frac{2}{5}$, what is the value of $\frac{UV}{MN}$?

Solution: Since the triangles are similar, $\frac{MN}{UV} = \frac{LM}{TU} = \frac{2}{5}$.
Thus, $\frac{UV}{MN} = \frac{1}{2/5} = \frac{5}{2}$.

Example 12   Using the information in Example 11, let LQ represent a median of $\triangle LMN$ and TZ represent a median of $\triangle TUV$. If $LQ = 7$, what is the value of TZ?

Solution: By direct substitution, $\frac{2}{5} = \frac{7}{TZ}$. Then by cross-multiplication, $(2)(TZ) = 35$, so $TZ = 17.5$.

Two congruent triangles will have the same area and the same perimeter.

Let's investigate the relationships for perimeter and area of two similar triangles. Our intuitive feeling would be that the ratio of the perimeters of two similar triangles would match the ratio of corresponding sides. This intuitive feeling would be 100% correct!

Suppose one triangle has sides 4, 7, and 9. A second triangle has sides 12, 21, and 27. These two triangles are similar since $\frac{4}{12} = \frac{7}{21} = \frac{9}{27}$, which reduces to $\frac{1}{3}$. The perimeters of these two triangles are 20 and 60; note that $\frac{20}{60}$ is also equivalent to $\frac{1}{3}$.

The ratio of the areas for similar triangles is somewhat different. Look at Figure 4.24, in which $\triangle DEF$ is similar to $\triangle HJK$.

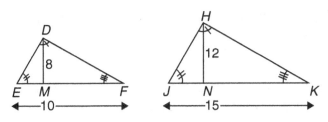

Figure 4.24

The ratio of corresponding sides is $\frac{10}{15}$, which reduces to $\frac{2}{3}$. As expected, the ratio of the corresponding altitudes, $\frac{8}{12}$, also reduces to $\frac{2}{3}$. The area of ΔDEF is $(\frac{1}{2})(10)(8) = 40$ and the area of ΔHJK is $(\frac{1}{2})(15)(12) = 90$. So the ratio of the areas is $\frac{40}{90}$, which reduces to $\frac{4}{9}$. Even though $\frac{2}{3}$ is not equal to $\frac{4}{9}$, we observe that $\left(\frac{2}{3}\right)^2 = \frac{4}{9}$. This would lead us to conclude that for two similar triangles the ratio of the areas is the square of the ratio of corresponding sides. (The proof can be found in most geometry textbooks.) By extension, if we are given two similar triangles, then the ratio of any pair of corresponding sides is equal to the square root of the ratio of the areas.

Example 13   Using the information in Example 11, where the ratio of corresponding sides is $\frac{2}{5}$, if the perimeter of ΔLMN is 12, what is the perimeter of ΔTUV?

Solution: Let x represent the perimeter of ΔTUV. Then $\frac{2}{5} = \frac{12}{x}$. Cross-multiplying leads to $2x = 60$, so $x = 30$.

Example 14   Using the information in Example 11, if the area of ΔTUV is 100, what is the area of ΔLMN?

Solution: Let x represent the area of ΔLMN. Then $(\frac{2}{5})^2 = \frac{x}{100}$. Simplified this equation becomes $\frac{4}{25} = \frac{x}{100}$. Then $25x = 400$, so $x = 16$.

Geometric Constructions Using Compass and Straightedge

There are seven basic constructions that can be performed with just a compass and a straightedge. Historically, compass-straightedge constructions have given mathematicians the opportunities to explore mathematical relationships geometrically and have led to interesting ideas related to straightedge-only constructions as well as "impossible" constructions. Related to teaching middle level mathematics, this connects well to the use of paper folding and computer software construction tools to support student exploration of examining geometric relationships.

Construction 1: Copying a given segment length

Given line segment $\overline{AB}$ and a point C not on the segment, construct a segment congruent to $\overline{AB}$ with C as an endpoint.

> **Solution:** Place the point of your compass at point A and stretch the radius of the compass to point B. Without changing the radius, move the compass to point C and draw an arc. Then select a point on the arc (name it D), and using your straightedge, connect point D to point C. Now you have $AB = CD$ thus $\overline{AB} \cong \overline{CD}$, as shown in Figure 4.25.

Figure 4.25

Construction 2: Perpendicular to a line through a point on the line

Given line l_1 and point P on l_1, construct line l_2 that is perpendicular to l_1 and contains P.

Solution: With your compass, use P as the center of a circle and draw a semicircle so that $\overline{AB}$ is a diameter, where A and B lie on l_1. Figure 4.26 illustrates this construction.

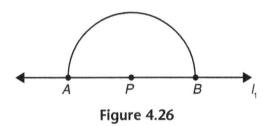

Figure 4.26

Second, use your compass, with each of A and B as a center, and make two intersecting arcs directly above P. Call this intersection point Q. This is shown in Figure 4.27.

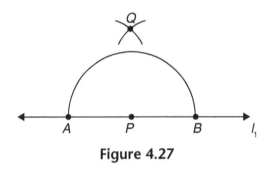

Figure 4.27

Third, draw a line that contains points P and Q. This is the required line l_2. Figure 4.28 shows the final step.

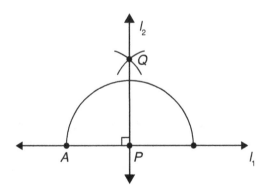

Figure 4.28

Construction 3: Perpendicular to a line through a point not on the line

Given line l_1 and point P not on l_1, construct line l_2 that is perpendicular to l_1 and contains P.

Solution: From point P, use your compass to draw an arc large enough to intersect l_1 at points A and B. Figure 4.29 shows this construction.

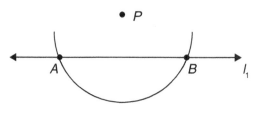

Figure 4.29

Second, use you compass, with each of A and B as a center, and make two intersecting arcs directly below P. Call this intersection point Q. This is shown in Figure 4.30.

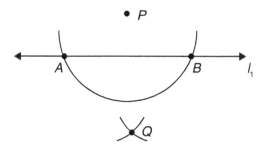

Figure 4.30

Third, draw a line that contains the point of intersection, Q, of the two arcs and point P. This is line l_2 and the construction is complete. Figure 4.31 illustrates this final step.

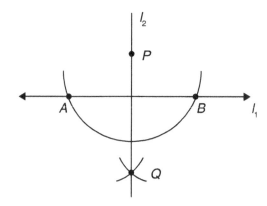

Figure 4.31

Construction 4: **Perpendicular bisector of a line segment**

Given line segment $\overline{AB}$, construct line l that is the perpendicular bisector of $\overline{AB}$.

Solution: From each of points A and B, use your compass to draw an arc both above and below $\overline{AB}$, such that there are two intersecting points, P and Q. The length of the arcs should be the same. Figure 4.32 shows this construction.

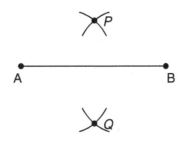

Figure 4.32

Second, draw line l that contains points P and Q. This is the perpendicular bisector of $\overline{AB}$. Figure 4.33 shows the final step.

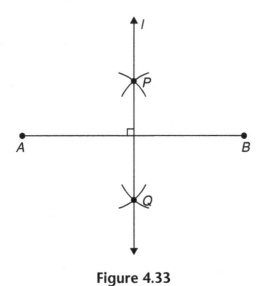

Figure 4.33

Construction 5: Copy an angle

Given ∠*ABC*, and any point *E* not on this angle, construct ∠*DEF* such that ∠*ABC* is congruent to ∠*DEF*.

Solution: Use your compass at point *B* and draw an arc so that it intersects both rays of the angle at points *A* and *C*. Figure 4.34 shows this construction.

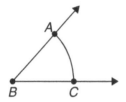

Figure 4.34

Second, draw any ray $\overrightarrow{EF}$, where neither *E* nor *F* are points of ∠*ABC*. Draw the same size arc at point *E* that was used at point *B*. This is shown in Figure 4.35.

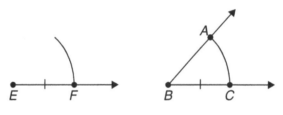

Figure 4.35

Third, using your compass to measure the opening between *A* and *C*, place the compass at point *F* and duplicate this opening on the arc formed at *F*. Call this point *G* on this arc. Figure 4.36 shows the location of point *G*.

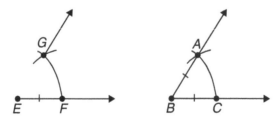

Figure 4.36

Fourth, draw ray $\overrightarrow{EG}$. Then ∠*GEF* is congruent to ∠*ABC*.

Figure 4.37 shows the final step.

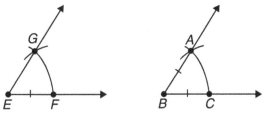

Figure 4.37

Construction 6: Bisect an angle

Given $\angle ABC$, construct ray $\overrightarrow{BD}$ that bisects $\angle ABC$.

Solution: Position your compass at point B and draw an arc to extend from $\overrightarrow{BC}$ to $\overrightarrow{BA}$, as shown in Figure 4.38.

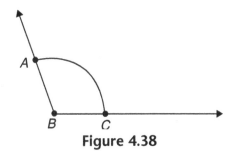

Figure 4.38

Second, construct two arcs of equal size from points A and C so that they intersect at a point D. This is illustrated in Figure 4.39.

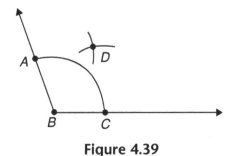

Figure 4.39

Third, draw $\overrightarrow{BD}$, which will be the angle bisector of $\angle ABC$, as shown in Figure 4.40.

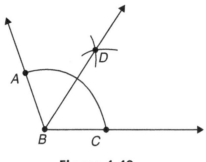

Figure 4.40

Construction 7: Construct a line parallel to a given line

Given any line l_1 and point P not on l_1, construct line l_2 that contains P and is parallel to l_1.

Solution: Draw any line m that contains point P and intersects line l_1 at point A. Figure 4.41 shows line m.

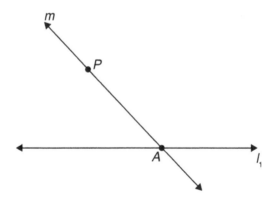

Figure 4.41

Second, using another point B on line l_1, use the techniques of the fifth construction to duplicate $\angle BAC$ at point P. Figure 4.42 shows all steps up to here.

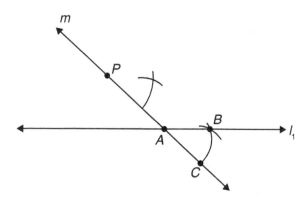

Figure 4.42

Third, complete the construction of the duplicated angle at P to form ray $\overrightarrow{PD}$. Then draw line $\overrightarrow{PD}$ and call it line l_2. This is the required line that is parallel to l_1, as shown in Figure 4.43. (Note that $\angle DPE \cong \angle BAC$.)

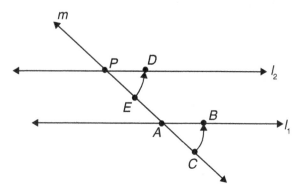

Figure 4.43

It is important to be able to explain or justify why each of the constructions is valid. Most can be justified using congruent triangles. As an example, let's look at Construction 6. You will notice that if you connect A to D and C to D, you form two triangles, $\triangle ABD$ and $\triangle CBD$. We know that $\overline{AB} \cong \overline{BC}$, since they are radii of the same circle. We can determine that $\overline{AD} \cong \overline{DC}$, since they represent radii of equivalent circles. Also, $\overline{BD} \cong \overline{BD}$ (Reflexive property), which means that $\triangle ABD \cong \triangle CBD$ by the Side-Side-Side congruency theorem. Thus, their corresponding parts are congruent. This implies that $\angle ABD \cong \angle CBD$, so that $\overrightarrow{BD}$ bisects $\angle ABC$ by the definition of an angle bisector.

The seven basic constructions can be used to complete many other constructions such as (a) inscribing a circle in a given triangle, (b) circumscribing a circle about a given triangle, (c) finding the centroid (intersection of the medians), and (d) finding the orthocenter (intersection of the altitudes) of a triangle. Additionally, we can construct a variety of different angle measures, such as 30° and 45° degree angles. Moreover, we can construct scalar products, sums, and differences of both line segments and angles.

With respect to geometric figures, these basic constructions can be used to (a) justify congruent triangle relationships, (b) construct equilateral and isosceles triangles, and (c) construct various tangent lines to circles. Let's look at some examples.

Example 15   Given an equilateral triangle, construct a 75° angle using only a compass and a straightedge.

Solution: Each angle of the given equilateral triangle ABC has a measure of 60°. Use Construction 3 to form a perpendicular from B to $\overline{AC}$. Call D the point at which the altitude from B intersects $\overline{AC}$. Since an altitude of an equilateral triangle also serves as an angle bisector, we note that $m\angle ABD = 30°$. Figure 4.44 shows the steps up to here.

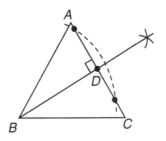

Figure 4.44

Next, we use Construction 6 to bisect $\angle BDA$. This will result in two 45° angles. In Figure 4.45, ray $\overrightarrow{DE}$ bisects $\angle ADB$, which means that $m\angle ADE = 45°$.

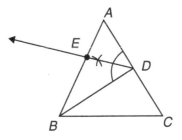

Figure 4.45

Finally, use Construction 5 to copy $\angle ADE$ onto $\overline{BA}$ so that $\angle ABF \cong \angle ADE$. In Figure 4.46, $m\angle DBF = 75°$.

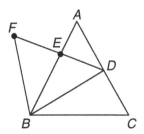

Figure 4.46

Example 16   Given $\triangle LMN$, construct the circle that circumscribes this triangle.

Solution: We need to identify the center of the required circle, which will be equidistant from each of points L, M, and N. The first step is to use Construction 4 to draw the perpendicular bisectors of two of the triangle segments, $\overline{LM}$ and $\overline{LN}$. Figure 4.47 shows these two perpendicular bisectors and their point of intersection, P.

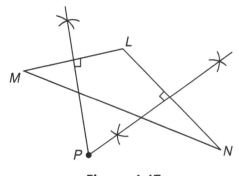

Figure 4.47

Using point P as the center, draw the circle with $\overline{LP}$ as the radius. (Any of $\overline{LP}$, $\overline{MP}$, or $\overline{NP}$ can be used as a radius.) This is the required circle, as shown in Figure 4.48.

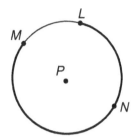

Figure 4.48

Example 17   Construct the line tangent to Circle O at point P.

Solution: We begin with circle O and a point P that lies on O. This is shown in Figure 4.49.

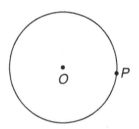

Figure 4.49

Next, use Construction 2 to draw a perpendicular to $\overleftrightarrow{OP}$ through P. Note that $\overleftrightarrow{OP}$ has been extended to accommodate this construction. Finally, $\overleftrightarrow{SP}$ is the required tangent line, as shown in Figure 4.50.

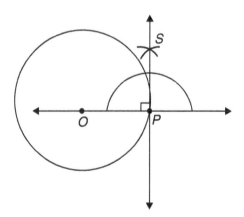

Figure 4.50

Quadrilaterals

While triangles have been discussed in length and various other polygons have been briefly addressed, it is important to further discuss quadrilaterals. A **quadrilateral** is any four-sided figure. There are categories of quadrilaterals that describe their specific properties.

A **parallelogram** is a quadrilateral with both pairs of opposite sides parallel. Additional properties include (a) opposite sides and opposite angles are congruent, (b) consecutive angles are supplementary, and (c) the diagonals bisect each other. These statements can be proven by drawing a diagonal and showing that the triangles formed are congruent. Figure 4.51 shows various types of parallelograms.

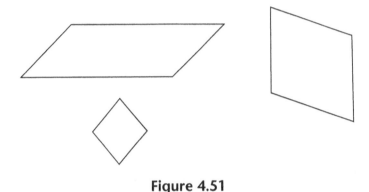

Figure 4.51

If a parallelogram has one right angle, then all its angles will be right angles. This type of parallelogram is called a **rectangle**. Figure 4.52 illustrates a few rectangles. Another property of a rectangle is that its diagonals are congruent.

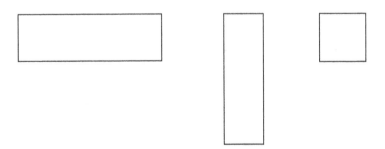

Figure 4.52

A **rhombus** (plural is **rhombi** or **rhombuses**) is a parallelogram with all sides congruent. Figure 4.53 shows three rhombi. Other properties include (a) the diagonals are perpendicular, and (b) the diagonals bisect the opposite angles.

Figure 4.53

A **square** is a parallelogram with all sides congruent and four right angles. This makes it a rhombus and a rectangle; therefore it has all the properties of a parallelogram, a rectangle, and a rhombus! Two examples of squares are shown in Figure 4.54.

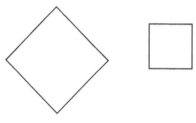

Figure 4.54

A **trapezoid** has exactly one pair of parallel sides. The parallel sides are referred to as bases and the two nonparallel sides are called **legs**. If the two legs are congruent, then it is called an **isosceles trapezoid**. In an isosceles trapezoid, the base angles and diagonals are congruent.

Figure 4.55 illustrates three different trapezoids, the first two of which are isosceles trapezoids.

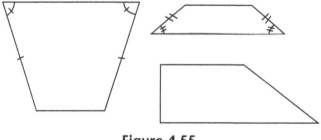

Figure 4.55

You may also recall that the midsegment of a triangle is a segment that joins the midpoint of two sides of the triangle. The **midsegment of a trapezoid** is the segment that joins the midpoint of the legs. It can be proven that the midsegment of a trapezoid is parallel to the bases, and its length is one half the sum of the two bases. This is a great one to explore using patty paper or a dynamic geometry software computer tool, such as Geometer's Sketchpad. In Figure 4.56, we show trapezoid *WXYZ* with midsegment *MN*.

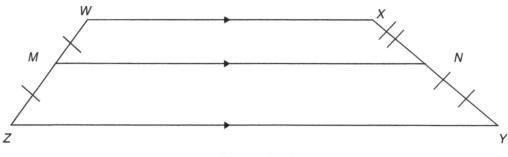

Figure 4.56

A **kite** has two pairs of consecutive congruent sides, but the opposite sides are not congruent. The diagonals of a kite are perpendicular, and exactly one pair of opposite angles is congruent. Figure 4.57 shows a kite for which $TU = TW$ and $UV = WV$.

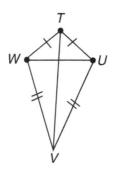

Figure 4.57

Additionally, (a) the longer diagonal ($\overline{TV}$) is the perpendicular bisector of the shorter diagonal ($\overline{WU}$), and (b) $\overline{TV}$ is the angle bisector for $\angle T$ and $\angle V$.

Example 18   The figure shown is a parallelogram. What are the values of *x* and *y*?

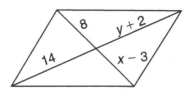

Solution: The diagonals bisect each other, so that $8 = x - 3$ and $14 = y + 2$. Thus, $x = 11$ and $y = 12$.

Example 19 A student is given the information that in quadrilateral $LMNO$, $\overline{LM} \parallel \overline{NO}$ and $\angle LMN$ is a right angle. The student concludes that the quadrilateral must be a rectangle. Explain why the student cannot make this conclusion.

Solution: The figure might be a trapezoid with one right angle, as shown below.

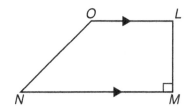

If the figure contained two pairs of parallel sides and one right angle, then the student could have concluded that the figure must be a rectangle.

Example 20 Use a Venn Diagram to show how to classify the quadrilaterals listed below by their properties. Parallelograms, trapezoids, kites, rhombi, rectangles, and squares.

Solution:

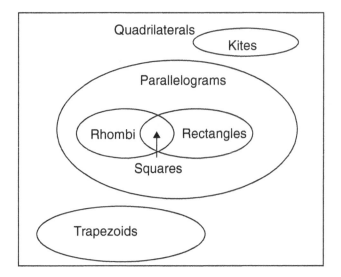

Measurement

The skills and process of measurement are begun early in elementary grades, but often measurement is an area of mathematics for which middle school students still struggle. They have difficulty making decisions about appropriate measurements in context, precision, and application of various formulas and their relationships. In part, this struggle comes from measurement's integral relationship to other content areas such as variables and rational numbers.

Perimeter and Area of Polygons

The **perimeter of a polygon** is the sum of the lengths of the sides, and thus is given in linear units such as inches, feet, or meters. The perimeter of a triangle is found by adding the lengths of the three sides. The properties of special quadrilaterals lend themselves to general formulas that may be helpful when finding perimeter. Let P represent the perimeter.

Perimeter of a rectangle: $P = 2l + 2w$, where l is the length and w is the width.

Perimeter of a square or rhombus: $P = 4s$, where s is the length of the side.

The **area of a polygon** is the number of square units contained within the polygon, and thus is measured in square units such as square inches or square meters. Here is a list of some formulas that are used in middle level mathematics related to the area of polygons:

Triangle: $A = \dfrac{1}{2}bh$, where b is the base and h is the height

Rectangle: $A = lw$, where l is the length and w is the width

Square: $A = s^2$, where s is the length of the side

Parallelogram: $A = bh$, where b is the base and h is the height

Rhombus: $A = \dfrac{1}{2}d_1 d_2$, where d_1 and d_2 are the diagonals

Trapezoid: $A = \dfrac{1}{2}h(b_1 + b_2)$, where h is the height and b_1 and b_2 are the two bases

Interestingly, if you know and understand the formula for finding the area of a rectangle, you can find most area formulas for other polygons! For example, suppose you only knew how to find the area of a rectangle but were asked to find the area of the parallelogram below with base b and height h, shown as Figure 4.58.

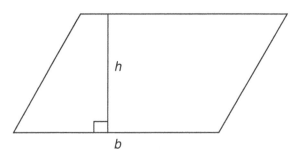

Figure 4.58

If you slide the height to the left such that it forms a right triangle, and then cut it off, you could then slide that triangle to the right, and it would then form a rectangle that would have the same area as the given parallelogram. Since the rectangle area would be bh, then so would the parallelogram, as shown in Figure 4.59.

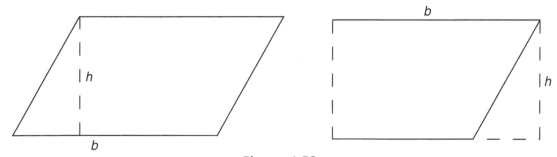

Figure 4.59

Circumference and Area of a Circle

The distance around the circle is called its **circumference**, and it is the same type of linear measurement as the perimeter is in a polygon. One key element related to circles is the use of π (Pi). As noted in Chapter 2, *pi* (denoted with the symbol π) is an irrational number that represents the ratio of the circumference of a circle to its diameter. That is, $\pi = \dfrac{C}{d}$, where C represents the circumference of a circle and d the diameter of that circle. The approximate value of π to 5 decimal places is 3.14159, but in middle school, we often use a two decimal approximation of 3.14 for computational purposes. Another useful approximation for π is the fraction $\dfrac{22}{7}$ (which is approximately 3.14). Remember that these are only approximations, not the exact value of π! Depending on the context, more decimal places in the computation might be appropriate to address error in measurement. We can find the circumference of a circle with the formula $C = \pi d$ or $C = 2\pi r$ where r represents the radius and the diameter d is equal to the length of two radii.

Example 21   If $r = 3$ cm, find the circumference of Circle O.

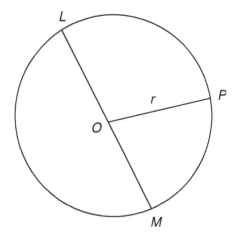

Solution: Using the formula $C = 2\pi r$, we get $C = 2\pi(3\text{cm})$. Thus $C = 6\pi$ cm, or using the approximation of $\pi \approx 3.14$, we get $C \approx 18.84$ cm.

It may important for you to consider an informal investigation to examine the relationship of the circumference of a circle to its diameter. One method that is useful when teaching middle level mathematics is to gather a variety of round objects and have students measure the distance around the object (circumference) and the diameter of each object. Create a recording chart, and have the students record the circumference and diameter for each object. Then the students can determine the ratio $\dfrac{C}{d}$ for each object. Students can then understand that the ratio $\dfrac{C}{d}$ is constant in each case. Be sure they use the same unit of measure for each object (such as centimeters or inches). It is also interesting to have one group of students use inches and a second group use centimeters to see that the ratio is independent of the unit! Following is an example of a recording chart.

Object	Circumference (C)	Diameter (d)	$\dfrac{C}{d}$
Plastic lid			
button			
Frisbee			
Paper plate			

Another idea is to give students a round object and string; then have them use the string to determine how many diameters it takes to go around the circle (that is, its circumference). You could also have the students investigate the ratio $\dfrac{C}{d}$ by using a geometry software tool, such as Geometer's Sketchpad. Any or all of these activities can help students understand circumference and π. Maybe you as a teacher should try it, too!

The **area of a circle** is found using the formula $A = \pi r^2$ where r is the radius of the circle. Informal investigations can help students understand how the formula is derived. One such investigation is to take a circle, slice it like a pie into equal serving pieces and then lay them side by side so that they fit together to form a parallelogram-type figure. Since the area of a parallelogram is found by $A = bh$, you might notice that the base (b) is actually half the circumference of the original circle, and the height (h) is the radius of the circle. Thus, the formula for the area of the circle could be found by substitution to get $A = (\pi r)(r)$, which simplifies to $A = \pi r^2$! Look at Figure 4.60 below:

 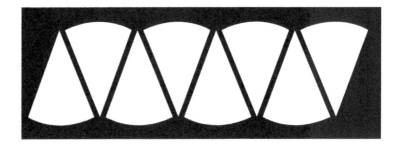

Figure 4.60

The above-mentioned illustration connects to calculus and the idea of limits. While the example shown is only 8 slices, if you were to continue to divide the circle into infinitely smaller slices and align them, the shape would get closer to a rectangle. This would show the relationship between the area of a rectangle (special case of parallelogram) and that of a circle. The length and width of the rectangle formed coincide with half of the circumference of the original circle and the radius, respectively.

Example 22   You have 30 yards of fencing to enclose a rectangular area that is adjacent to a house. You can use the house wall as one side, but will need to enclose the other three sides with fencing. The area should be 100 square yards. Find the length and width of the fenced-in area.

Solution: Let l be the length of the fence side opposite the house wall and w be the width of the fencing needed for the other two sides. Then $30 = 2w + l$ represents the formula for the fencing that is needed and $100 = lw$ is the formula for the area. Solving the first equation for l we get $l = 30 - 2w$. Substituting $30 - 2w$ into the area equation, we get $100 = (30 - 2w)(w)$, which becomes $100 = 30w - 2w^2$. Bringing all terms to one side of the equation, then dividing by 2, we get $w^2 - 15w + 50 = 0$. By factoring the left side, we get $(w - 10)(w - 5) = 0$.

Thus the width can be either 5 or 10 yards. If the width is 5 yards then the length is $30 - 2(5)$ or 20 yards. If the width is 10 yards the length is $30 - 2(10)$ or 10 yards, making it a square. Thus the two possible answers are

(a) 20 yards long by 5 yards wide, or (b) 10 yards long by 10 yards wide.

Example 23   The area of a triangle is 15 cm^2 with a base of 9 cm. Find the height of the triangle.

Solution: Use the formula $A = (\frac{1}{2})(b)(h)$. Then $15 = (\frac{1}{2})(9)(h)$, which simplifies to $15 = 4.5h$. Thus, $h = \dfrac{15}{4.5} = 3\dfrac{1}{3}$ cm.

Example 24   The area of a trapezoid is 372 in^2 with a height of 12 in. If one of the bases is 9 inches, find the length of the other base.

Solution: Use the formula $A = \dfrac{1}{2}h(b_1 + b_2)$. Let b_2 represent the unknown base. By substitution, $372 = \left(\dfrac{1}{2}\right)(12)(9 + b_2)$. Then

$372 = (6)(9 + b_2)$, which simplifies to $372 = 54 + 6b_2$. So, $318 = 6b_2$. Thus, $b_2 = \dfrac{318}{6} = 53\,\text{in.}$

Example 25 An ice-resurfacing machine is used to smooth the ice at a rectangular NHL hockey rink that is 200 feet by 84 feet. If the machine can resurface an area of about 300 square yards in a minute, approximately how many minutes does it take the machine to resurface the entire rink?

Solution: The area of the hockey rink is $(200)(84) = 16{,}800$ square feet. Since there are 9 square feet per square yard, 16,800 square feet is equivalent to $\dfrac{16{,}800}{9} = 1866\dfrac{2}{3}$ square yards. Thus, the number of required minutes is $\dfrac{1866\dfrac{2}{3}}{300} = 6.\overline{2}$ minutes. Thus, it would take just over 6 minutes to resurface the rink. (The exact answer is 6 minutes $13\dfrac{1}{3}$ seconds.)

Example 26 Find the circumference of a round flying disk that has an area of 16π square inches.

Solution: Substituting into the area formula of a circle, we get $\pi r^2 = 16\pi$. Then $r^2 = 16$, so $r = 4$. Thus, the circumference $= (2\pi)(4) = 8\pi$ inches.

Pythagorean Theorem

The **Pythagorean theorem** is used to find a missing length in a right triangle, when the other two sides are known. This theorem states that the sum of the squares of the two legs (shorter sides) is equal to the square of the hypotenuse (the longer side) such that in $\triangle ABC$, $a^2 + b^2 = c^2$. The quantities a and b represent the two legs; c represents the hypotenuse. The Pythagorean theorem is also related to various trigonometric relationships and finding distance in the coordinate plane, both of which will be discussed later in this chapter. Each of a, b, and c represents the side opposite vertices A, B, and C, respectively, as shown in Figure 4.60.

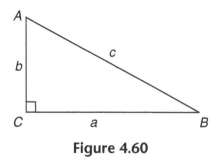

Figure 4.60

One area of interest in middle school mathematics is substantiating this relationship. Often it is shown geometrically using grid paper to form the squares on each side of the triangle. These squares are formed using the length of each side of the triangle. This is shown in Figure 4.61.

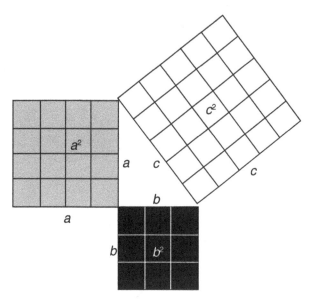

Figure 4.61

Other methods that can be used are the geoboard, grid paper, or a geometric drawing software tool.

Distance Formula

Related to the Pythagorean theorem is the **Distance formula**. This is often helpful when looking at points in the Cartesian coordinate plane discussed in Chapter 3.

Suppose you have two points graphed in the coordinate plane, and you want to find the distance between them. In general if the points are (x_1, y_1) and (x_2, y_2) we can find the distance using the formula

$$D = \sqrt{(x_2 - x_1)^2 + (y_2 - y_1)^2}$$ where D is the distance from (x_1, y_1) to (x_2, y_2).

Example 27   What is the distance between $(-2, 4)$ and $(5, -7)$?

Solution: By substitution, we get $D = \sqrt{(5 - (-2))^2 + (-7 - 4)^2}$

$$= \sqrt{49 + 121} = \sqrt{170} \approx 13.04.$$

In order to understand the connection to the Pythagorean theorem, we'll graph the two points and draw dotted line segments to make a right triangle (the horizontal and vertical lines shown). We can then find the distance for each side and use the Pythagorean theorem to find the length of the hypotenuse. This is shown in Figure 4.62.

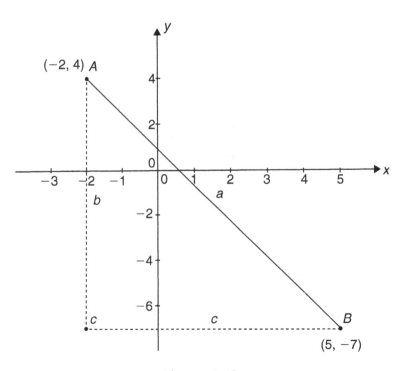

Figure 4.62

We can see that the length of b is 11 by calculating the distance between the y-coordinates of the two points (difference in the y coordinates) and the length of a is 7, which is found by calculating the distance between the x-coordinates (difference in the x coordinates). Essentially, we are using the Pythagorean theorem to find the distance (c) between the two given points.

Applications of the Pythagorean theorem to Special Right Triangles

Figure 4.63 shows a $45° - 45° - 90°$ right triangle. Each of the congruent legs has been labeled as x, and the hypotenuse is labeled c.

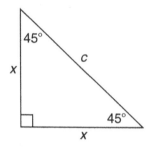

Figure 4.63

We can prove that the hypotenuse is $\sqrt{2}$ times as long as either leg. By the Pythagorean theorem, $x^2 + x^2 = c^2$. Then $2x^2 = c^2$, which means that $c = \sqrt{2x^2} = x\sqrt{2}$.

Figure 4.64 shows a $30° - 60° - 90°$ right triangle. The side opposite $30°$ has been labeled x and the side opposite $90°$ has been labeled why $2x$. The longer side has been labeled b.

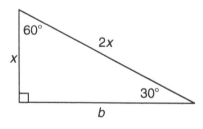

Figure 4.64

Using the Pythagorean theorem, we can prove that the longer leg is $\sqrt{3}$ times as long as the shorter leg. We have $x^2 + b^2 = (2x)^2$, which simplifies to $x^2 + b^2 = 4x^2$. Then $b^2 = 3x^2$, so $b = \sqrt{3x^2} = x\sqrt{3}$.

Basic Trigonometric Functions

For the following three definitions, we are referencing an acute angle in the following right triangle *DEF*, as shown in Figure 4.65.

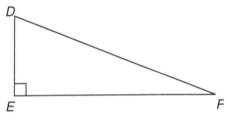

Figure 4.65

The **tangent** function represents the ratio of the side opposite the given angle to the side adjacent to this angle. The tangent of $\angle F$, abbreviated as $\tan \angle F$, equals $\dfrac{DE}{EF}$. Similarly, we could also write $\tan \angle D = \dfrac{EF}{DE}$.

The **cosine** function represents the ratio of the side adjacent to the given angle to the hypotenuse. The cosine of $\angle D$, abbreviated as $\cos \angle D$, equals $\dfrac{DE}{DF}$. Similarly, we could also write $\cos \angle F = \dfrac{EF}{DF}$.

The **sine** function represents the ratio of the side opposite the given angle to the hypotenuse. The sine of $\angle D$, abbreviated as $\sin \angle D$, equals $\dfrac{EF}{DF}$. Similarly, we could also write $\sin \angle F = \dfrac{DE}{DF}$.

Let's look at a few real-world examples in which either the Pythagorean theorem or one of these basic trigonometric functions can be directly applied.

Example 28   On a baseball diamond, the distance between consecutive bases is 90 feet. To the nearest hundredth of a foot, what is the distance from home plate to second base?

Solution: Here is a diagram of a baseball diamond.

The distance from home plate to second base represents the hypotenuse of an isosceles right triangle, with sides of 90 feet. Therefore the required distance is $90\sqrt{2} \approx 127.28$ feet.

Example 29 A 48-foot ladder is leaning against the side of a building at a 46-degree angle from the ground. To the nearest hundredth of a foot, how far is the bottom of the ladder from the base of the building?

Solution: Here is a diagram for illustrative purposes, where d represents the unknown distance.

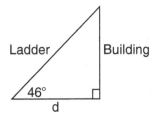

Based on this diagram, we can write $\cos 46° = \dfrac{d}{48}$. Thus, $d = (48)(\cos 46°) \approx 33.34$ feet.

Example 30 A 30-foot tree is casting a 12-foot shadow. To the nearest degree, what is the angle of elevation?

Solution: Here is a general diagram.

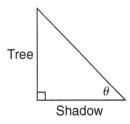

In the diagram, θ represents the angle of elevation. Then $\tan \theta = \dfrac{30}{12} = 2.5$. Thus, $\theta = \tan^{-1}(2.5) \approx 68°$. (Note that the symbol "$\tan^{-1}$" means "inverse tangent.")

NOTE:

These trigonometric functions and inverse trigonometric functions may be found on your TI-30 calculator.

The Unit Circle

We introduce the meaning of an angle in **standard position**. This is an angle whose initial ray lies on the positive *x*-axis. Its terminal ray may lie in any quadrant or on any axis. Angles in standard position are always measured in a counterclockwise direction. Figures 4.66 − 4.69 illustrate various angle measures for angles in standard position.

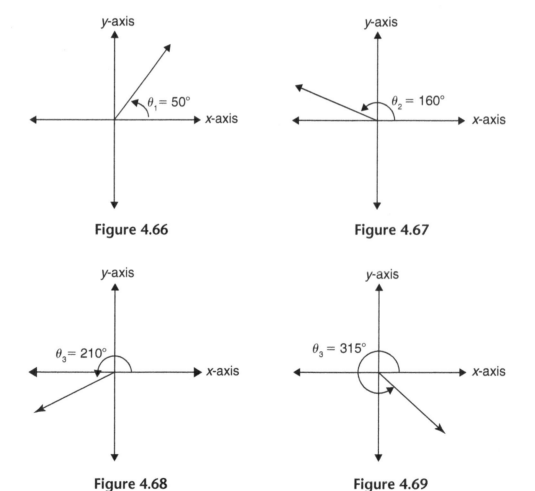

Figure 4.66   **Figure 4.67**

Figure 4.68   **Figure 4.69**

For any angle in standard position, there is a corresponding **reference angle**. This reference angle is the acute angle that is formed by the terminal side and the *x*-axis. Figures 4.70 − 4.73 illustrate the standard position angles (θ_i) and the corresponding reference angles (α_i). Note that when the given angle is acute, the angle in standard position is identical to the reference angle.

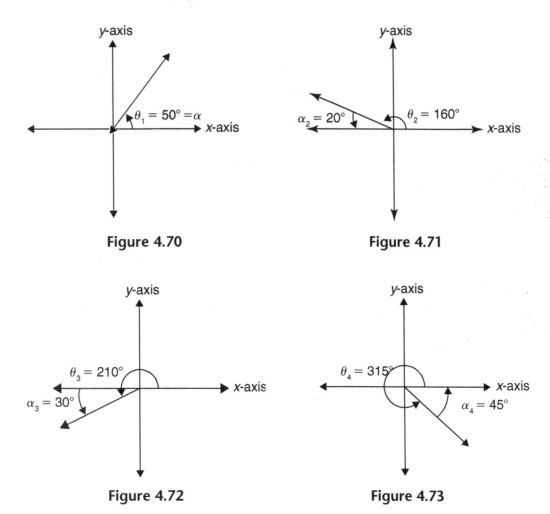

Figure 4.70   Figure 4.71

Figure 4.72   Figure 4.73

The **unit circle** is a circle with radius of 1 and center at (0, 0). Let *P* represent any point on this circle with coordinates (*a*, *b*). Let θ represent an angle in standard position whose terminal ray passes through (*a*, *b*), as shown in Figure 4.74.

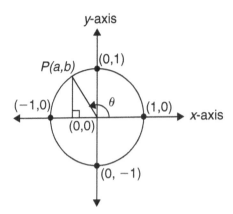

Figure 4.74

Since the hypotenuse is 1, the following identities exist:

$$\sin \theta = b, \cos \theta = a, \text{ and } \tan \theta = \frac{b}{a}.$$

These relationships hold regardless of the quadrant in which point P occurs. The only restriction is that $a \neq 0$ for the tangent ratio. Figures 4.75 and 4.76 illustrate key points on the unit circle. Figure 4.75 shows the xy-coordinates, and Figure 4.76 shows angle measures that correspond to the terminal side of an angle in standard position.

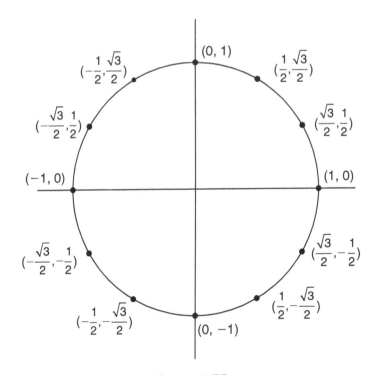

Figure 4.75

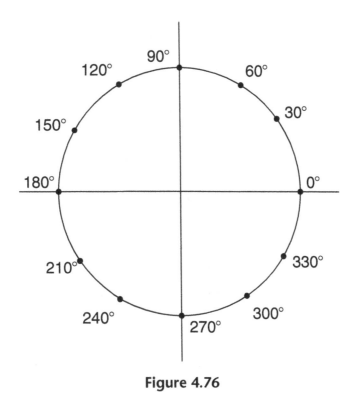

Figure 4.76

Sine and cosine functions can be applied to numerous real-world situations such as sound waves, electrical currents, temperature cycles in weather, ocean tides, and respiratory cycles.

Transformations

Transformations of geometric figures occur when movement or motion is applied to a figure. The result will be a change in size, orientation, and/or direction. There are four different types of transformations that we will consider: translations, reflections, rotations, and dilations.

Translations

A **translation** changes the location but not the size or orientation of a figure. Every point of the original figure is moved the same distance in the same direction along a straight path. Informally, a translation is referred to as a glide. Figures 4.77 and 4.78 illustrate translations. The direction of a translation (movement) is shown with an arrow.

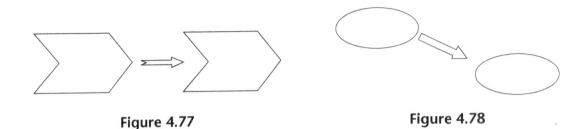

Figure 4.77   Figure 4.78

You can also see this in the *xy*- coordinate plane where a translation moves the given figure a specific distance left or right and up or down such that $(x, y) \rightarrow (x + a, y + b)$ indicates a point (x, y) that has been translated horizontally *a* units and vertically *b* units.

Example 31   Given $\triangle ABC$ with coordinates A: $(-2,5)$, B: $(-5,1)$, and C: $(-1,1)$, what will be the coordinates of the new triangle after the translation $(x, y) \rightarrow (x + 8, y - 3)$?

Solution: Call the new vertices D, E, and F, that result from the translation from A, B, and C, respectively. The translation means changing the three vertices by adding 8 to the *x*-coordinate and subtracting 3 from the *y*-coordinate. The coordinates after the translation become D: $(6, 2)$, E: $(3, -2)$, and F: $(7, -2)$. This translation is shown below.

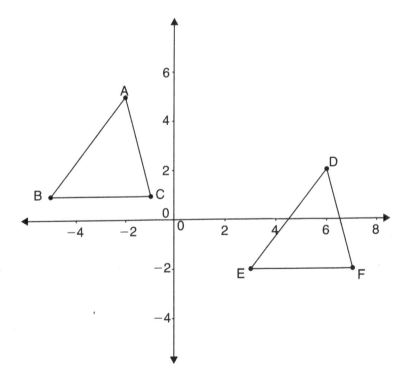

Reflections

A **reflection** (informally referred to as a "flip") of a geometric shape changes location and orientation but not size. A reflection is a mirror image of the shape about a given line called the **axis of reflection**. This can be a horizontal or vertical reflection and within the coordinate plane is typically the x-axis or y-axis. Figures 4.79 and 4.80 illustrate reflections of a line and a trapezoid, respectively. For either figure, the original shape and its reflection are interchangeable. Thus, either figure is a mirror image of the other.

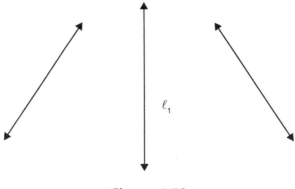

Figure 4.79

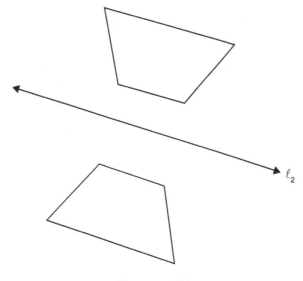

Figure 4.80

In the xy-coordinate system, the points of the reflection can be determined by multiplying either the y or x coordinate by -1 if the figure is reflected about the x-axis or y-axis.

Example 32   The vertices of a quadrilateral are (1, 6), (3, 4), (6, 5), and (5, 8). If this quadrilateral is reflected about the *x*-axis, what will be the coordinates of the reflected quadrilateral?

Solution: The *x*-coordinates remain the same, but the *y*-coordinates are multiplied by −1. The new vertices are (1, −6), (3, −4), (6, −5), and (5, −8).

Example 33   Using the vertices of the original quadrilateral in Example 32, suppose that the quadrilateral is reflected about the *y*-axis. What will be the coordinates of the midpoint of the reflection of the side that contains (1, 6) and (3, 4)?

Solution: The point (1, 6) becomes (−1, 6), and the point (3, 4) becomes (−3, 4). The midpoint of the segment with endpoints (−1, 6) and (−3, 4) is $\left(\dfrac{-1-3}{2}, \dfrac{6+4}{2} \right) = (-2, 5)$.

Rotations

A **rotation** is a movement of a figure by a number of degrees around a point (called the **center of rotation**) either in a clockwise or counterclockwise direction. A rotation changes location and orientation but not size. When rotations are done in the coordinate plane the origin is usually the center of rotation. Let's look at a few examples in the coordinate plane.

Figure 4.81 shows a counterclockwise rotation of 90° about the origin. (The original figure is located in quadrant I.)

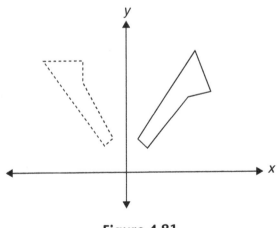

Figure 4.81

Figure 4.82 shows a 90-degree clockwise rotation of line segment l_1 about the origin to become l_2.

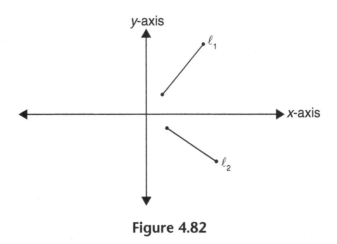

Figure 4.82

Dilations

A **dilation** is a movement that stretches or shrinks a figure. A dilation causes a change in size, but not in orientation. Two key related ideas are the center of the dilation and the **scale factor** of the dilation. The center of the dilation is the point from which the figure is enlarged or shrunk, and the scale factor indicates the ratio of the length of the sides of the original figure to those of the new figure after the dilation.

Example 34 ΔDEF is a dilation of ΔABC by a scale factor of 2. The coordinates of the vertices of ΔABC are $(-2, 1)$, $(1, 1)$, and $(-2, 5)$, and the center of dilation is $(-2, 1)$. What will be the coordinates of the vertices of ΔDEF?

Solution: ΔABC is a right triangle, with a right angle at $(-2, 1)$. The lengths of its sides are 3 and 4. By the Pythagorean theorem, we can verify that the hypotenuse is 5. Using a scale factor of 2 means that the horizontal side of ΔDEF becomes 6 and its vertical side becomes 8. The coordinates of D will match those of point A, namely $(-2, 1)$. The horizontal leg DE is 6 units, so the coordinates of E are $(-2 + 6, 1) = (4, 1)$. The vertical leg DF is 8 units, so the coordinates of F are $(-2, 1 + 8) = (-2, 9)$. Here is the diagram that shows the two triangles.

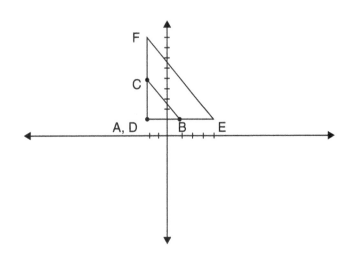

Example 35 Determine whether the transformation illustrated is a translation, rotation, reflection, or dilation. The original triangle is represented by the solid line, and the transformation is represented by the dotted line(s).

a.

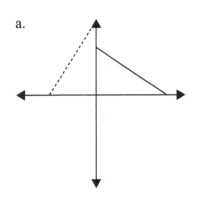

b.

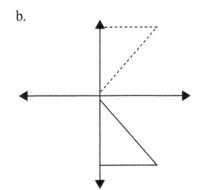

c.

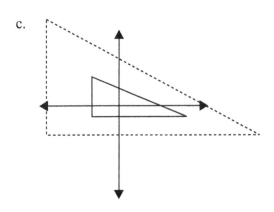

d.

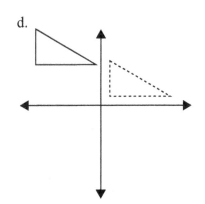

Solutions:

a. rotation (90° counterclockwise rotation)

b. reflection (about the *x*-axis)

c. dilation (enlarged by a scale factor)

d. translation (shift downward and to the right)

Tessellations

A **tessellation** is a set of shapes that "tile" (or cover) a plane such that there are no overlaps or gaps. Tessellations are also an application of transformations. Many artists and designers make use of tessellations in their creations. Perhaps most notable is the artist M. C. Escher. A regular tessellation is made from congruent regular polygons. However, all regular polygons do not tessellate, and there are shapes that tessellate that are not regular as well! Figure 4.83 represents a series of equilateral triangles that tessellate. Figure 4.84 represents a series of regular octagons that do not tessellate. Notice that there are square gaps within the regions covered by the octagons.

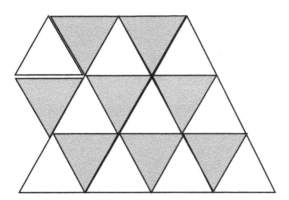

Figure 4.83

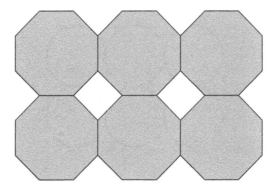

Example 36   Determine whether the given shape tessellates, and if it does tessellate, state whether it would create a regular tessellation.

a. Regular Hexagon   b. circle   c. trapezoid

 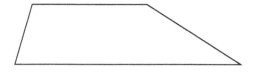

Solutions:

a.   The regular hexagon does tessellate, and it is a regular tessellation.

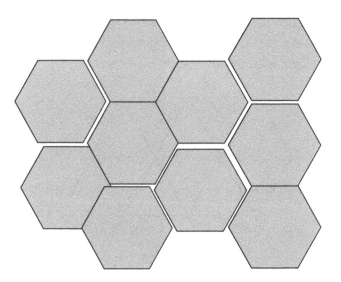

b.   The circle does not tessellate as there are gaps between the circles.

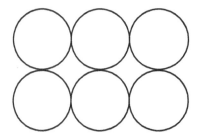

c. The trapezoid does tessellate, but since it is not a regular polygon it does not form a regular tessellation. Note that the tessellation is formed by applying transformations such as glides and reflections.

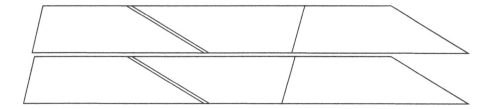

There are many real-world objects that are tessellations. Examples include checkerboards, floor tiles, wallpaper patterns, and quilt designs. Middle school students can explore tessellations with pattern blocks, dynamic drawing software packages, and paper folding activities.

Three-Dimensional Geometric Shapes

When looking at 3-dimensional shapes, we can compare their relationships to 2-dimensional shapes. In particular, we will look at cylinders, cones, prisms, pyramids, and spheres by investigating cross sections, and nets, as well as their volume and surface area. It is helpful when teaching about these shapes and their relationships to use real-world objects as well as geometric models of the shapes. Additionally, there are dynamic drawing software packages that allow students to draw these shapes and manipulate them in a variety of ways.

A **net** is the 2-dimensional representation of a 3-dimensional figure that is unfolded. A **cross-section** of a 3-dimensional figure is the resulting shape when a plane is passed horizontally or vertically through it. **Volume** is the amount a 3-dimensional shape can hold, and the **surface area** is the sum of the areas of the 2-dimensional shapes that enclose the 3-dimensional shape.

Cylinders

A **cylinder** is a three dimensional shape with two circular bases. We will restrict our discussion to right circular cylinders, as they have parallel bases and the axis of rotation is perpendicular to the bases. This is shown in Figure 4.85.

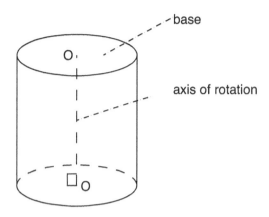

Figure 4.85

The **net** for a cylinder is shown in Figure 4.86 and is similar to a rectangular sheet of paper that is rolled up. Its net consists of two circles and a rectangle.

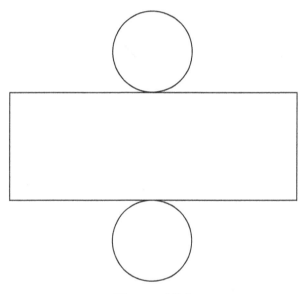

Figure 4.86

The **volume** of a cylinder is found by using the formula $V = \pi r^2 h$. Basically, you are finding the area of the base, which is a circle, and then multiplying it by the height of the cylinder. In effect, the height is the number of circular "layers." Often we see the formula as $V = Bh$ which is a general form, indicating B as the area of the base. **The total surface area** (SA) is the sum of the areas of the two bases (which are congruent) and the outer side (recall that it forms a rectangle when unfolded). The formula for the surface area is $SA = 2\pi r^2 + 2\pi rh$. The **lateral surface area** is the area of only the outer side, thus excluding the area of the two bases. The lateral surface area is given by the expression $2\pi rh$.

Example 37 To the nearest hundredth, find the volume and total surface area of the following cylinder, with a radius of 3.5 cm and a height of 12 cm.

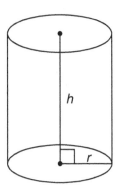

Solution: $V = (\pi)(3.5)^2 (12) = 147\pi \approx 461.81$ cubic cm.
$SA = (2\pi)(3.5)^2 + (2\pi)(3.5)(12) = 108.5\pi \approx 340.86$
square cm.

Note that volume is in cubic units and surface area in square units!

Cones

A **cone** is a three-dimensional shape with a circular base and a vertex. The height (h) of a cone is the distance from the vertex to the center of the circular base. The slant height (l) is the distance from the vertex down the side of the cone to the circular base. We will limit our discussion to **right circular cones** where the height is perpendicular to the base. Figure 4.87 shows a right circular cone.

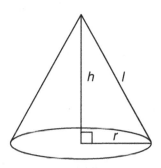

Figure 4.87

The net for a cone is shown in Figure 4.88. It consists of a sector of a circle and a smaller circle.

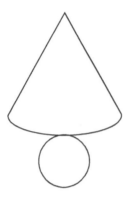

Figure 4.88

The formula for finding the **volume** of a cone is $V = \frac{1}{3}Bh$ or $V = \frac{1}{3}\pi r^2 h$. An interesting observation is that the volume of a cone is one-third the volume of a cylinder with the same size base and height. One informal investigation that middle grade students can do to understand this relationships is to have open containers in the shape of a cylinder and a cone that have the same base and height. Fill the cone with beans or popcorn kernels. Ask how many cones would it take to fill the cylinder. Often students guess that it will take two, but when they actually conduct the experiment, they find it takes three!

To find the **surface area** of a cone, we use the formula $SA = \pi r^2 + \pi rl$. Notice that the surface area is simply the sum of the area of the base, which is a circle and the "side" of the cone (see the net of the cone).

Example 38   To the nearest hundredth, find the volume and the surface area of a right circular cone whose radius is 7 feet and whose slant height is 15 feet.

Solution: We will need to find the height of the cone by using the Pythagorean theorem. The radius is one of the legs and the slant height is the hypotenuse. We get $h = \sqrt{15^2 - 7^2} = \sqrt{176} \approx 13.27$ feet. Then $V = (\frac{1}{3})(\pi)(7)^2(13.27) \approx 216.74\pi \approx 680.92$ cubic feet. The surface area is found by $SA = (\pi)(7)^2 + (\pi)(7)(15) = 154\pi \approx 483.81$ square feet.

Prisms

A **prism** is a three-dimensional figure that has two congruent polygonal **bases** that lie in parallel planes; the remaining faces are rectangles. (The base is also considered a face.) A prism is named by the shape of its two bases. Our discussion will be limited to right prisms, for which the bases and lateral faces are perpendicular to each other. Figures 4.89, 4.90 and 4.91 illustrate a few types of prisms.

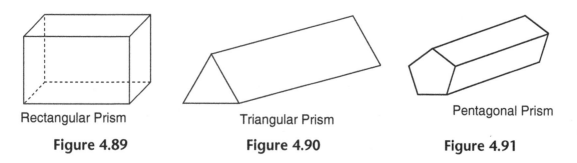

Rectangular Prism

Figure 4.89

Triangular Prism

Figure 4.90

Pentagonal Prism

Figure 4.91

The **cube** is a special prism in that all of its faces are square, as shown in Figure 4.92.

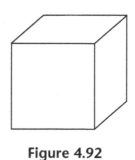

Figure 4.92

Figure 4.93 is a net of a rectangular prism and Figure 4.94 is a net of a cube.

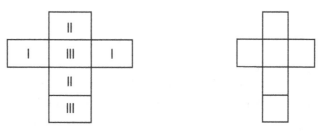

Figure 4.93

Figure 4.94

Note that for the net of a rectangular prism, the identically marked faces are opposite each other.

The **volume** of a rectangular prism is found using the formula $V = lwh$. In general, the volume of a prism is found by finding the area of the base and multiplying it times the height ($V = Bh$ where B represents the area of the base). The **total surface area** of a prism is the sum of the area of all its faces. For the special case of a cube, we have $V = e^3$ and $SA = 6e^2$ where e is the length of the edge, and all the edges are congruent. An edge is the segment formed by two intersecting faces.

Example 39   Given that the volume of a cube is 350 in³, find the total surface area, to the nearest hundredth.

Solution: First we find the length of the edge of the cube since we know the volume. We have $350 = e^3$, so $e = \sqrt[3]{350} \approx 7.047$. Thus, $SA \approx (6)(7.047)^2 \approx 297.96$ square inches.

Example 40   The dimensions of the bottom of a rectangular lap pool are 10 ft, by 6 ft, and the pool is 4 ft deep. The owner would like to paint the inside surface of the four walls and the bottom with a blue paint that costs \$12.50 per quart. A quart of paint covers 14 square feet. How much will it cost to paint all the surfaces?

Solution: The area of each of two walls is 24 (6×4) square feet and the area of each of the other two walls is 40 (10×4) square feet. The area of the bottom is 60 (10×6) square feet. The total surface area is $(2)(24) + (2)(40) + 60 = 188$ square feet. Since each quart of paint can cover 14 square feet, the owner will need $\frac{188}{14} \approx 13.42$ quarts. Because he cannot buy a fraction of a quart, he will need 14 quarts. The cost is therefore $(14)(\$12.50) = \$175$.

Pyramids

A **pyramid** is a three-dimensional figure with triangular faces and a polygonal base. The faces meet at a point called the **vertex**. A pyramid is named by the shape of its base. We will restrict our discussion to pyramids in which the base is a regular polygon. Figure 4.95 is an example of a regular pyramid with a square base. The **vertex** is point V, the square base is $ABCD$, the perpendicular **height** is h, and the **slant height** is l.

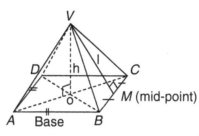

Figure 4.95

Figure 4.96 is the net of a regular pyramid with a square base.

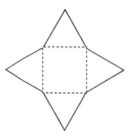

Figure 4.96

The **volume** of a regular pyramid is determined by the formula $V = \frac{1}{3}Bh$ where B is the area of the base and h is the length of the perpendicular height of the pyramid. A pyramid is much like a cone, so the volume relationship of a cylinder to a cone is similar to the volume relationship of a prism to a pyramid. The **surface area** of a pyramid is the sum of the areas of the triangular faces and the base. If the base is a square, then the surface area is given by the formula $SA = 2sl + s^2$, where s is the length of one side of the base and l is the lateral height.

Example 41   Find the total surface area of a square pyramid whose base has a side of 6 and whose perpendicular height is 4.

Solution: The area of the base would be 36, but to find the area of each triangular face, we will need to find the slant height. A right triangle is formed when we connect the vertex of the pyramid to the base of the perpendicular height to the midpoint of one of the sides of the base. Using the Pythagorean theorem, slant height is $\sqrt{3^2 + 4^2} = \sqrt{25} = 5$. Then the total surface area is $(2)(6)(5) + 6^2 = 96$.

Example 42 A regular pyramid with a square base has a volume of 250 cubic meters. Each side of the base is 9 meters. To the nearest hundredth, what is the perpendicular height?

Solution: The area of the base is $9^2 = 81$. Then $250 = \left(\dfrac{1}{3}\right)(81)(h) = 27h$. Thus, $h \approx 9.26$ meters.

Spheres

A **sphere** is a three-dimensional figure that represents all the points in space that are at a fixed distance from a given point. This fixed distance is called its radius.

Figure 4.97 illustrates a sphere.

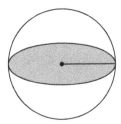

Figure 4.97

Since it is impossible to make a "perfect" sphere from a piece of paper we cannot make an exact **net** of a sphere. If you wanted to simulate the net of a sphere, it would be like making a polyhedron with a large number of sides and then unfolding it.

The **volume** of a sphere is given by the formula $V = \dfrac{4}{3}\pi r^3$, and the **surface area** is given by the formula $SA = 4\pi r^2$. In each case, r is the radius.

Example 43 Zorbing, also known as sphereing, is a favorite form of recreation of people all over the world including New Zealand, England, and most recently, the United States. It is constructed with one spherical ball inside another, with a layer of space between them. A person gets inside the inner inflatable ball and rolls down a hill! The outer ball is about 3 meters in diameter. Find the surface area of the outer ball, to the nearest hundredth.

Solution: Since the diameter is 3 meters, then the radius of the sphere would be 1.5 meters. Thus, the surface area is $(4\pi)(1.5)^2 = 9\pi \approx 28.27$ square meters.

Example 44 For a certain sphere, the numerical value of its volume is five times the numerical value of its surface area. What is the length of the radius?

Solution: Let r represent the radius. Then $\frac{4}{3}\pi r^3 = (5)(4\pi)(r^2)$. Dividing both sides of this equation by πr^2, we get $\frac{4}{3}r = 20$. Thus, $r = (20)\left(\frac{3}{4}\right) = 15$.

Cross-Sectional Areas

The intersection of a plane and a three-dimensional figure is called a **cross-section**.

Let's investigate the cross-sections for the three-dimensional figures we have studied in this chapter.

1. If a plane is parallel to the bases of a cylinder, the cross-section is a circle.

2. If a plane is parallel to the base of a cone and does not pass through the vertex, the cross-section is a circle. The longer the distance between the vertex and the plane, the larger the circle.

3. If a plane is parallel to the bases of a prism, the cross-section is congruent to the bases.

4. If a plane is parallel to the base of a pyramid, the cross-section is similar to the base. The longer the distance between the vertex and the plane, the larger the cross-section.

5. The cross-section of a plane and a sphere is a circle. The largest possible circle occurs when the plane passes through the center of the sphere.

Precision of Measurement

When we have students measure, we usually ask them to measure with accuracy to a specific unit of measure. As examples, we might ask them to measure to the nearest inch, centimeter, or nearest tenth of a centimeter; the **unit of measure** would be inch, centimeter, or tenth of a centimeter, respectively. It is important that students measure as precisely as possible, so that their measurement error is minimal. In fact the "**greatest possible error**" of a measurement should be equal to one half the unit of measure. The ratio of the greatest possible error to the measured length is called the **relative error of a measurement**. The smaller the relative error is, the more accurate the measurement.

Accuracy refers to the closeness of a measurement to the exact value and **precision** refers to the closeness of a measurement to the "real" value. Generally, the smaller the unit that you use to measure, the more precise the measurement is. The smaller the difference between your measurement and the accepted measurement, the more accurate your measurement.

Example 45   A football field is 360 feet, and the width of the upright goal post is 18.5 feet wide. Find the relative error of each measurement. Which measurement is more accurate?

Solution:

	Football Field-360 ft	Goal post-18.5 ft
Unit of measure	1 ft	0.1 ft
Greatest possible error	½(1 ft) = 0.5 ft	½(0.1 ft) = 0.05 ft
Relative error	$\dfrac{0.5\,\text{ft}}{360\,\text{ft}} \approx 0.00138889 \approx .1\%$	$\dfrac{0.05\,\text{ft}}{18.5\,\text{ft}} \approx 0.00270270 \approx .3\%$

The football field has the smaller relative error, so it is more accurate.

Quiz For Chapter 4

1. Which one of the following shows all the correct markings for the construction of the perpendicular bisector of $\overline{RT}$?

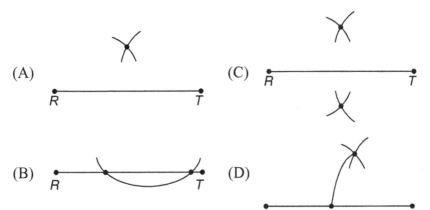

2. A wire is connected from the top of a vertical telephone pole to a stake in the ground. The height of the telephone pole is 80 feet, and the angle of elevation is 36°. To the nearest hundredth of a foot, what is the length of the wire?

    (A) 74.04

    (B) 98.89

    (C) 108.80

    (D) 136.10

3. Which one of the following could represent the measures of two angles of a triangle that is both acute and isosceles?

    (A) 58° and 64°

    (B) 41° and 41°

    (C) 56° and 60°

    (D) 35° and 55°

4. In a given trapezoid, one base is 7 units larger that the other base. If the height is 14 units and the area is 315 square units, what is the length, in units, of the shorter base?

    (A) 12

    (B) 19

(C) 26

(D) 33

5. If the surface area of a sphere is 25π square units, what is the volume, in cubic units?

(A) 4.5π

(B) 12.9π

(C) $20.8\overline{3}\pi$

(D) $18.1\overline{6}\pi$

6. Which one of the following diagrams illustrates a reflection of ΔABC to its image $\Delta A'B'C'$ over line l_1?

(A)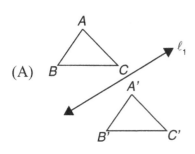

(C)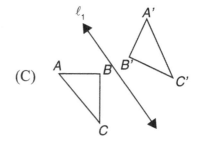

(B)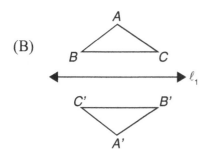

(D)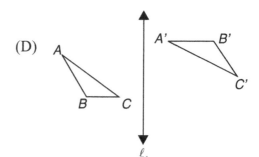

7. The sum of the interior angles of a regular polygon is 2880°. What is the measure of each exterior angle?

(A) 20°

(B) 24°

(C) 30°

(D) 36°

8. Consider the following statement: An angle consists of two rays. This definition of an angle is incomplete. Which one of the following should be added to the above definition so that it is a correct definition of an angle?

    (A) going in opposite directions

    (B) with a common endpoint

    (C) that are congruent

    (D) with different endpoints

9. Triangles *GHJ* and *LMN* are similar. The lengths of the sides of $\triangle GHJ$ are 14, 18, and 30. If the largest side of $\triangle LMN$ is 75, what is the difference of the perimeters of these triangles?

    (A) 31

    (B) 93

    (C) 135

    (D) 155

10. The area of each base of a cylinder is 100π square units. If the height is 13 units, what is the total surface area, in square units?

    (A) 460π

    (B) 400π

    (C) 360π

    (D) 300π

Solutions

1. (C)

   In order to construct the perpendicular bisector of a line segment, a set of congruent arcs must be made above and below the line segment.

2. **(D)**

Let x represent the length of the wire. Then $\sin 36° = \dfrac{80}{x}$. Thus, $x = \dfrac{80}{\sin 36°} \approx 136.10$ feet.

3. **(A)**

If two of the angles are $58°$ and $64°$, then the third angle is $180° - 58° - 64° = 58°$. A triangle with these angle measurements is both acute and isosceles. Answer choice (B) is wrong because the third angle measurement is $100° - 41° - 41° = 98°$; this means that it has an obtuse angle. Both answer choices (C) and (D) represent scalene triangles.

4. **(B)**

Let x and $x + 7$ represent the two bases. Then $315 = \left(\dfrac{1}{2}\right)(14)(x + x + 7)$. This equation simplifies to $315 = (7)(2x+7)$, which becomes $315 = 14x + 49$. Then $266 = 14x$, so $x = 19$.

5. **(C)**

Since $4\pi r^2 = 25\pi, r = \sqrt{\dfrac{25}{4}} = 2.5$. Thus, the volume is $\left(\dfrac{4}{3}\right)(\pi)(2.5)^3 = 20.8\overline{3}\pi$.

6. **(C)**

Each vertex A', B', C' is a mirror image over line l_1 of A, B, and C, respectively.

7. **(A)**

Let n represent the number of sides. Then $2880 = (n - 2)(180)$, which simplifies to $2880 = 180n - 360$. Then $3240 = 180n$, so $n = 18$. Thus, the measure of each exterior angle is $\dfrac{360}{18} = 20°$.

8. (B)

The definition of an angle requires a common endpoint for its two rays.

9. (B)

The ratios of the perimeters is $\dfrac{30}{75} = \dfrac{2}{5}$. This means that each side of the larger triangle is 2.5 times the corresponding side of the smaller triangle. Besides 75, the other two sides of $\triangle LMN$ are $(2.5)(14) = 35$ and $(2.5)(18) = 45$. The perimeter of $\triangle LMN$ is $75 + 35 + 45 = 155$, and the perimeter of $\triangle GHJ$ is $14 + 18 + 30 = 62$. Thus, the difference in perimeters is 93.

10. (A)

The total surface area is represented by $100\pi + 100\pi + (2\pi)(r)(13) = 200\pi + 26\pi r$. Additionally, we know that $100\pi = \pi r^2$, so $r = 10$. Thus, the total surface area is $200\pi + 26\pi(10) = 460\pi$.

CHAPTER 5

Probability and Statistics

Introduction

This chapter deals with Domain IV Competencies 012–014 related to data analysis and probability theory. This domain emphasizes data collection through experiments and simulations and explores various methods of data displays, measures of central tendency, and the role of sampling in analysis. The domain requires that the teacher be able to demonstrate an understanding of sampling techniques, calculate and interpret percentiles and quartiles, and use a variety of techniques to make predictions and draw conclusions based on data collection.

Displaying Data

Once data is collected, it is often useful to present or display the data in some type of graphical representation. This aids in organizing the data for analysis and interpretation by providing a visual representation. Examples will be provided to illustrate the various types of graphical representations. Some data can be presented in multiple graph forms, but there are times when a particular graph will be more useful when answering a particular question about the data. It is important for students to apply appropriate graphical representations when interpreting data sets.

Example 1 Suppose a family decided to make the allocations indicated below for the 2011 budget.

2011 Family Budget	
Percent Allocated	**Category of Allocation**
24%	Housing
15%	Food
16%	Transportation
10%	Utilities
10%	Clothing
4%	Insurance
6%	Entertainment
5%	Savings
10%	Non-Profit Contributions

How can this data be represented in a pie chart?

Solution: A **pie chart or circle graph** is a circle divided into sections that represent the different categories. The parts or sections make up the whole and the sizes of the sections reflect the related information. The size of the central angle of each section is calculated by multiplying the corresponding percent by 360. Recall that there are 360° in a circle. Figure 5.1 shows the pie chart.

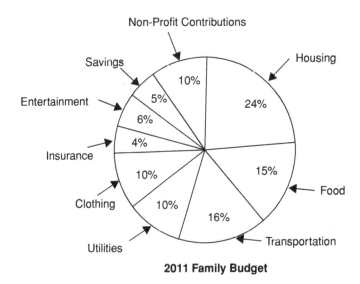

2011 Family Budget

Figure 5.1

Example 2   How can the data in Example 1 be shown as a bar graph?

Solution: A **bar graph** uses both a horizontal and a vertical axis. One of these axes is labeled with the individual categories, and the other axis is labeled with the corresponding numerical value. Figure 5.2 shown below illustrates a bar graph, in which the categories are listed on the vertical axis. The numbers along the horizontal axis indicate the corresponding percents.

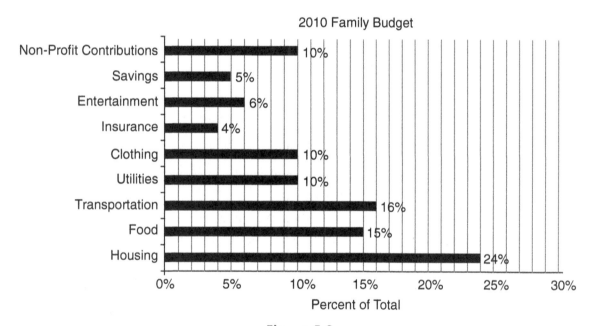

Figure 5.2

A **line graph** can also be used to display data. This type of graph is most appropriate when we wish to show a trend of some quantity over a period of time. Similar to a bar graph, a line graph uses the horizontal and vertical axes. The horizontal axis is labeled as a unit of time and the vertical axis is labeled with the quantity being measured.

Example 3   The population of the United States for the years 1860 to 1960 is shown in the following table.

Year	Population in millions
1860	31.4
1870	39.8
1880	50.2
1890	62.9
1900	76.0
1910	92.0
1920	105.7
1930	122.8
1940	131.7
1950	151.1
1960	179.3

How is this information displayed as a line graph?

Solution: We will label the horizontal axis as "Year" and label the vertical axis as "Population." The line graph is shown below in Figure 5.3.

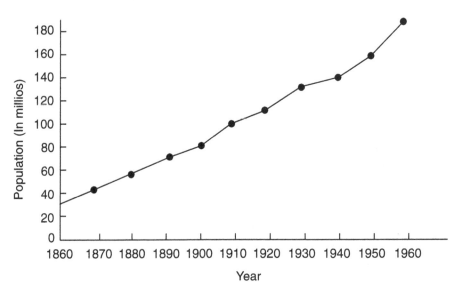

Figure 5.3

A line graph relates two pieces of information and indicates how they vary as one depends on the other. You may recall this discussion related to independent and dependent variables with line graphs in Chapter 3. In this case, the total population is dependent on the year.

Example 4   How can the data in Example 3 be displayed as a bar graph?

Solution: Although not as popular for showing trends over time, a bar graph may also be used. Simply replace the data points with bars, as shown below in Figure 5.4. Note that these bars are constructed vertically, whereas the bars in Example 2 were constructed horizontally.

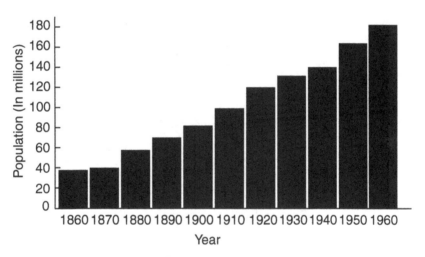

Figure 5.4

Example 5   Twenty students are enrolled in the foreign language department, and their major fields are as follows: Spanish, Spanish, French, Italian, French, Spanish, German, German, Russian, Russian, French, German, German, German, Spanish, Russian, German, Italian, German, and Spanish.

(a) Construct a frequency distribution table.

(b) Construct a bar graph.

Solution: (a) We can use a two-column table. The individual languages (major fields) are listed in the left column, and the corresponding number of students is listed in the right column, as shown.

Major Field	Number of Students
German	7
Russian	3
Spanish	5
French	3
Italian	2
Total	20

(b) Figure 5.5 shown below is the bar graph for Example 5. Note that each major field is represented by a rectangle, and that all rectangles have the same width. A number on the vertical axis identifies the height of each rectangle, and this number corresponds to the number of students who specialize in these fields.

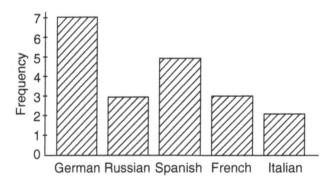

Figure 5.5

As a follow-up exercise, students can answer questions related to the graph, such as which language has the most or least number of students enrolled. Students could be asked to determine the percentage of students who take each language. This would require students to compute the percentage based on the total number of students. For example since 7 out of 20 students are enrolled in German, this means that $\frac{7}{20}$ or 35% of the students enrolled in the foreign languages department are majoring in German.

Before we introduce the next type of graph, we must explain the meaning of **percentiles**. These numbers correspond to the approximate percent of data that is equal to or less than a particular number. For example, suppose that a national exam has scores that range from 100 to 300. Furthermore, suppose that you receive a score of 270 and are informed that this score represents the 80th percentile. This means that 80% of the students who took this test scored 270 or lower. By extension, we can also conclude that 20% of the students scored higher than 270.

We now introduce the **box-and-whisker plot** (also known as a **boxplot**). In this type of graph, five statistics are displayed. In order from lowest to highest, these five statistics are minimum score, 25th percentile, 50th percentile (median), 75th percentile, and maximum score. From left to right, here are the elements of the graph.

(a) A horizontal segment ("whisker") whose endpoints are the minimum score and the 25th percentile.

(b) A rectangle ("box") that extends from the 25th percentile to the 75th percentile. The 50th percentile is identified with a vertical segment from the top to the bottom of the rectangle.

(c) A horizontal segment whose endpoints are the 75th percentile and the maximum score.

Example 6   For a particular set of scores on a class test, the minimum score is 70, the 25th percentile is 78, the median is 82, the 75th percentile is 90, and the maximum score is 94.
Construct the box-and-whisker plot.

Solution: Figure 5.6 shows the completed box-and-whisker plot. Note that a delineated horizontal scale is shown below it. This scale provides more readability for the data.

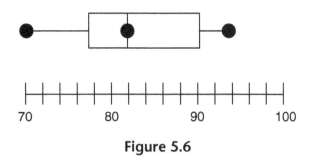

Figure 5.6

As a follow-up exercise, students can answer questions related to (a) the range and (b) the interquartile range. The **range** is the difference between the maximum and minimum scores. The **interquartile range** is the difference between the 75th percentile and the 25th percentile. For Figure 5.6, the range is $94 - 70 = 24$ and the interquartile range is $90 - 78 = 12$. With only the boxplot given, we cannot determine each score, nor can we determine the number of scores.

A **stem-and-leaf plot** is a system by which individual data items can be displayed in groups. This is most advantageous when (a) the range of data is not too large, (b) the total number of data items is fairly small, and (c) when there are repetitions of data items.

Example 7   There is a parking lot on your school campus that the administration is considering eliminating, but they want more information concerning the number of people that park in that lot. Suppose you were given the following information that was collected three times each week by counting the number of cars in a particular parking lot over a period of 4 weeks. Here are the car counts: 58, 43, 23, 69, 69, 44, 70, 53, 78, 63, 35, 41. Create a stem-and-leaf plot.

Solution: The first step is to list the numbers from smallest to largest. Notice the minimum number is 23, and the maximum number is 78. The list would then appear as follows:

23, 35, 41, 43, 44, 53, 58, 63, 69, 69, 70, 78.
The "stems" are listed in the left-hand column, which contains the tens digit. The "leaves" are listed in the right-hand column, which represents the ones digit. Finally, for the benefit of readability, a vertical line is drawn to separate the stems and leaves. Here is the stem-and-leaf plot for this set of data. Notice that the leaves have been organized in ascending order.

Stem	Leaf
2	3
3	5
4	1 3 4
5	3 8
6	3 9 9
7	0 8

Note that with stem-and-leaf plots, all of the data can be viewed. Besides identifying the highest and lowest data, students could be asked to calculate quantities such as the 25th percentile, mean, and standard deviation. (These calculations have not yet been discussed in this book.)

Another type of graph is a **histogram**. A histogram represents data frequency with bars. The constant width of each bar represents the interval (or class) of data, and each bar shows the frequency for that interval or class. The bars in a histogram do not have spaces between them as bars do in a bar graph.

Example 8   Suppose you gave a test to your students for which the grade distribution was as follows:

Student	Grade
Angela	79
Tina	84
Devon	96
Janique	67
Horatio	75
Evan	88
Shania	63
Madison	92
Malike	77
Eduardo	58
Angela	60
Dwight	89
Sara	84
Ben	72
Arethea	86
Monique	91

Construct a histogram for this data.

Solution: There is no automatic way in which the intervals must be chosen. Since the lowest score is 58 and the highest score is 96, we'll use the following five intervals: 50 − 59, 60 − 69, 70 − 79, 80 − 89, and 90 − 99. Each of these intervals has a **lower limit** and an **upper limit**. For example, the interval 70 − 79, has 70 as its lower limit and 79 as its upper limit. Because the bars must be connected, we will need to use the **lower boundary** and the **upper boundary** for each interval. These numbers are found by simply subtracting one-half unit from each lower limit and adding one-half unit to each upper limit. For example, the interval 70 − 79 becomes 69.5 − 79.5. Likewise, the interval 60 − 69 becomes 59.5 − 69.5. In this way, all the bars will be connected. The vertical axis will be labeled as "Frequency " and the horizontal axis will be labeled "Grades." Figure 5.7 shows the histogram for this data.

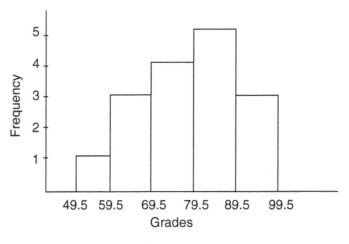

Figure 5.7

Our final graph is the **scatter plot**. This is a graph of (*x, y*) coordinates that shows the strength of the relationship between the quantities *x* and *y*.

Example 9   Look at the following table, in which *x* represents grade level and *y* represents the corresponding average number of hours of homework each week.

Grade Level (*x*)	1	2	3	4	5	6	7	8	9	10	11	12
Average Hours of Homework	2	3	3	6	4	10	7	10	12	9	14	15

Construct a scatter plot.

Solution: The grade levels are listed along the horizontal axis, and the hours of homework each week are listed along the vertical axis. Figure 5.8 shows the scatterplot.

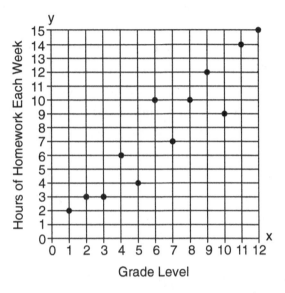

Figure 5.8

You will notice that as the grade level goes up, the number of hours of homework increases, and it closely follows a straight line. This shows a **correlation** between the grade level and the number of hours. In fact it shows a **positive correlation**, which means that as one variable changes, the other variable tends to change proportionally.

A **negative correlation** means that as one variable increases, the other variable tends to decrease proportionally. A zero correlation means that the two variables are not related to each other in a linear sense. Figures 5.9, 5.10, and 5.11 illustrate these three correlations.

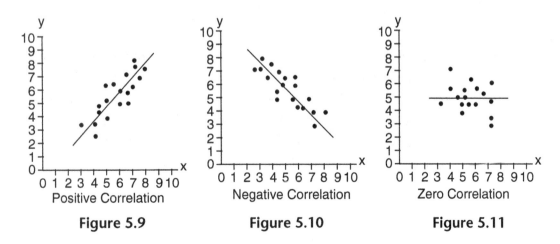

Figure 5.9 **Figure 5.10** **Figure 5.11**

When middle grade students are learning about graphs, not only is it important that they be able to construct graphs that have been discussed thus far, but it is also important that they be able to determine which type of graph is most useful in understanding data that is collected or provided. For example, suppose students had collected data on the ages of the members of their 7th grade mathematics class and wanted to construct a graph to display the data. Most likely the ages would be in the range of 11 to 13. A circle or pie graph could be beneficial in readily seeing what percentage or proportion each of the three ages represent. Also, a bar graph could display the total number of each age as would a histogram. A scatterplot would not be useful because you are not looking for the relationship between 2 sets of data. A line graph would not be useful because the data is not continuous and would be clustered around just three age levels. Providing students, throughout middle school, multiple opportunities to work with data and graphs is extremely important. This affords them opportunities to collect data and to interpret the related graphs. Students would learn which graph(s) would be most useful to answer questions about the data.

One final comment about drawing graphs and displaying data should be mentioned. While we have approached the examples as if you would be constructing them by hand, you should also be reminded that there are various technology tools that can aid in displaying data. For example, graphing calculators have functions that allow for construction of graphs such as scatter plots, line graphs, and histograms. Some calculators can also draw bar graphs and box-and-whisker graphs. There are computer software packages, from spreadsheets to commercial graphing software, which are specifically designed for graphing. In addition, there are on-line internet-based graphing tools. In considering this from a teaching perspective, the teacher should think about the purpose of the task or activity as to whether it would be beneficial to use a graphing tool. Graphing tools aid in construction, which allows more time to be spent on data interpretation, answering questions, and drawing conclusions.

Example 10 In a 6th grade classroom of 20 students, the teacher had the students write their hair color on a chart on the blackboard. Here are the data:
brown, black, blonde, blonde, red, brown, black, black, brown, brown, blonde, red, blonde, brown, brown, brown, black, black, red, brown
Construct a frequency table (or distribution) for the data, and use this to construct a bar graph.

Solution: We'll use a two-column table with four rows. Figure 5.12 shows the associated bar graph.

Hair Color	Frequency
brown	8
blonde	4
black	5
red	3

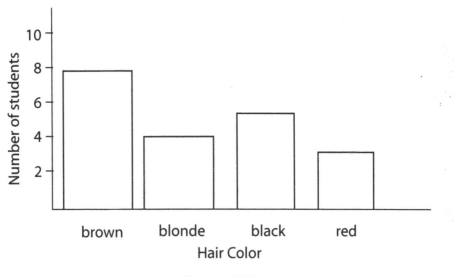

Figure 5.12

Example 11   Tracey enjoys bowling so much that she decided to keep track of her bowling scores for 20 games. Her results were as follows:
288, 205, 212, 189, 131, 169, 205, 230, 162, 188, 209, 160, 150, 200, 195, 182, 200, 167, 175, and 195. Construct a box-and-whisker plot to display the data.

Solution: We will arrange the data from least to greatest.

131, 150, 160, 162, 167, 169, 175, 182, 188, 189, 195, 195, 200, 200, 205, 205, 209, 212, 230, and 288

We now know the minimum and maximum values, which are 131 and 288, respectively; so we have the endpoints of the whiskers. In order to construct the box-and-whisker plot, we also need to find the median, 25th percentile (also called the lower quartile), and the 75th percentile (also called the upper quartile).

Since there is an even number (20) of data, the median falls midway between the 10th and 11th numbers. Thus, the position of the median is 10.5. The corresponding value is the arithmetic average of the 10th and 11th numbers, which is $\frac{189+195}{2} = 192$.

Next we look at the numbers on the left side of the median (192), in order to find the 25th percentile. There are ten numbers that are less than 192, so the 25th percentile falls midway between the 5th and 6th numbers of this group. Thus, the value of the 25th percentile is the arithmetic average of 167 and 169, which is $\frac{167+169}{2} = 168$.

Next we look at the data on the right side of the median (192), in order to find the 75th percentile. For the ten elements in this group, the value of the 75th percentile will be the arithmetic average of the 5th and 6th numbers. For this second group, the 5th and 6th numbers are each 205. Thus, the 75th percentile is 205. Now we can construct the box-and-whisker plot!

We can use a scale of 20 on the horizontal axis. Figure 5.13 shows the box-and-whisker plot.

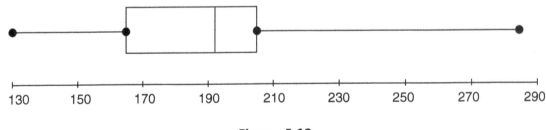

Figure 5.13

As a quick review, we mentioned the range and the interquartile range following the solution for Example 6. For Example 11, the range is $288 - 131 = 157$. The interquartile range is $205 - 168 = 37$.

Measures of Central Tendency and Dispersion

There are many statistics that are useful when addressing questions related to the data you have collected. We have already discussed maximum and minimum values, as well as the range for a set of data. While these values are important, they are limited in what they tell us about the data. **Central tendencies** provide additional insight because these relate to how the data are distributed or spread. The three most common measures of central tendency are mean, median, and mode. We avoid the word "average" because it could apply to mean, median, or mode.

The **mean** refers to the **arithmetic mean** and is found by adding the numbers in the data set, then dividing by the total frequency (or number of data). The symbol commonly used is $\overline{X}$.

The **median** of a set of data is the middle number of all the data when it is arranged in order from least to greatest. The position of the median is always given by $\frac{n+1}{2}$, where n represents the number of data. If there is an odd number of data, the median will always be one of the actual data values. If there is an even number of data, the median will be the mean of the two middle data values, and may not be one of the actual date values. The mode, if it exists, is (are) the number(s) that occur(s) most frequently in the data set. The mode would not exist if every data given had a frequency of 1. There can be more than one mode.

Example 12   Suppose the ages of a group of 20 students in a combined elementary-middle school choir were given as follows: 12, 12, 13, 14, 10, 15, 11, 11, 14, 14, 14, 13, 13, 12, 12, 12, 12, 15, 13, 12.

Calculate the mean, median, and mode. Also, create a frequency table.

Solution: The sum of the 20 numbers is 254, so $\overline{X} = \frac{254}{20} = 12.7$. That is, the mean age of a student in the middle school choir is about midway between $12\frac{1}{2}$ and 13 years old. When the numbers are arranged in ascending order, they appear as follows: 10, 11, 11, 12, 12, 12, 12, 12, 12, 12, 13, 13, 13, 13, 14, 14, 14, 14, 15, 15. By using the expression $\frac{n+1}{2}$, the position of the median is $\frac{20+1}{2} = 10.5$. This value is determined by calculating the mean of the 10th and 11th numbers, which is 12.5. Finally, the mode is 12 because 12 occurs more than any other data item.

You can either look at the data list above in ascending order or create a frequency table, which appears below.

Age	Frequency
10	1
11	2
12	7
13	4
14	4
15	2

When selecting or designing tasks and problems for student to do related to measures of central tendency, it is important to have them develop a conceptual understanding of these measures and how they are used. It is not sufficient to simply provide a computational skill. As an example, let's revisit Example 12. One way a teacher might engage the students in this problem is to have them construct a bar graph of the data; that is, have them line up the bars on a graph according to their ages. Then you can have them actually count each data item in order to find the median. In addition, they will easily see the mode.

Skewness relates to the frequency distribution in data. This is easily seen in the graphs of data. Look at the histogram in Example 8, which shows the scores of a class test. We can see that the data is slightly negatively skewed (or skewed to the left) since the majority of the data lie further to the right of the mean (which is 78.8). In a negatively skewed distribution, the mean is less than the median, which is less than the mode. For this example, the mean is 78.8, the median is 81.5, and the mode is 84. In order to illustrate a positively skewed distribution, consider the following example.

Example 13   A standardized test was administered to a class of 30 students. Scores ranged from 75 to 120. Here are the scores, arranged in ascending order. 75, 76, 77, 79, 79, 79, 79, 80, 80, 82, 84, 84, 84, 85, 86, 88, 90, 90, 91, 92, 95, 95, 98, 101, 102, 106, 108, 112, 116, 120.

Determine the mean, median, and mode.

Solution: The sum of all 30 data values is 2713, so the mean is $\frac{2713}{30} \approx 90.43$. The median is the number in the 15.5th position, which becomes $\frac{86 + 88}{2} = 87$. The mode is 79, since it occurs most frequently.

We note that the mode is less than the median, which is less than the mean. This is a characteristic of a positively skewed distribution. Furthermore, we can illustrate this data set by using a histogram. We'll use the following five intervals: 75 − 84, 85 − 94, 95 − 104, 105 − 114, and 115 − 124. The corresponding boundaries for these intervals become 74.5, 84.5, 94.5, 104.5, 114.5, and 124.5. Figure 5.14 shows the histogram.

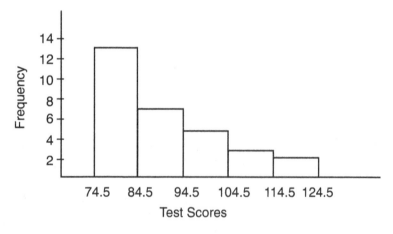

Figure 5.14

If the data is evenly distributed then the histogram will be show a symmetrical distribution of the data. If a vertical line is drawn at some point in the histogram so that the shape on the left and right of the line is the same (mirror images of each other), then it is a symmetrical distribution. For a symmetrical distribution, the mean, median, and mode are identical.

Example 14   Suppose the following data distribution related to scores on a test is given as follows:

Score Group	Frequency
30-39	3
40-49	6
50-59	12
60-69	18
70-79	13
80-89	7
90-99	3

Determine the mean, median, and mode of this distribution. Also, create a histogram.

Solution: To calculate the mean, we use the midpoint of each group and multiply by the corresponding frequency. Thus, we have

$$\overline{X} = \frac{(34.5)(3) + (44.5)(6) + (54.5)(12) + (64.5)(18) + (74.5)(13) + (84.5)(7) + (94.5)(3)}{62}$$

$$= \frac{4029}{62} \approx 64.98$$

The median is a bit complicated to find in grouped data and beyond the scope of this book. However, for completeness, it lies in the $\frac{62}{2} = 31^{st}$ position. (Its actual value is $65.0\overline{5}$.) Finally the mode, which is referred to as the "modal class" since the data is grouped, is 60-69. Figure 5.15 shows the histogram that represents this data. Note that the mean, median, and mode are nearly equivalent.

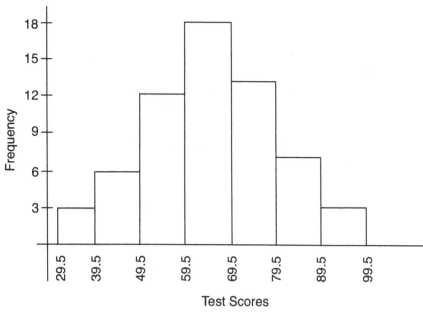

Figure 5.15

What may be of interest and important to students as they study skewness is to consider what happens to a set of data should a value change or a value be added. The change would be considerable should an unusually large or small value be added. However, the change would not be significant if a value close to the mean were added. A good exercise would be to apply this concept to some of the examples in this chapter.

Our next topic is the **Standard Deviation and Variance** of a data set. The standard deviation reflects how the data is distributed about the mean. The deviation of a number x from its mean $\overline{x}$ is defined as $x - \overline{x}$. The standard deviation is calculated by taking the square root of the average of the sum of the squared differences between each data value and the mean. Thus, for the set x_1, x_2, x_3, x_4, ..., x_n of n numbers, the standard deviation, symbolized as σ is given by the following formula:

$$\sigma = \sqrt{\frac{\sum_{i=1}^{n}(x_i - \overline{x})^2}{n}}$$, where σ refers to the population standard deviation. If a sample of

the population were used, the formula is modified to

$$s = \sqrt{\dfrac{\sum_{i=1}^{n}(x_i - \bar{x})^2}{n-1}}$$, where s denotes the sample standard deviation. If the values of n are large, the difference between the two definitions is negligible. The higher the value of the standard deviation, the greater the spread of the data will be. **Variance** is the square of the standard deviation, which is written symbolically as either $\sigma^2 = \dfrac{\sum_{i=1}^{n}(x_i - \bar{x})^2}{n}$ (for a population) or as $s^2 = \dfrac{\sum_{1}^{n}(x_i - \bar{x})^2}{n-1}$ (for a sample).

Example 15 A simple manual task was given to six children, and the time each child took to complete the task (x_i) was measured (in minutes). The results are shown in the following table.

x_i	$x_i - \bar{x}$	$(x_i - \bar{x})^2$
12	2.5	6.25
9	−0.5	0.25
11	1.5	2.25
6	−3.5	12.25
10	0.5	0.25
9	−0.5	0.25
Total 57	0	21.5

Determine the sample variance and the sample standard deviation.

Solution: The mean equals 9.5, which can be checked by dividing 57 by 6 (the number of data) or by inspecting any row. For instance, on the third row, the value of x_i is 11 and the value of $x_i - \bar{x}$ is 1.5. This implies that $\bar{x} = 9.5$. Thus, the sample variance (s^2) = $\dfrac{21.5}{5}$ = 4.3 minutes. Then the sample standard deviation (s) = $\sqrt{4.3} \approx 2.07$ minutes.

Example 16 A couple has five children whose ages are 4, 7, 11, 15, and 23. What is the variance for this sample?

Solution: $\bar{x} = \dfrac{4+7+11+15+23}{5} = 12$. Then

$$\sum_{1}^{5}(x-\bar{x})^2 = (4-12)^2 + (7-12)^2 + (11-12)^2 + (15-12)^2 + (23-12)^2$$

$$= 64 + 25 + 1 + 9 + 121 = 220. \text{ Thus, } s^2 = \frac{220}{4} = 55.$$

Linear Regression

Earlier in the chapter we discussed a **scatterplot** graph. The purpose of the scatter plot is to examine the relationship between the **independent** (x) and **dependent** variables (y). If that relationship appears linear, we could imagine a straight line through most of the points. We can then look at how close the points are to the imaginary line, and thus can consider the strength of that relationship. The closer the points are to the line, the stronger the relationship between the two variables. While the actual calculations for determining the equation of the regression line is detailed and complex (and beyond the scope of this book), the focus at the middle school level is not on the actual calculation, but rather on the interpretation of its meaning. One way to informally examine the **regression line** (also called the **line of best fit**) is to plot the data points and lay a string down in such a way as to reflect the general direction of the points. Students can then write an equation based on the slope and y-intercept (or the point-slope form). Often, middle school students use graphing calculators to compute the linear regression equation based on the input of the data. It will actually yield the slope and y-intercept, so that the required equation can be determined. A graphing calculator will also reveal the correlation coefficient. The calculation of this quantity is beyond the scope of this book, but the concept is centered on how close the **correlation coefficient** is to 1. The closer this value is to 1, the better the equation models or fits the data. To better understand this relationship, let's look at an example.

Example 17   Crickets make their chirping sounds by rapidly sliding one wing over the other. Data collected concerning the number of chirps crickets make per second and the temperatures in Fahrenheit are recorded in the table below. Scientists wonder if there is any relationship between the number of chirps a cricket makes per second and the temperature. Based on the data, determine if there is a correlation between the number of chirps and the temperature and explain your reasoning. In your explanation, include any graphical representation and computations you use as support.

Chirps/second	Temp in F°
20.0	88.7
16.1	71.5
19.5	93.4
18.2	84.1
17.0	80.7
15.6	75.0
14.8	69.8
17.2	82.1
15.3	69.3
16.1	83.2
15.0	79.7
17.3	82.5
16.0	80.8
17.1	83.6
14.2	76.1

Solution: Consider making a scatter plot of the data. You may notice that as the temperature gets hotter, there are fewer chirps made by the crickets. In fact, it seems to be a linear relationship. Thus, we could use the linear regression function on the graphing calculator to determine how good a fit it is. Figure 5.16 shows the scatter plot.

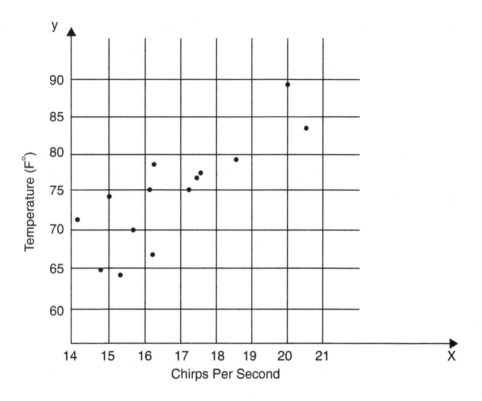

Figure 5.16

It appears that the data is linear, so we could use two of the points (18.2, 84.1) and (15.6, 75.0) to estimate a line of best fit. Then $m = \dfrac{75.0 - 84.1}{15.6 - 18.2} = 3.5$. Using the point-slope form for a linear equation and substituting the point (18.2, 84.1), we get $y - 84.1 = 3.5\,(x - 18.2)$, which simplifies to $y = 3.5x + 20.4$, which is the equation for the line of best fit.

NOTE:

A TI-83 calculator would reveal that the linear regression equation is $y = 3.326x + 24.728$. In addition, the correlation coefficient, called r, has a value of approximately 0.82. This number is considered to indicate a fairly strong positive correlation.

You will notice in the graph that the points are not too far from the line, which indicates a fairly good fit. But suppose there were another data point that had been collected, such as (17.9, 58). If you graph this point, you will notice that is far away from the line and from the other points. This point would be called an **outlier** because it appears isolated from the other data. Sometimes statisticians will omit such a point, as it greatly affects or possibly skews your results. However, this must be considered with great caution. It might also cause you to wonder why it happened. In the case of the crickets it may be an error in the data collection or just an anomaly!

At times, middle school students misunderstand outliers. Consider the point (21.3, 110). This point lies very far away from the other points, so some students might think it is an outlier. In reality, it is actually modeled well by the line! But in the context of the problem, it is not necessarily a real point on this line. Consider the fact that 110° F is very hot, so perhaps the crickets may actually die at that temperature!

We could also use the graph or the linear regression equation to predict how many chirps there would be at a particular temperature or what the temperature would be for a specific number of chirps. As an example, using the equation $y = 3.326x + 24.728$, if the number of chirps is 19, we would estimate that the temperature would be $(3.326)(19) + 24.728 \approx 87.9°$ Fahrenheit. Likewise, given a temperature of 73° (F), we would solve the equation $73 = 3.326x + 24.728$ to determine the number of chirps. In this case, $x \approx 14.5$.

Probability

Probability is defined as the likelihood or chance that a particular event will occur. It is an area common to everyday life and includes areas of application such as weather forecasting, the stock market, various board and card games, and playing a lottery. There are two types of probability, theoretical and experimental. **Theoretical probability** is determined by the ratio of the number of outcomes of an event to the total number of possible outcomes.

$$P(E) = \frac{\text{Number of outcomes for an event } E}{\text{Total number of possible outcomes}}$$

Experimental probability is based on the actual experience or experiment conducted for the event. It is determined by the ratio of the number of times the event actually occurred in the experiment to the total number of possible outcomes.

A **sample space** (*S*) indicates the set of all possible outcomes of an experiment. For example, the sample space for flipping a coin contains two possibilities. It will either be heads (H) or tails (T), that is $S = \{H, T\}$. As a second example, consider a spinner that has 3 equal sections, labeled red, yellow, and green. There are three possible outcomes, so we can write the sample space as $S = \{$red, yellow, green$\}$.

An **event** is a subset of a sample space. For example, let the sample space consist of the 52 cards of a deck. The experiment consists of drawing one card. If drawing a red queen from a deck of cards represents the event E, then the two possible outcomes are the queen of diamonds and the queen of hearts. This can be represented symbolically as $E = \{Q_D, Q_H\}$, where $Q_D =$ queen of diamonds and $Q_H =$ queen of hearts.

As another example of an event, let the sample space consist of the outcomes of tossing an ordinary die once. Then $S = \{1, 2, 3, 4, 5, 6\}$. If event F is described by the die landing on the numbers 1 or 3, then $F = \{1, 3\}$.

A critical assumption for sample spaces is that each outcome is assumed to be equally likely. Thus, if we are selecting one card from a deck, it is assumed that the probability of drawing the queen of hearts is the same as the probability of drawing the ace of clubs. Similarly, in tossing a die once, the probability of getting the number 1 is the same as the probability as getting the number 5. If a bag has one red, one green, and two blue marbles in it, it is more likely that a blue marble will be drawn than a red one.

Example 18   Determine the sample space when two coins are tossed one at a time.

> **Solution:**   Since either coin could land heads up or tails up, the possible outcomes are
>
> $TT =$ both tails up
>
> $HH =$ both heads up
>
> $HT =$ first coin with heads up and second coin with tails up
>
> TH = first coin with tails up and second coin with heads up

Thus, $S = \{TT, HH, HT, TH\}$. Note that HT and TH appear to be the same but they are actually two <u>different</u> outcomes since you are using two different coins. If the same coin were to be tossed twice, HT and TH would still represent different outcomes.

Example 19   Determine the probability of drawing a green marble from a bag that has 3 red marbles, 6 green marbles, 1 blue marble, and 4 yellow marbles in it.

Solution:

$$P(Green) = \frac{\text{Total number of green marbles in the bag}}{\text{Total number of marbles in the bag}} = \frac{6}{14} \approx 0.429$$

Computing Probabilities

Every probability value lies between 0 and 1 inclusively; that is $0 \leq P(E) \leq 1$, where 0 represents absolute certainty that an event *will not occur* and 1 represents absolute certainty that an event *will occur*.

Mutually exclusive events are two events from the same sample space that have no common outcomes. These events cannot occur simultaneously. To find the probability that one or the other of the two mutually exclusive events will occur, we add their individual probabilities.

Example 20   Two ordinary dice are tossed. What is the probability that the sum of the dice is either 3 or 7?

Solution: In this example, there are $(6)(6) = 36$ outcomes in the sample space. We'll use the notation $(1, 2)$ to indicate that the first die shows a 1 and the second die shows a 2. Let D represent the event that the sum of the dice is 3 and let F represent the event that the sum of the dice is 7. Then $D = \{(1, 2), (2, 1)\}$ and $F = \{(1, 6), (2, 5), (3, 4), (4, 3), (5, 2), (6, 1)\}$. Thus, $P(D \text{ or } F) = P(D) + P(F) = \frac{2}{36} + \frac{6}{36} = \frac{8}{36}$, which can be reduced to $\frac{2}{9}$. The answer may also be expressed as approximately 0.22.

At this point, we need to introduce some notation. The probability of either A or B (or both) is designated as $P(A \cup B)$, where the symbol $\cup$ means "union." The probability of both A and B is designated as $P(A \cap B)$, where the symbol $\cap$ means "intersection."

For any two events A and B, the following formula applies:

$P(A \cup B) = P(A) + P(B) - P(A \cap B)$. Note that whenever A and B are mutually exclusive, $P(A \cap B) = 0$. So, for mutually exclusive events A and B, the previous formula reduces to $P(A \cup B) = P(A) + P(B)$.

Example 21   One card is to be drawn from a deck. What is the probability that the selected card is either a king or a heart?

> **Solution:** $P(\text{King or Heart}) = P(\text{King}) + P(\text{Heart}) - P(\text{King \& Heart})$
> $= \dfrac{4}{52} + \dfrac{13}{52} - \dfrac{1}{52} = \dfrac{16}{52}$, which reduces to $\dfrac{4}{13}$. The decimal equivalent is approximately 0.31.

Note that the reason for subtracting $\dfrac{1}{52}$ is that the king of hearts was counted as both a king and a heart. If the fraction $\dfrac{1}{52}$ were not subtracted, then the king of hearts would have been counted twice.

Two (or more) events are **independent** if the occurrence of one event has no effect on whether or not the other event occurs. The probability that both events occur is the product of the probability for each event to occur. Thus, if D and F are independent events, then $P(D \cap F) = P(D) \times P(F)$.

Example 22   An ordinary six-sided die is rolled twice. What is the probability that the first number is even and the second number is odd?

> **Solution:**   If D represents the event of getting an even number on the first roll and F represents the event of getting an odd number on the second roll, then
>
> $P(D) = \dfrac{3}{6} = \dfrac{1}{2}$ and $P(F) = \dfrac{3}{6} = \dfrac{1}{2}$. Since these events are independent,.
> $P(D \cap F) = \dfrac{1}{2} \times \dfrac{1}{2} = \dfrac{1}{4}$.

Events D and F are called **dependent** if the occurrence of one event will affect the probability of the occurrence of the other event. To determine the probability that event D occurs and event F occurs when D and F are dependent we will see a similar multiplication but with a caveat! We introduce the symbol $P(F \mid D)$ to mean the probability that event F occurs, given that event D has already occurred. The formula for the probability that both D and F occur becomes $P(D \cap F) = P(D) \times P(F \mid D)$. Furthermore, since $P(D \cap F) = P(F \cap D)$, we can also write $P(F \cap D) = P(F) \times P(D \mid F)$. We note that $P(D \mid F)$ means the probability that event D occurs, given that event F has already occurred. Be extremely careful that you do <u>not</u> equate $P(F \mid D)$ and $P(D \mid F)$. These two probabilities have two distinct meanings! As with independent events, the concept of dependence can apply to more than two events.

Example 23   In a bag of jellybeans, there are 6 red, 8 yellow, 4 green, and 7 black ones. Two jellybeans will be randomly drawn, one at a time, with no replacement. What is the probability of selecting a red jellybean, followed by a black jellybean?

Solution: Let M represent the event of selecting a red jellybean on the first draw and let N represent the event of selecting a black jellybean on the second draw. Then $P(M) = \dfrac{6}{25}$, and since there are 24 jellybeans available for the second draw, $P(N \mid M) = \dfrac{7}{24}$. Thus, $P(M \cap N) = P(M) \times P(N \mid M) = \dfrac{6}{25} \times \dfrac{7}{24} = \dfrac{42}{600}$, which reduces to $\dfrac{7}{100}$.

Example 24   Four cards are drawn from a deck, one at a time, with no replacement. What is the probability that the first is a king, the second is an ace, the third is a queen, and the fourth is a king?

Solution: Let A = ace, Q = queen, K_1 = the first king, and K_2 = the second king.

Then $P(K_1, A, Q, K_2) = P(K_1) \times P(A \mid K_1) \times P(Q \mid K_1 \text{ and } A) \times P(K_2 \mid K_1 \text{ and } A \text{ and } Q)$

$= \dfrac{4}{52} \times \dfrac{4}{51} \times \dfrac{4}{50} \times \dfrac{3}{49} = \dfrac{192}{6,497,400}$, which reduces to $\dfrac{8}{270,725}$. The decimal equivalent is approximately 0.00003.

While we have discussed and provided examples of ways of computing probabilities, in particular theoretical probabilities, it is essential for middle school students to conduct hands-on experiments. By doing so, they will have a clearer understanding of probability and its associated formulas. For example, when a coin is flipped, there is a 0.5 probability that "tails" will show. It would be important for students to actually conduct an experiment to test this statement.

Suppose a student flips a coin 10 times and gets 3 heads and 7 tails. Then the experimental probability of tails is 0.3, even though the theoretical probability is 0.5. Next, suppose you ask all the students do the same experiment but flip the coin 100 times! What happens now is that the results are more likely to approximate the theoretical probability due to the greater number of trials. Of course, it gets tedious doing so many coin flips; for this reason, it is also useful (and much faster) to use various technological devices or programs to simulate the act of tossing a coin. Such applications exist for graphing calculators as well as for computer software and virtual manipulatives on the Internet. While the coin toss was provided as an example, there are many other such simulations that can be conducted by students to gain a better understanding of the relationship between theoretical and experimental probability.

Example 25   One card is drawn from a deck of cards. What is the probability of drawing a number card (that is, with a number from 2 to 9) or a king?

Solution: Let N represent the event of drawing a number card and let K represent the event of drawing a king. There are 32 number cards from 2 to 9 and there are 4 kings, so $P(N) = \dfrac{32}{52} = \dfrac{8}{13}$ and $P(K) = \dfrac{4}{52} = \dfrac{1}{13}$. These events are mutually exclusive, so $P(N \cup K) = \dfrac{8}{13} + \dfrac{1}{13} = \dfrac{9}{13}$, or approximately 0.69.

Example 26   There are 50 color tiles in a bag, in which 20 are red, 15 are blue, 10 are green, and the rest are yellow. Jessica will randomly pull out 2 color tiles, one at a time, with replacement. What is the probability that at least one of the tiles she pulls out is red?

Solution: Let R represent the event that the first tile is red and let T represent the event that the second tile is red. The phrase "at least one" is equivalent to "one or both." This implies that we need to determine the value of $P(R \cup T)$. These events are independent, but they are not mutually exclusive, so we need to include $P(R \cap T)$ in our calculation. You recall that for independent events, $P(R \cap T) = P(R) \times P(T)$. In our current example, $P(R) = P(T) = \dfrac{2}{5}$

Now, $P(R \cup T) = P(R) + P(T) - P(R \cap T) = \dfrac{2}{5} + \dfrac{2}{5} - \left(\dfrac{2}{5}\right)\left(\dfrac{2}{5}\right) = \dfrac{4}{5} - \dfrac{4}{25} = \dfrac{16}{25}.$

SPECIAL NOTE:

There is an alternative method for solving Example 26. We need to introduce the **complement** of an event. Given an event E', its complement (denoted as E') consists of all outcomes in the sample space that are not in E. As an example, if the sample space consists of the outcomes of tossing a die once, then $S = \{1, 2, 3, 4, 5, 6\}$. Let E represent the event of getting a 3. Then E' represents the event of getting any number except 3. Note that $P(E) = \dfrac{1}{6}$ and that $P(E') = \dfrac{5}{6}$, which is equivalent to $1 - P(E)$. With respect to Example 26, let's determine the probability that neither the first tile nor the second tile is red. This probability is calculated as $\dfrac{3}{5} \times \dfrac{3}{5} = \dfrac{9}{25}$. Then the probability that at least one of the tiles is red is $1 - \dfrac{9}{25} = \dfrac{16}{25}$.

Methods of Counting

Permutations and combinations are another aspect of probability that provide ways of counting. In the examples we have discussed to this point, we were able to list all possible outcomes of a sample space. However, for fairly large sample spaces, the process of listing them is not feasible. This is why the **Fundamental Counting Principle** is important. The Fundamental Counting Principle can be describes as follows:

Let D and E be two events. Suppose that event D can occur in n different ways. After D has occurred, event E can occur in m different ways. The number of ways the two events can both occur is $n \times m$. Consider the number of ways that a triangle with vertices A, B, and C can be named. There are 3 ways to pick the first letter, 2 ways to pick the second letter, and only 1 way to pick the third letter. We now have $3 \times 2 \times 1 = 6$ ways to write the name of the triangle. The six ways are listed below.

$\triangle ABC$ $\triangle ACB$ $\triangle BCA$ $\triangle BAC$ $\triangle CAB$ $\triangle CBA$

While this one is easy to list, it illustrates how the principle works.

Example 27   Suppose a car's license plate has 5 characters that are either numbers or letters. The first character must be a letter, but can be any letter from the English alphabet. Each of the second, third, and fourth characters can be either a letter or a digit from 0 to 9. The fifth character of the license plate must be a digit from 0 to 9. How many possible license plates are there?

(It is assumed that repetition of any letter or number is allowed.)

Solution: The following table illustrates the elements of the car's license plate. The number inside each box represents how many different characters are possible for each position.

26	36	36	36	10

Thus there are $26 \times 36 \times 36 \times 36 \times 10 = 12{,}130{,}560$ possibilities!

There are two applications of the Fundamental Counting Principle that we should consider. The first is a permutation of elements, and the second is a combination of elements. A **permutation** is a set of objects in which order matters or is a consideration.

Example 28   How many permutations are possible with the letters A, B, C, D, and E?

Solution: For the first position, there are 5 available letters. For the second position, there are 4 remaining letters because one of the five has already been used. For the third position, there are 3 remaining letters because two of the five letters have already been used. Continuing with this approach, there are 2 remaining letters for the fourth position, and finally only 1 remaining letter for the fifth position. Thus, we have a total of $5 \times 4 \times 3 \times 2 \times 1 = 120$ permutations.

You should note that Example 28 also represents a special product of numbers referred to as **factorial**. The product $5 \times 4 \times 3 \times 2 \times 1$ can be written as 5! In general n!, read as "*n* factorial," is the product $(n)(n-1)(n-2)(...)(2)(1)$. You can usually find this function on a calculator, which will simplify the calculation. Often we refer to permutations of *n* objects taken *r* at a time denoted as $_nP_r$, which is equal to

$$\frac{n!}{(n-r)!} = \frac{(n)(n-1)(n-2)(...)(n-r)(n-r-1)(...)(1)}{(n-r)(n-r-1)(...)(1)} = (n)(n-1)(n-2)(...)(n-r+1)$$

As a special case, if $n = r$, then $_nP_n = \dfrac{n!}{(n-n)!} = \dfrac{n!}{0!} = n!$

Students often have difficulty understanding why 0! is 1. It seems odd at first and students are usually told it is a definition. However, you can actually provide a method to show why 0! = 1 is a logical statement. Consider the following sequence of identities.

$5! \div 5 = 4!$
$4! \div 4 = 3!$
$3! \div 3 = 2!$
$2! \div 2 = 1!$

Based on this pattern then $1! \div 1$ should be 0!. But we also know that 1! = 1 so this implies that 0! = 1 as well! You can also check 0! on your calculator, and you will get 1.

Example 29   The Jackson family has won 11 trophies in tennis. They would like to display all of them on a shelf in the living room. Unfortunately, there is only room for 5 of them on the shelf. In how many ways can they select and arrange any 5 of these 11 trophies?

Solution: From left to right, any one of the 11 trophies can be placed first, any one of the remaining 10 trophies can be placed second, any one of the remaining 9 trophies can be placed third, and so forth. The answer is $11 \times 10 \times 9 \times 8 \times 7 = 55,440$. We recognize that this is equivalent to $_{11}P_5$.

For any examples that deal with permutations, we can see that order is important. In Examples 28 and 29, the elements were all different (such as 4 different letters of the alphabet). Suppose though that you are asked to find how many different ways the letters in the word *BROOM* can be arranged. In this case, not all of the letters are distinguishable. Let's label the two O's as O_1 and O_2. Note that the permutations BRO_1O_2M and BRO_2O_1M would appear identical. So would the permutations RO_1BO_2M and RO_2BO_1M appear alike. The solution is to divide 5! by 2!. Basically, we use the factorial of the total number of letters and then divide by the factorial of the number of repetitions of each letter. Here, the letter O appears twice. No other letter in the word $BROOM$ is repeated. Thus, the number of permutations is $\dfrac{5!}{2!} = \dfrac{120}{2} = 60$.

Example 30 In how many different ways can the letters of the word *BANANAS* be arranged?

Solution: There are a total of 7 letters, including 3 A's and 2 N's. Thus, the answer is $\dfrac{7!}{(3!)(2!)} = \dfrac{5040}{12} = 420$.

Example 31 In how many different ways can the letters of the word *MISSISSIPPI* be arranged?

Solution: There are not too many words in the English language with this many repetitions of letters! There are a total of 11 letters, including 4 S's, 4 I's, and 2 P's. Thus, the answer is $\dfrac{11!}{(4!)(4!)(2!)} = \dfrac{39,916,800}{(24)(24)(2)} = 34,650$.

A **combination** is a set of objects for which order does <u>not</u> matter. We use the notation $_nC_r$ as the number of combinations of n objects taken r at a time. The formula is

$$_nC_r = \frac{n!}{(n-r)! \times r!} = \frac{(n)(n-1)(n-2)(\bullet\bullet\bullet)(n-r+1)}{r!}.$$

It should also be noted that since $_nP_r = \dfrac{n!}{(n-r)!}$, we can also write $_nC_r = \dfrac{_nP_r}{r!}$.

Example 32 Heena is the personnel coordinator for an international company of 32 people. She needs to choose a committee of 10 people to travel to India for an important conference. How many different committees are possible?

Solution: For a committee, the order in which a particular selection is made is not important. Therefore, we need to compute the number of combinations of 10 people from 32.

The answer is $_{32}C_{10} = \dfrac{32!}{(22!)(10!)} = \dfrac{2.6313 \times 10^{35}}{(1.124 \times 10^{21})(3,628,800)} = 64,512,240.$

Example 33 You are forming a 10-member diving team from 12 girls and 14 boys. The team must have 4 girls and 6 boys. How many different 10-member teams are possible?

Solution: Our method of solving this problem is to determine the number of combinations of girls and boys separately, then multiply these numbers. Therefore, the answer will be the product of $_{12}C_4$ and $_{14}C_6$, which is $\dfrac{12!}{(8!)(4!)} \times \dfrac{14!}{(8!)(6!)} = 495 \times 3003 = 1,486,485.$

Real-Life Applications

It is helpful to consider actual applications of probability, permutations, and combinations within real-world situations. We have offered a few throughout the chapter but let's consider a few others.

Example 34 A combination lock will open when the correct choice of three numbers in order from 1 to 20 is selected. How many different "combinations" are possible?

Solution: We note that a combination lock really involves the Fundamental Principle of Counting, not combinations. The reason is that the order in which the numbers is selected does matter. Assuming that a number may be repeated, the answer is $20 \times 20 \times 20 = 8000.$

Example 35 There are 5 different stations in an assembly line for completing a particular product and the station processes can be performed in any order. The company is trying to determine which sequencing of stations is the most efficient. How many different orders will need to be tested?

Solution: There are 5 ways to begin the assembly line, then four ways to select the next station, then 3 ways to select the next station, and so forth. Thus, the answer is $_5P_5$, which is equivalent to $5! = 120$.

Example 36 In a group of 12 buildings, there are 5 ranch homes, 4 condominiums, and 3 apartments. Each building has a different shape so that no two buildings are alike. Linda is a real-estate agent and will visit 3 ranch homes, 2 condominiums, and 1 apartment. How many different selections of the 12 buildings can Linda visit?

Solution: For any particular category of building, the order in which she makes her selection is not important. Thus, the answer will be $(_5C_3)(_4C_2)(_3C_1) = 10 \times 6 \times 3 = 180$.

Example 37 Suppose you have a square dartboard with a circle inside it. The circle has a radius of 2 inches, and the length of each side of the square is 12 inches. What is the probability, to the nearest thousandth, that a dart lands inside the circle?

Solution: The area of the circle is $(\pi)(2^2) = 4\pi$ square inches, and the area of the square is $(12)(12) = 144$ square inches. The requested probability is the ratio of the area of the circle to the area of the square, which is $\frac{4\pi}{144} \approx 0.087$.

Probability Distributions

We have discussed skewness in relation to distributions. In this section we will explore three types of distributions, namely binomial, normal, and geometric in relation to solving problems involving statistics. A **binomial distribution** is a list of the outcomes of a binomial experiment and their associated probabilities. The experiment consists of n trials where the outcome for each trial is either a success or a failure. The probability of exactly N successes, ($N \le n$), in which p equals the probability of a success on a single trial is given by the formula $P(N) = (nC_N)(p)^N (1-p)^{n-N}$. The trials are independent, which means that one trial's outcome does not affect another trial's outcome.

Example 38 A coin is flipped 15 times. Assuming that the probability of landing on heads or tails is 0.5, what is the probability of getting tails exactly 6 times?

Solution: Let N represent the variable for the number of successes. Then $n = 15$, $N = 6$, and $p = 0.5$. Thus, $P(N = 6) = (_{15}C_6)(0.5)^6(0.5)^9 \approx (5005)(.015625)(.00195) \approx 0.1527$.

Example 39 A bag contains ten marbles, of which 4 are red and the rest are blue. Kenny will randomly select 3 marbles, one at a time with replacement. What is the probability that he selects exactly 2 red marbles?

Solution: The probability of selecting a red marble is $\frac{4}{10} = 0.4$, which becomes the value of p. In this example, $n = 3$ and $N = 2$. Thus, the answer is given by $(_3C_2)(0.4)^2 (0.6)^1 = (3)(0.16)(0.6) = 0.288$.

Note that for middle school students, the application of this formula is beyond their usual curriculum expectations. However, conducting actual experiments for students to test hypotheses is definitely within their experience and understanding.

A special case of the binomial distribution is the **geometric distribution**. In this type of distribution, we determine the probability for the first success in a binomial distribution. The actual number of trials is not used. The probability that the first success will occur on the xth trial is given by the expression $p(1-p)^{x-1}$.

Example 40 Suppose a card is drawn from a deck, then replaced before the next card is drawn. What is the probability that the first time either a 5 or 6 number card is drawn is on the fifth draw?

Solution: There are 8 cards in the deck that are either a 5 or a 6, so $p = \frac{8}{52} = \frac{2}{13}$. Thus, the required probability is $\left(\frac{2}{13}\right)\left(\frac{11}{13}\right)^4 \approx 0.0789$.

Again, this calculation is beyond the scope of middle school curriculum, but have students conduct experiments. This will help them understand the actual calculation.

Finally, the most common statistical distribution is the **normal distribution**. A normal distribution reflects continuous variables and how they cluster around the mean. It is bell-shaped, so that its maximum value is the mean. A set of data that is normally distributed, when graphed, will be similar to a symmetric histogram. Thus, the mean, median, and mode are identical. Examples of data that resemble normal distributions are the heights of all adult men and the highest daily temperature in a given city over a period of time. Figure 5.17 illustrates a normal distribution.

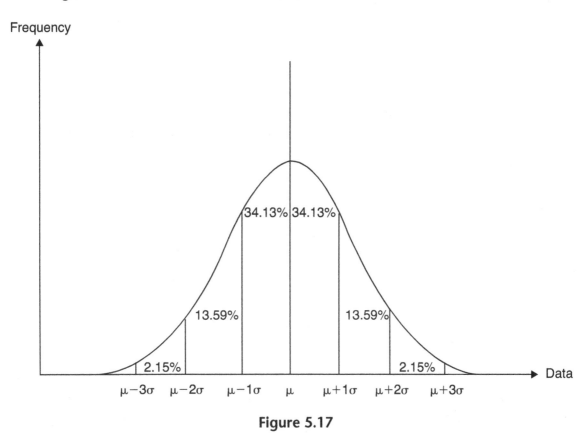

Figure 5.17

The curve is continuous but never intersects the x-axis, and all the dependent variable values (y) are positive. The main ingredients that affect the shape of a normal distribution are the mean and standard deviation. Both of these have been discussed earlier in this chapter. It may be helpful to look at cases related to mean and standard deviation differences and how they impact the graph.

The values on the x-axis represent a number of standard deviations from the mean. For example, $\mu + 1\sigma$ represents the value that lies one standard deviation above the mean. Likewise, $\mu - 2\sigma$ represents the value that lies two standard deviations below the mean. The percents shown represent the approximate amount of data that lies between two given x values. As examples, about 34.13% of the data lies between μ and $\mu + 1\sigma$, and about 47.72% (13.59% + 34.13%) lies between $\mu - 2\sigma$ and μ. If you add up the given percents that correspond to all data that lie between $\mu - 3\sigma$ and $\mu + 3\sigma$, the total is 99.74%. This means that only 0.26% of all the data lies either below $\mu - 3\sigma$ or above $\mu + 3\sigma$.

Example 41   Given a normal distribution in which the mean is 15 and the standard deviation is 4, what percent of the data lies between the values of 11 and 15?

Solution: The number 15 corresponds to the mean. The number 11 lies four units below 15, so it corresponds to one standard deviation below the mean. Using Figure 5.17, the answer corresponds to the percent of data between $\mu - 1\sigma$ and μ is 34.13%.

Example 42   Given a normal distribution in which the mean is 60 and the standard deviation is 5, what percent of the data lies between 65 and 75?

Solution: The number 65 lies one standard deviation above the mean and the number 75 lies three standard deviations above the mean. ($75 - 60 = 15$ and $15 = 3 \times 5$). Using Figure 5.17, the answer corresponds to the percent of data between $\mu + 1\sigma$ and $\mu + 3\sigma$, which is 13.59% + 2.15% = 15.74%.

Example 43   Given a normal distribution of 1000 data items in which the mean is 100 and the standard deviation is 12. How many data lie between 88 and 124?

Solution: Since 88 is 12 units below 100, it corresponds to $\mu - 1\sigma$. The number 124 lies 24 units above 100 and since $24 = 2 \times 12$, this means that 124 corresponds to $\mu + 2\sigma$. Using Figure 5.17, the percent of data between $\mu - 1\sigma$ and $\mu + 2\sigma$ is 13.59% + 34.13% + 34.13% = 81.85%. Finally, the required number of data is (0.8185)(1000) = 818.5, which can be rounded off to 819.

Figure 5.18 shows two normal distributions where the means are the same, but the standard deviations are different.

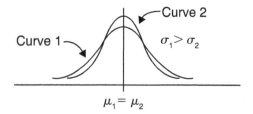

Figure 5.18

Figure 5.19 shows two normal distributions for which the means are different but the standard deviations are the same.

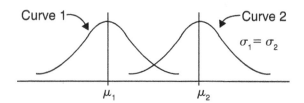

Figure 5.19

Figure 5.20 shows two normal distributions with different means and different standard deviations.

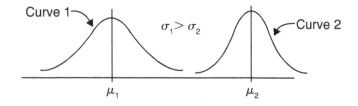

Figure 5.20

Figure 5.21 shows a normal distribution with a mean of 50 and a standard deviation of 10. Notice that most of the data falls between 20 and 80, indicating that values less than 20 or greater than 80 are very rare.

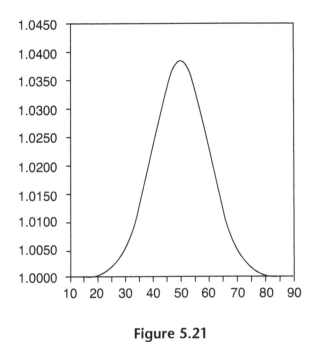

Figure 5.21

Figure 5.22 shows a normal distribution with a mean of 50 and a standard deviation of 2.

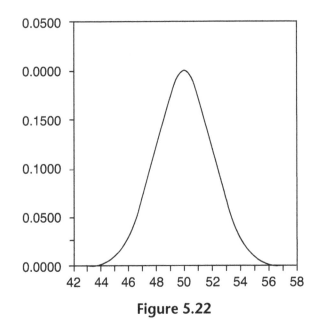

Figure 5.22

In Figure 5.22, notice that most of the data falls between 44 and 56. Even though Figures 5.21 and 5.22 both represent data with the same mean, the standard deviation is smaller in Figure 2.22.

Inferential Statistics

There are occasions in which we wish to make an educated guess about a population quantity based on the results of a corresponding sample quantity. In particular, suppose we calculate the mean and standard deviation of a sample. If our sample is reasonably large (at least 30), we can state a range of values that we expect will include the actual population mean. This range of values is called the confidence interval. The values that correspond to the **confidence interval** will change as our level of confidence changes. As the level of confidence increases, so does the corresponding interval of values. The actual expression for the confidence interval is given by $\bar{x} \pm (z_c)\left(\dfrac{\sigma}{\sqrt{n}}\right)$. As a review, $\bar{x}$ represents the sample mean, σ represents the population standard deviation, and n represent the number of data in the sample. Sometimes we do not know the population standard deviation. In that case we use s, which is the sample standard deviation. In that case, the above expression becomes $\bar{x} \pm (z_c)\left(\dfrac{s}{\sqrt{n}}\right)$.

In order to explain the meaning of z_c, we must mention that a **standard normal distribution** has a mean of zero and a standard deviation of 1. Then z_c represents a value on the standard normal distribution such that a given percent of the data lies between $-z_c$ and z_c. The term "critical z value" is often used to label z_c. The derivation of z_c values is beyond the scope of this course, but certain z_c values are the most popular. They are shown in the following table.

Percent Confidence	80%	90%	95%	98%	99%
z_c value	1.28	1.645	1.96	2.33	2.575

Example 44 One hundred English professors at various colleges were asked how many minutes they required to grade a student's final exam. The responses showed that the mean time was 9 minutes, with a standard deviation of 1.5 minutes. Assuming that a normal distribution exists for the time required by all English professors to grade a student's final exam, what is the 95% confidence interval for the population mean? Round off answers to the nearest hundredth.

Solution: Since we have the value of s (the sample standard deviation) and not σ {sigma} (the population standard deviation), we will use the expression

$\bar{x} \pm (z_c)\left(\dfrac{s}{\sqrt{n}}\right)$. By substitution, we have $9 \pm (1.96)\left(\dfrac{1.5}{\sqrt{100}}\right) \approx 9 \pm 0.29$.

The two values associated with 9 ± 0.29 are 8.71 and 9.29. Our answer is $8.71 < \mu < 9.29$.

Note that the final answer yields an inequality for the value of the population mean. We are asserting that we are 95% sure that the actual value of the unknown population mean lies between 8.71 and 9.29.

Example 45 Using the information in Example 44, what would be the 99% confidence interval for the population mean? Round off answers to the nearest hundredth.

Solution: The new z_c value becomes 2.575, so the expression for the confidence interval becomes $9 \pm (2.575)\left(\dfrac{1.5}{\sqrt{100}}\right) \approx 9 \pm 0.39$. The two corresponding values for 9 ± 0.39 are 8.61 and 9.39. Thus, the final answer is $8.61 < \mu < 9.39$.

It is important to note that the 99% confidence interval is wider than the 95% confidence interval. This is logical because as the interval becomes larger (wider), the more confident we can be that the actual value of μ does lie in that interval. As we would expect, as the percent confidence level decreases, the corresponding confidence interval becomes narrower. As an additional exercise, you are encouraged to determine the 90% confidence interval for Example 44. (Your answer should be $8.75 < \mu < 9.25$.)

Quiz for Chapter 5

1. The following graph depicts the relationship between grade level and amount of time a student spends watching television in a week. You observe that the relationship seems linear.

   The table of actual values is as follows.

Grade Level	1	2	3	4	5	6	7	8	9	10	11	12
Hours of Watching TV	8	7	6	14	8	21	17	20	24	23	30	32

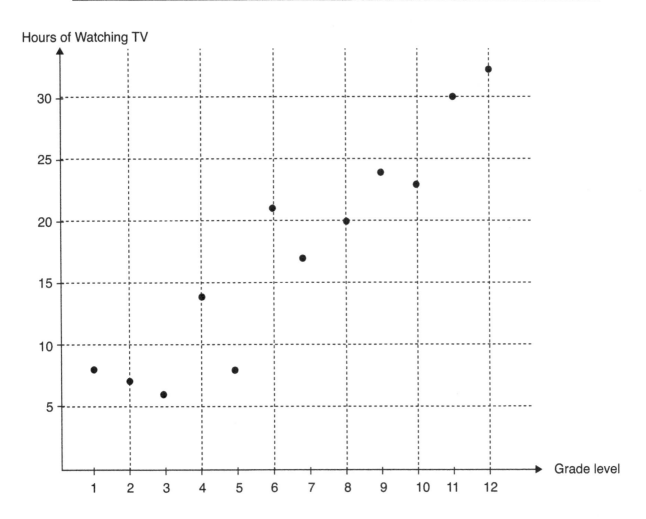

Which one of the following equations provides the best linear regression model for the scatter plot?

(A) $y = 2.43x + 2.14$

(B) $y = -x + 9$

(C) $y = 5.18x + 5.82$

(D) $y = 2x$

2.   For which one of the following box-and-whisker plots is the value of the median one-half the sum of the values of the first and third quartiles?

(A)
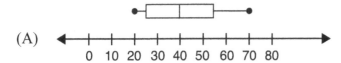

(B)
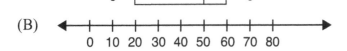

(C)
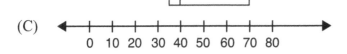

(D)
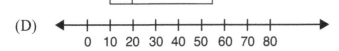

3.   A seven-sided die is rolled twice. The numbers on the die are 1 through 7. What is the probability that the die will show a prime number on the first roll or an even number on the second roll, or both of these outcomes?

(A) $\dfrac{8}{49}$

(B) $\dfrac{2}{7}$

(C) $\dfrac{37}{49}$

(D) $\dfrac{6}{7}$

4. Look at the following summary of classifications of students in a small college.

	Freshmen	Sophomores	Juniors	Seniors
Males	75	90	150	125
Females	105	170	200	85

The name of each student is put on a slip of paper and placed into a box. One slip of paper is randomly drawn. Given that the name drawn is that of a female student, to the nearest hundredth, what is the probability that the individual is a sophomore or junior?

(A) 0.37

(B) 0.56

(C) 0.61

(D) 0.66

5. Look at the following histogram.

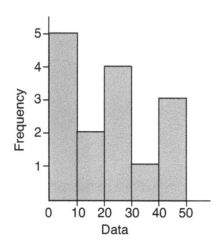

What is the arithmetic mean?

(A) 10

(B) 21.67

(C) 26.67

(D) 80

6.   A math teacher wants to provide her students with a practical example of a data set that illustrates the normal curve. Which of the following is her best choice?

   (A)   The shoe sizes of the 15 students in her class

   (B)   The weight of all the 17 year olds in the country

   (C)   The number of times out of 50 that a flipped penny will land on heads

   (D)   The height of the students in the high school

7.   Which of the following groups of data has two modes?

   (A)   2, 2, 3, 3, 4, 4, 5, 6, 7

   (B)   2, 2, 2, 3, 3, 4, 4, 4, 5

   (C)   2, 3, 3, 4, 4, 4, 5, 5, 6

   (D)   2, 3, 3, 3, 3, 4, 5, 6, 6

8.   A computer manufacturer interviews 10 people for three openings in the research and development area of the company. Four of the ten people are women. If all 10 are equally qualified, in how many ways can the employer fill the three openings if exactly two of those selected are women?

   (A)   6

   (B)   36

   (C)   120

   (D)   720

9.   Given the seven numbers 26, 30, 32, 32, 28, 21, 21, which one of the following can be added to this group of numbers so that the median of all eight numbers is 27?

   (A)   23

   (B)   27

   (C)   29

   (D)   31

10. The mean of a group of 20 numbers is 9. If one number is removed, the mean of the remaining numbers is 7. What is the value of the removed number?

(A) 16

(B) 25

(C) 40

(D) 47

Solutions

1. (A)

There are several ways to approach the problem. First, choice (B) can be eliminated as it reflects a negative correlation and the trend is certainly positive. Choice (D) can be eliminated easily as you can quickly graph it using 0 as the y-intercept and slope of 2, you find that the line that results rises in such a way as to be well above most of the points. That leaves choices (A) and (C). Choice (C) represents a line whose graph has a slope of 5, which is too steep to model the given data points. Thus, choice (A) is best. In fact, using the points (2, 7) and (12, 33), the equation becomes $y = 2.6x + 1.8$. This is a very close approximation for choice (A).

2. (A)

The vertical segment in the box represents the median, which is 40. The left-most vertical segment (left side of the box) and the right-most segment (right side of the box) represent the first and third quartiles, respectively. For Choice (A), their values are 25 and 55.

$40 = (1/2)(25 + 55)$. This relationship is not true for the other answer choices.

3. (C)

The prime numbers between 1 and 7 inclusive are 2, 3, 5, and 7; so the probability of getting a prime number on the first roll is $\frac{4}{7}$. Since the even numbers are 2, 4, and 6, the probability of getting an even number on the second roll is $\frac{3}{7}$. The probability of getting at least one of these outcomes (and possibly both) is given by $\frac{4}{7} + \frac{3}{7} - \left(\frac{4}{7}\right)\left(\frac{3}{7}\right) = \frac{37}{49}$.

4. (D)

There are a total of 560 female students. Of that total, 370 are either sophomores or juniors. Then $\frac{370}{560} \approx 0.66$.

5. (B)

To find the arithmetic mean, $\overline{x}$, multiply each different number by its associated frequency. The numbers to be used are the midpoints of the intervals, since we do not know the individual values. Add the products and then divide by the total frequency of numbers. $\overline{x} = [5(5) + 2(15) + 4(25) + 1(35) + 3(45)] \div 15 \approx 21.67$.

6. (D)

The students in the statistics class have a reasonable chance at being able to sample a large enough portion of the students at their high school to get a reasonable estimate of the population. The data collected would produce a normal curve under these circumstances. This choice provides a concrete and mathematically correct option. Choice (A) would not provide enough students, and the data collected is unlikely to yield a normal curve over such a small, homogenous sample. Choice (B) is problematic as there is no practical way to collect the data for such a large sample. The data in Choice (C) would not produce a normal curve.

7. (B)

The two modes are 2 and 4. Choice (A) has three modes. Choices (C) and (D) each have only one mode.

8. (B)

Using the Fundamental Counting Principle, there are $_4C_2 \cdot {_6C_1}$ ways of choosing two women and 1 man. Thus, the number of ways to fill the three openings is $_4C_2 \cdot {_6C_1} = \dfrac{4!}{2!2!} \cdot \dfrac{6!}{1!5!} = 6 \cdot 6 = 36$.

9. (A)

When 23 is added to the list, the numbers will appear in ascending order as follows: 21, 21, 23, 26, 28, 30, 32, 32. The median will equal the mean of the two middle numbers 26 and 28, which would be 27. Choice (B) would give a median of 27.5. Choice (C) would give a median of 28.5. Choice (D) would give a median of 29.

10. (D)

The sum of the original group of 20 numbers is $(9)(20) = 180$. The sum of the new group of 19 numbers is $(7)(19) = 133$. The difference between the two sums 180 and 133 is 47, which is the value of the removed number.

Mathematical Processes and Perspectives

Introduction

This chapter deals with Domain V Competencies 015–016 related to mathematical processes that include problem solving, communication, connections, and reasoning. Throughout each of Chapters 2–5, as specific content has been addressed, the mathematical processes have also been integrated. In this way, the reader understands these processes with respect to mathematical content. Thus, in this chapter, we will review some ideas related to the processes and encourage the reader to revisit each chapter as it relates to these processes. While the processes are presented in individual sections in this chapter, remember that they are connected rather than independent. They support one another and are integral to gaining a deep understanding of mathematics. For example, when applying problem solving approaches, you may consider the type of representations that may be useful. Then you should be able to justify their solutions through the use of appropriate mathematical language. We must recognize that the processes are not isolated events, but rather interconnected!

Role of Problem Solving in Mathematics

For many students in mathematics, **problem solving** is the cornerstone of understanding mathematics and approaching problems as presented in the mathematics classroom or encountered in everyday life. When a problem is presented or encountered, students must understand the problem or question being asked, consider what information given is pertinent, and recognize what additional information needs to be considered. Students then work on organizing this information, devising a plan or strategy for solving the problem, and then taking steps to actually solve the problem. If the selected strategy does not yield a successful solution, then perhaps you need to revisit the problem and the given information in order to consider other options. Further, the student needs to examine if the solution obtained is reasonable within the context of the problem's parameters. This may come in the form of remembering to include units of measure, considering the domain or range of a function, or determining whether the solution is realistic when given as a decimal or whole number.

Another aspect that is related to reasonableness is student use of **estimation**. When a student encounters a problem, it is often helpful to consider what would be a reasonable estimate of the solution. Then, when the problem is solved, the student will have a good idea whether his/her approach was correct. If not, then perhaps a calculation error was made or the student misunderstood the given information.

Often, middle school students (and teachers, too!) get a solution, write it down, and fail to consider if the solution is **reasonable**. This reflection process is central to a deeper understanding of mathematics. Even if a reasonable and correct solution is reached, sometimes students miss opportunities for strengthening their mathematical understanding. This can be achieved by extending the problem, looking at other strategies, or investigating connections that the problem may have to other mathematical ideas. It is important that you encourage students to revisit the problem, examine the solution in relation to the problem, and then look for connections to other mathematical concepts. You should remember that these ideas and approaches to problem solving do not necessarily come naturally or automatically to all students; thus, you should strive to teach these ideas and incorporate activities that allow students to develop effective problem solving skills.

Finally a note about types of problem solving strategies and skills is in order. The following is a list of possibilities, but certainly is not exhaustive!

- Draw a picture or diagram

- Find a pattern

- Make it a simpler problem

- Make a list

- Construct a table

- Work backwards

- Apply guess and check

- Estimate the solution

- Apply logical reasoning

- Act it out

So as you approach a problem, consider what type of strategy might work best for it. You may want to return to exercises and quizzes in the content chapters to examine more closely how you solved the problems and the approaches that you used that were effective. Reflect on whether there were other useful strategies to consider. And finally, connected to teaching about problems solving, do not assume your students will just naturally know all the strategies as mentioned previously. Select tasks and plan instruction in such a way to support your students in becoming flexible, effective, and confident problem solvers!

Example 1   Consider problem #10 in the Chapter 3 quiz. How did you solve the problem? Did you use a proportion or an inequality? Did you consider using a table or making an estimate? This problem can be approached using a variety of different strategies. The solution provided shows the use of direct variation with proportions, but there are other approaches. If you used inequalities, your solution may have looked like this

$$\$2.95x \leq (\$2.75)(8)$$
$$\$2.95x \leq 22$$
$$x \leq 7.46$$

where x represents the number of gallons Jolene buys at \$2.95 per gallon.

Thus Jolene can purchase approximately 7.46 gallons.

Another approach could be creating a table of values for the \$2.75 per gallon price up to 9 gallons and then creating a table for the \$2.95 per gallons price.

# of gallons	Price in $
1	2.75
2	5.50
3	8.25
4	11.00
5	13.75
6	16.50
7	19.25
8	22.00

# of gallons	Price in $
1	2.95
2	5.90
3	8.85
4	11.80
5	14.75
6	17.70
7	20.65
8	23.60

You might notice from the first table that you must stay under $22, because that is the amount of money you had for purchasing gas. Looking at the second table, we see that $22 falls between 7 and 8 gallons, but is closer to 7 gallons. In fact, the difference is $1.35, which is just under the price of a half-gallon, Thus, from the given answer choices, 7.46 is the closest.

Another approach would be to work backwards using the gallons in each response choice and then calculating the cost for each amount to see which is closest to $22. You will notice that choices (C) and (D) are over $22, while (A) and (B) are both under $22, (B) is the closest to $22.

Role of Communication in Mathematics

It is necessary for both you and your students to effectively and meaningfully communicate mathematically. Mathematics is a language that involves contextual vocabulary, definitions, syntax, and grammar. It is essential that students, as well as teachers, use appropriate and precise vocabulary, descriptions, and definitions. Careless or ambiguous use of mathematical language does not support understanding and often fosters misunderstandings.

At times it may be a simple matter of direct translation of word to a symbol such as "is" to "=," but more often it is much more complex. You may need to provide support for your students when decoding and interpreting information. These could include the use of symbols, formulas, equations, diagrams, and graphs. Thus, it is essential that you understand the role of representations when communicating mathematically. Representations may be graphical, numerical, symbolic, pictorial, verbal, or written. In addition, there may be concrete materials that support both geometric and algebraic approaches. Again, you may want to review Chapters 2–5 and examine the use of representations in communicating mathematical ideas. You will find examples of various types such as the use of algebra tiles, graphing calculators, dynamic computer drawing tools, equations, and formulas.

The chart below identifies problems from previous chapters that you may want to revisit. They illustrate the use of various representations to communicate mathematical ideas and understanding.

Location	Type of Communication and/or representation
Chapter 2 Figure 2.2	Tree diagram for categories of numbers
Chapter 2 Figures 2.3 and 2.4	Pattern blocks with fractional relationships
Chapter 3 Example 3	Algebra tiles in working with polynomials
Chapter 3 Figure 3.18	Graph for solving a system of equations
Chapter 4 Example 16	Compass and straightedge to construct a circle
Chapter 4 Example 8	Formal mathematical proof
Chapter 4 Example 20	Venn diagram for categories of quadrilaterals
Chapter 5 Example 44	Application of a formula
Chapter 5 Example 27	Design a simulation to communicate understanding

The ability to communicate mathematically is essential when connected to justification and proof, particularly when these are examined with respect to assessment of student understanding. If the student cannot communicate effectively, you will be challenged to understand what a student knows. In the same way, if you cannot communicate effectively, then the students will struggle to understand mathematics. Students need opportunities in both written and verbal form to communicate what they understand mathematically, including the use of various technological tools such as graphing calculators.

Example 2   Ernest, a 7th-grade student, is asked to compute $-6 + 4$ and gets -2 as the answer. The teacher checks and affirms that his solution is correct. With no further questioning or explanation, the teacher assumes the student understands how to compute the sum of two integers with different signs. But, what if the teacher asked Ernest to explain why -2 is the solution and he responds by saying,

> "I subtracted 6 and 4 and got 2. Since a negative and a positive is a negative, the answer is negative. So I got -2 for my answer."

In this case, if the student had been given $(6) + (-4)$ and used his same reasoning he would also have answered -2, which would have been incorrect. Also, in his explanation, it is unclear what is meant by "a negative and a positive is a negative." This is not precise and appropriately mathematical language. In the first case, since no communication was required other than the final answer, the teacher would not have known the misuse of rules that perhaps had been applied. The teacher may have followed up with having Ernest revisit the problem using a number line or color tiles to demonstrate his understanding of the problem.

You need to also consider special communication challenges that English Language Learners (ELL) encounter related to understanding mathematical language in English. ELL students are also learning English in a social context. Some mathematical terms require the learner to understand how that word meaning may change, depending on the context. For example, the interpretation of the word "mean" will vary, depending on whether we are talking about finding the "average" of a set of data or if we are asking about the interpretation of a particular problem. Furthermore, the word "mean" can also refer to the personality of an individual. Even a word such as "table" can have multiple meanings depending on the context.

Role of Connections in Mathematics

Connections in mathematics relate to both applications of mathematics to real world/real-life situations and to relationships between mathematical concepts and ideas. Throughout Chapters 2–5, you will find examples of mathematical problems within the context of applications such as art, business, science, and the social sciences. While some of the application areas may seem too sophisticated for (or not in the experience of) the middle school student, it is important to incorporate applications throughout the instruction of the content. In this way, students can see the relevancy and importance of understanding the concepts and skills that they are studying. Finding areas of interests, connecting to community resources, and integrating authentic experiences into the instructional sequence are vital for students to build mathematical connections. The following table identifies specific problems in Chapters 2–5 that illustrate real-world applications that the reader may want to revisit.

Location	Application Type
Chapter 3 Examples 42–45	Linear graph on water height
Chapter 3 Example 46	Quadratic equation for area and perimeter of a fence
Chapter 3 Example 52	System of equations for ticket sales
Chapter 3 Example 66	Digital video sales based on a quadratic function
Chapter 4 Example 25	Area of an ice-surfacing machine
Chapter 4 Example 45	Measurement error and football field
Chapter 5 Example 34	Combination locks
Chapter 5 Example 37	Probability with dartboards

The second type of connection that relates to mathematical ideas will aid the student in understanding the structure of mathematics and help build a coherent view of mathematics. These connections may be about

(a) understanding the relationship between a graphical representation of data and its corresponding table of values,

(b) recognizing that "completing the square" relates to deriving the quadratic formula,

(c) realizing that the method for finding the area of a circle is related to finding the area of a parallelogram.

Understanding the connections between the symbolic and concrete representation of a mathematical idea provides a means for students to see that mathematics makes sense and is not something that just "magically" happens. For example, students should understand how the use and manipulation of algebra tiles aids in developing an understanding of factoring. Without any deliberate connection of the tiles to the factoring process, students may view the tiles as "toys" and not as a means for understanding the principles of factoring. Creating models from data collected and understanding the relationship between algebraic and geometric concepts help students view mathematics as a coherent structure. These examples, as well as many others, have been shown throughout Chapters 2–5, within the context of the content being studied. As you review those chapters, you may want to do so with the lens of looking for and understanding the connections. Understanding these connections will aid you in lesson planning and task selection when providing instruction. The following table provides examples of connections between mathematical ideas found in Chapters 2–5.

Location	Mathematical Connection
Chapter 2 Example 11	Connection of decimals, percents, and fractions
Chapter 3 Example 3	Connection of algebra tiles to symbolic representation
Chapter 3 Examples 28–32	Connection between methods for solving quadratic equations and graphical interpretations
Chapter 4 Example 28	Connection of a geometric diagram to the Pythagorean theorem
Chapter 4 Figures 4.51, 4.52	Connection between the area of a parallelogram and the area of a rectangle
Chapter 4 Figure 4.60	Connection between the area of a rectangle and the area of a circle
Chapter 5 Example 20	Connection between sample space and probability

Role of Reasoning in Mathematics

Reasoning and proof are fundamental to understanding and communicating mathematical concepts. The ability to conjecture, investigate, and draw valid conclusions based on sound reasoning are important in developing mathematical understanding. Types of reasoning include

- Indirect proofs (proof by contradiction)

- Deductive reasoning (conclusion follows from set of premises)

- Inductive reasoning (specific examples leading to a generalization)

Each of these was specifically discussed in detail, and examples were provided in Chapter 5 with respect to geometry. These approaches are equally valid within numeric, algebraic, geometric, and statistical situations. You will find examples of the two most common types of reasoning used in middle school math, namely deductive and inductive reasoning, as you review Chapters 2–5. The following table provides specific examples in which we have studied deductive and inductive reasoning.

Location	Type of Reasoning or Proof
Chapter 2 Example 1	Deductive reasoning (Categories of numbers)
Chapter 4 Example 8	Deductive Reasoning (Two-Column Proof)
Chapter 3 Examples 1 and 2	Inductive Reasoning

Quiz For Chapter 6

1. What is the primary purpose of a mathematical counterexample?

    (A)   To justify a general claim based on a given set of statements

    (B)   To provide new examples that do not resemble a given set of statements

    (C)   To provide a different approach to solving a given equation

    (D)   To negate a general claim based on a given set of statements

2. Which one of the following is an example of deductive reasoning?

    (A)   The first term of a sequence of numbers is 1, the second term is 3, and the third term is 5. Thus, the nth term is $2n - 1$.

    (B)   The sum of the angles in ΔTUV and in ΔXYZ is 180°. Therefore, the sum of the angles in any triangle is 180°.

    (C)   All rectangles have four right angles. Since $ABCD$ is a rectangle, it must have four right angles.

    (D)   Line l_1 has a slope of 5 and line l_2 has a slope of 4. Line l_1 is closer to the appearance of a vertical line than l_2. Thus, the larger the slope of a line, the more vertical the line will appear.

3. Consider the following three statements:

(a) $1 + 3 = 2^2$,   (b) $1 + 3 + 5 = 3^2$,   and   (c) $1 + 3 + 5 + 7 = 4^2$.

Using inductive reasoning, which one of the following would apply?

    (A)   The sum of the first n consecutive positive odd integers equals n^2.

    (B)   The sum of any consecutive odd integers equals n^2.

(C)   The sum of the squares of the first n positive odd integers equals $(n-1)^2$.

(D)   The sum of the squares of any consecutive odd integers equals $(n+1)^2$.

4.   Look at the following diagram.

	x	x	1	1	1
x	x^2	x^2	x	x	x
1	x	x	1	1	1
1	x	x	1	1	1
1	x	x	1	1	1
1	x	x	1	1	1

This is an example of using algebra tiles to represent the factoring of which polynomial?

(A) $2x^2 + 3x + 3$

(B) $3x^2 + 8x + 3$

(C) $2x^2 + 11x + 12$

(D) $3x^2 + 11x + 7$

5.   Melissa decided to invest $2,000 into Bank One for a period of five years. This bank pays an annual interest rate of 6%, compounded annually. Her friend Rocco chose to invest some money into Bank Two for five years. Bank Two also pays an annual interest rate of 6%, but the money is compounded quarterly. To the nearest dollar, how much money should Rocco invest in order for his amount to match Melissa's amount at the end of five years?

(A) $1990

(B) $1987

(C) $1984

(D) $1981

6. Mrs. Parallel teaches an algebra class. She asked her students to write the following statement using algebraic symbols. "Given three consecutive numbers, the sum of the first two is three times the third number." Which of the following is the correct equation to use for finding the three numbers?

    (A) $x + (x + 2) = 3(x + 4)$

    (B) $(x)(x + 2) = 3(x + 4)$

    (C) $(x)(x + 1) = 3(x + 2)$

    (D) $x + (x + 1) = 3(x + 2)$

7. Mr. Perpendicular teaches a sixth-grade math class. He has asked his students to convert 50 miles per hour to a measure in yards per second. One of the students, Alicia, offered the following response:

    1760 yards is equivalent to one mile, so 50 miles is equivalent to $(50)(1760) = 88,000$ yards. There are 360 seconds in one hour, so 88,000 divided by $360 = 244.4$ yards per second. What should be Mr. Perpendicular's response?

    (A) Alicia's answer is incorrect. She should have divided 88,000 by 3600.

    (B) Alicia's answer is incorrect. She should have multiplied 50 by 5280.

    (C) Alicia's answer is incorrect. She should have multiplied 88,000 by 360.

    (D) Alicia's explanation is completely correct.

8. Which algebraic concept can be BEST used to illustrate a method by which $1002 \cdot 998$ can be calculated without the use of a calculator?

    (A) $(a - b)^2 = a^2 - 2ab + b^2$

    (B) $(a - b)(a + b) = a^2 - b^2$

    (C) $(a)(a + b) = a^2 + ab$

    (D) $(a + b)(a^2 - ab + b^2) = a^3 + b^3$

9. Steve wishes to estimate how many miles per gallon his Honda gets. When he last filled up his car with gas, his odometer reading was 20,000. He is about to fill up his car with gas today, with his odometer reading 20,180. Which of the following would be the BEST method?

    (A) Identify the number of gallons needed to fill up. Divide this number into the sum of 20,000 and 20,180.

    (B) Identify the number of gallons needed to fill up. Divide this number into the difference of 20,180 and 20,000.

    (C) Identify the cost to fill up. Divide this number into the difference of 20,180 and 20,000.

    (D) Identify the cost to fill up. Divide this number by the number of gallons. Then multiply this answer by the difference of 20,180 and 20,000.

10. In evaluating the expression $70 - 10 \times 3 + [(6^2 \div 4) + 3]$, which of the following steps should NOT be used?

    (A) Dividing 36 by 4

    (B) Multiplying 10 by 3

    (C) Subtracting 10 from 70

    (D) Adding 3 to 9

Solutions

1. **(D)**

    The purpose of a counterexample is to provide evidence that contradicts a general claim that is based on a given set of statements.

2. **(C)**

    In deductive reasoning, the validity of a general statement is applied to a specific case.

3. (A)

"The sum of the first n consecutive positive odd integers equals n^2" expresses the relationship that exists in each of the three examples.

4. (C)

There are two boxes labeled as "x^2", eleven boxes labeled "x," and twelve boxes labeled "1." The actual factors are shown by the horizontal and vertical representations that lie outside the boxes. They are $2x + 3$ and $x + 4$, respectively. Note that $2x^2 + 11x + 12 = (2x + 3)(x + 4)$.

5. (B)

At the end of five years, Melissa will have a total of $(\$2000)(1.06)^5 \approx \$2676.45$. Let x represent the amount that Rocco should invest in Bank Two. Since his money is being compounded quarterly, the interest per quarter is $\dfrac{0.06}{4} = 0.015$. In addition, there are $(5)(4) = 20$ compounding periods. Then $(x)(1.015)^{20} = \$2676.45$. Thus, $x = \dfrac{\$2676.45}{(1.015)^{20}} \approx \$1987$.

6. (D)

The three consecutive numbers are represented by x, $x + 1$, and $x + 2$. "The sum of the first two numbers" is expressed as $x + (x+1)$. "Three times the third number" is expressed as $3(x + 2)$.

7. (A)

There are 60 seconds in one minute and 60 minutes in one hour. This means that there are $(60)(60) = 3600$ seconds in one hour. Alicia should have divided 88,000 by 3600 to get the correct answer of $24.\overline{4}$ yards per second.

8. (B)

Rewrite $(1002)(998)$ as $(1000 + 2)(1000 - 2)$. This format resembles $(a + b)(a - b)$, which is equivalent to $a^2 - b^2$. Therefore, our answer becomes $1000^2 - 2^2 = 1,000,000 - 4 = 999,996$.

9. (B)

After Steve identifies the number of gallons he needs to fill up, he should divide this number into 180 (the difference of 20,180 and 20,000). The quotient represents the number of miles per gallon. For example, if he needs 8 gallons to fill up, then the number of miles per gallon is $\dfrac{180}{8} = 22.5$.

10. (C)

The operation of subtracting 10 from 70 should NOT be used.

The correct sequence of operations is as follows:

$70 - 10 \times 3 + [(6^2 \div 4) + 3] = 70 - 10 \times 3 + [36 \div 4 + 3] = 70 - 10 \times 3 + [9 + 3] = 70 - 10 \times 3 + 12 = 70 - 30 + 12 = 52.$

CHAPTER 7

Mathematical Learning, Instruction, and Assessment

Introduction

This chapter deals with Domain VI Competencies 017–019 related to learning, instruction, and assessment. Throughout each of Chapters 2–6, as specific content and processes have been addressed, approaches to learning mathematics, implications for instruction, and methods of assessment have also been integrated. In this way, you are able to develop a contextual connection within teaching and learning content. Thus, in this chapter, we will review some ideas related to the areas of learning, instruction, and assessment, and encourage you to revisit each chapter to examine these areas within the content and process areas.

Teaching and Learning Mathematics

Possibly the most important thing to remember regarding instruction is focusing on the learner. That may seem obvious, but often other things become the center of instruction such as curriculum documents, mandatory testing, or textbook frameworks. All of these are important and useful when planning, but the focus of instruction should be on the learner. This includes (a) the selection of a particular task to address the content, (b) the sequence and pacing related to the lesson, and (c) the determination of appropriate manipulatives and technological tools. As is often the case, there are many tasks one could choose to address a specific area of content. There are many variations in sequencing and pacing that would make a lesson effective. Also, there are multiple manipulatives and technological tools available to support a lesson. When making instructional decisions, always consider what would be best for the student to learn, and keep the instruction learner-centered. In the case of the test for which you are preparing, as you read a problem and the various options related to instruction (as well as learning and assessment), you should ask yourself what is the best choice that will focus on the learner. Several of the choices may seem reasonable, but analyze them carefully in terms of learner-centeredness.

Relationship of Content and Pedagogical Knowledge

Teaching mathematics is a journey that is exciting, rewarding, and challenging. To be an effective teacher of middle level mathematics, you must not only have a strong knowledge of the content at that grade level, but also have an understanding of the mathematics taught in the elementary grades and at the high school level. A major objective on the part of the middle grade math teacher is to strengthen the foundation that students bring to the middle grades, and to prepare them for a successful understanding of the mathematics that will be studied at the high school level. A deeper understanding of mathematics and its connectedness to everyday life will aid you in making instructional decisions.

As a math teacher, you need to not only know what to teach (the content), but also how to teach it. The "how to teach it" refers to pedagogical considerations, but recent research has shown that teachers need a specialized knowledge to teach mathematics, which is more than a knowledge of mathematics or pedagogy. This is often referred to as pedagogical content knowledge. It requires a specialized knowledge of the content that supports instructional decisions that consider the needs of students related to their prior knowledge, previous understandings, misunderstandings, learning styles, and developmental readiness. These decisions are reflected in areas such as

- **Choice of mathematical task:** Is the task or problem one that builds on previous experiences? Does it extend knowledge? Does it provide a discovery basis for a concept? Does it provide a relevant application? Will it take one class period or multiple class sessions? Is it accessible to all students? Can it be modified to address individual student needs?

- **Selection and implementation of manipulative and/or technology to support learning:** Does the tool (manipulative or technology) support student understanding? Does it provide a discovery experience? Does it allow for exploration? Does it give the student access to mathematical ideas that would not be accessible otherwise? Does the tool model the mathematics appropriately? Does it provide for movement from concrete to abstract? Is it the best approach for developing understanding? Is it available for all students? Do all students need the tool?

- **Choice of teaching strategy:** Is the concept best understood through a discovery approach? Is a discussion, demonstration, or lecture most appropriate? Will the selected strategy engage the learner? Does the instructional time and space available support the effectiveness of the strategy? Does it include opportunities for students to share understandings with the teacher and peers? Is there inclusion of a variety of levels of questions that include higher-level critical thinking? Is time for practice on a skill needed?

- **Type of grouping** (individual, partner, small group, whole class): What can students learn by working in small groups? Is their thinking better facilitated by working with others or independently? When should whole class instruction be used? Is there time needed for individual accountability? Is the task best approached with a student working with a partner? Does the grouping choice encourage discussion, question/answer, or dialogue?

The following table identifies problems from previous chapters that you may want to revisit that illustrate the consideration of these four decision-making areas related to instruction.

Location	Decision area
Chapter 3 Example 2; Chapter 2 Figures 2.3 and 2.4	**Selection and implementation of manipulative to support learning:** The use of color tiles and pattern blocks that allow for a discovery approach and accessibility to a variety of learners. These manipulatives also provide a venue for the movement from concrete to abstract.
Chapter 3 Examples 21, 22, and 23	**Selection and implementation of technology to support learning:** When exploring the horizontal and vertical shifts of the graph, the learner can use a graphing calculator. This method provides student accessibility to a concept with which the student might otherwise struggle.

Chapter 4 Example 9	**Choice of teaching strategy:** When determining the sum of the interior angles of the octagon, students may apply a formula. However, the explanation within the solution also provides a teaching strategy that would help a student understand how the formula was derived. If students were provided an activity to explore several polygons with a different number of sides and set up a table to look for a pattern, they may be able to inductively determine the formula. This technique would engage the learner at a higher level.
Chapter 4 Example 28	**Choice of mathematical task:** The use of a baseball diamond with the Pythagorean theorem illustrates a relevant application.
Chapter 5 Quiz Question #6	**Type of grouping:** When conducting a probability simulation, it is often beneficial to have students work in pairs. In this instance, the students can assist one another in collecting the data recording it, and discussing conclusions based on the data.

It is also important to know your students' strengths, struggles, interests, and learning preferences. While there is some debate as to the influence of learning styles, it is useful to understand the preferences strengths of your students and the nature of the tasks and content when planning instructional experiences. Learning styles include visual, auditory, and kinesthetic. Visual learners, tend to learn best from pictures, diagrams, and mental images. Auditory learners tend to learn best by hearing or listening to discussions, dialogues, or lectures, and may respond less through written communication. Kinesthetic learners (sometimes called tactile learners) tend to learn best with a hands-on approach, actively engaged in the physical activity related to the development of the concept. While these three are the most common styles, the teacher should be aware that some students gain a better understanding through reading and writing approaches. These approaches involve organizing and analyzing information, making lists, and constructing written justifications and descriptions. Remember that while a student may have a preferred or dominant learning style, students learn through a variety of modalities. Also, if a particular style is not strong, perhaps varied learning experiences can strengthen the student's learning in that modality.

The following table identifies problems from previous chapters that you may want to revisit that illustrate various learning styles of learners that are related to instruction.

Location	Learning Style
Chapter 3 Example 3	The use of algebra tiles related to polynomials, operations with polynomials, and factoring provides opportunities for kinesthetic as well as visual learners. These tiles enable students to understand polynomial relationships by connecting the concrete representations to the symbolic notations.
Chapter 3 Example 30	For the student who prefers reading and writing approaches, this example illustrates not only the algebraic solution, but also includes a written explanation of each step. It is followed by the graph of the function, which may aid visual learners in making necessary connections to the symbolic notation.
Chapter 4 Example 36	This example offers options for varied learner types and could encompass multiple approaches. In order to solve this problem, the student could draw the given polygons by hand or use a compute software drawing tool to determine if the shapes tessellate. This method would address the visual learner, but kinesthetic learners may benefit from having the actual physical shapes (i.e. pattern block hexagons), then positioning them to determine if the shapes tessellate. Alternately, a virtual manipulative experience could aid both the visual and kinesthetic learner.
Chapter 4 Figure 4.10	The teacher could offer a follow-up experience on the classification of triangles by dividing the class into groups of four and providing each group with a paper set of different types of triangles. Each group could be instructed to sort the triangles, reaching a group consensus regarding their reasoning for the classifications. This could be shared in written form or verbally through presentations to the whole class. Such an approach could address multiple learning styles including verbal, auditory, kinesthetic, and written.

Assessing Mathematical Understanding

When planning a lesson, clear goals and objectives should be devised and made apparent to the students. While most teachers have curriculum documents to guide their choice of objectives, it is equally important (if not more so) to assess your students' current level with respect to those objectives. In this way, effective instructional planning for reaching the stated goals and objectives can be based on those assessments. It is important that assessments reflect what is taught and how it is taught. Assessments can be formative or summative; they should be on-going and incorporate both informal and formal methods.

Informal and Formal Methods

An informal method is important during the instructional sequence in that it can be used to provide immediate feedback to students related to their understanding of a concept. This can be accomplished through the use of questioning and discussion with individual or small groups of students, as you walk around and monitor students as they work on problems, tasks, or projects. This is a time during which you can quickly scan student work, ask questions to have students further expand on their thinking, and address student questions that may lead to important discussions! It is also helpful when you provide written feedback on homework assignments and in-class tasks to assist students in monitoring their own understanding in preparation for more formal assessments.

Formal methods are used to inform both the student and you of a student's level of understanding on a specific concept or skill. These evaluations are often tests, quizzes, or culminating projects.

Formative and Summative Assessments

Formative assessments are on-going formal or informal methods that are used by the teacher to provide feedback to the student and inform instructional decision-making. These can occur when the teacher is observing students as they work, listening to student discussions, analyzing question and answer sessions, or providing feedback on practice problems or tasks.

Summative assessments, which are usually formal in nature, are generally used to make an evaluative judgment on the progress of a student based on a unit of study or over a course that spans an entire school year. They can also be used to evaluate instructional program effectiveness.

In order to illustrate both informal and formal methods, as well as formative and summative assessments, we will revisit Figure 4.10 in Chapter 4 and the description in the table on the previous page that was used to address learning styles. Here is the description:

"The teacher could offer a follow-up experience for students related to the classification of triangles by dividing the class into groups of four and providing each group with a paper set of different types of triangles. Each group could be instructed to sort the triangles, reaching a group consensus regarding their reasoning for the classifications. This could be shared in written form or verbally through presentations to the whole class. Such an approach could address multiple learning styles including verbal, auditory, kinesthetic, and written."

You could use a checklist assessment while the groups are working. This could serve as an informal assessment used in a formative manner to provide you with information on student understanding that could be used in planning future instruction. If the task were given at the end of a learning unit on triangle classification, the assessment might serve as a more formal, formative assessment as an evaluation of student understanding of the content.

The following table represents a potential checklist.

Student Name	Understands how to classify triangles according to side lengths	Understands how to classify triangles according to angle measures	Understands relationship between equilateral and equiangular triangles	Comments
1.				
2.				
3.				
4.				

√ indicates clear understanding

√- indicates partial understanding, with misunderstandings on some classification characteristics

x indicates significant misunderstandings as demonstrated through multiple errors in classifications

Comments: Provide examples to support assessment and other anecdotal evidence

It is essential that you use a variety of different types of assessments in order to better understand what students know and are able to do. This information can be used to evaluate student understanding, monitor progress, and plan future instruction. If you limit yourself to using assessments that focus only on skills or problems with one correct solution, then you are also limiting the information you can gather on what your students understand. Valuable evidence can be garnered from assessment opportunities that allow students to think critically, approach problems in multiple ways, and engage in complex tasks.

Types of assessment opportunities include performance-based tasks, open-ended questions, projects, portfolios, quizzes, tests, journals, checklists of expectations, homework, lab reports, and self-assessments.

When designing assessment protocols, it is important to consider several questions.

- Does the assessment accurately reflect the mathematical concept or skill?

- Does the assessment match the intended goals and objectives?

- Does the type of assessment parallel the instructional approach?

- Is the assessment clear and free of bias?

- Does the assessment take into account potential student errors and misunderstandings?

- Does the assessment provide an opportunity to learn?

- Does the assessment provide opportunities for communication and reasoning?

- Will the assessment provide an opportunity for the learner to demonstrate what s/he knows and understands about the particular mathematical concept or skill?

Student Errors and Misconceptions

One final topic related to assessment involves identifying and diagnosing student errors and misconceptions. Assessments often reveal not only what students know about a concept or skill, but also what they do not know based on a misunderstanding. What you may initially attribute to a "careless mistake" may actually result from a particular misunderstanding. Attending to student errors will allow you opportunities to design more effective instruction. When you anticipate potential errors and misunderstandings you can plan more effectively how and when to address these errors and their related misconceptions. If appropriate, some may be addressed during a lesson, but other times you will need to work with the individual or small group of students with similar misunderstandings. Consider the following examples:

Example 1 A student is working on solving the equation $2x + 4 = 18$ and writes $6x = 18$, so $x = 3$.

The student combined $2x$ and 4 to get $6x$. This problem may have occurred because the student does not understand what the variable x represents, and thus what the term $2x$ means and how it is different from the number 4.

Example 2   The student is asked to determine how many solutions there are for the equation $y = \frac{2}{3}x + 15$ by examining its graph. The student responds by stating it has no solution and provides the sketch of the graph shown below as Figure 7.1.

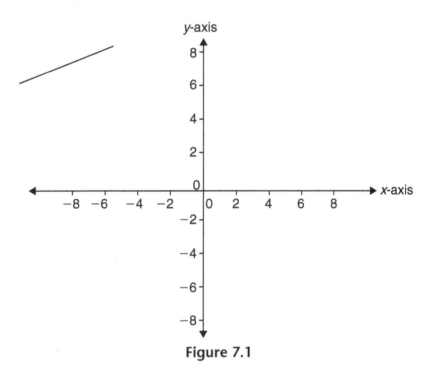

Figure 7.1

Perhaps the student used a graphing calculator to graph the equation. While the student may realize that the solution to the equation is where the graph crosses the x-axis, the graph does not show such an intersection. Therefore, the student concludes that there is no solution. What the student may not understand is that the graph provided does not provide the full view of this function. It is likely that the calculator screen has been set to a limited domain; thus the entire function is not visible. The student should have realized that the function is a line with a slope of $\frac{2}{3}$ and a y-intercept of 15. As such, it would eventually cross the x-axis. It would be a matter of adjusting the domain and range in the graphing window to be able to view the intersection and thus identify the solution. As an alternative approach, the student could recognize that the y value of the x-intercept can be determined by solving the equation $0 = \frac{2}{3}x + 15$. Then the student should be able to determine that the x-intercept is $(-22.5, 0)$.

Quiz For Chapter 7

1. Which one of the following illustrates the error of dividing by zero?

   (A) If $x = y$, then $x + 0 = y + 0$.

   (B) $\dfrac{5^3}{5^3} = 5^0$.

   (C) If $x = 3$, then $\dfrac{x}{x - 3} = \dfrac{3}{x - 3}$.

   (D) $(5)(4)(3)(2)(1)(0) = 0$.

2. Certain mathematical questions require a scoring rubric, whereby points are awarded for the method of approach solution as well as for the answer. For which one of the following should a scoring rubric be used?

   (A) Finding the area of a rectangle whose length is 12 units and whose width is 8 inches.

   (B) Finding the area of a sector of a circle for which the circumference is 18π and the central angle is $30°$.

   (C) Finding the perimeter of a triangle in which the sides are 8, 9, and 12.

   (D) Finding the measure of an interior angle of a regular hexagon.

3. Which of the following is the BEST rationale for creating small groups for learning a concept?

   (A) Students share their ideas and learn from each other.

   (B) Students discover which among them knows the most about the subject.

   (C) Students are forced to complete an assignment without the assistance of the teacher.

   (D) Students are given more time to reflect on their understanding of the material.

4. Auditory learners can respond BEST to a concept presenated by which of the following?

   (A) Diagram

   (B) Hands-on Approach

   (C) Discussion

   (D) Written Explanation

5.	A student asks a question that pertains to a concept that was just covered in yesterday's lesson. Which of the following would be the BEST approach on the part of the teacher?

(A)	Answer the student's question directly, but without a lengthy explanation.

(B)	Answer the student's question and remind the class that since this concept was covered in yesterday's lesson, it should have been learned.

(C)	Do not answer the student's question, but remind the class that this concept should have already been mastered.

(D)	Do not answer the student's question and assign additional homework on this concept.

6.	Four students are assigned to one of four different questions on the rules of exponents. Which one of the following miscalculations shows the LEAST amount of understanding of these rules?

(A)	$(5^3)(5^4) = 5^{12}$

(B)	$6^{10} \div 6^5 = 6^2$

(C)	$(7^3)^6 = 7^9$

(D)	$8^4 + 8^5 = 64^{20}$

7.	Ms. Anglewood teaches a geometry class. The results of the ten-question quiz she gave the class yesterday reveal that the majority of the class missed question #7, although overall the class scores were fairly good. Which of the following actions should Ms. Anglewood take?

(A)	Do not count the quiz and do not spend any more time with the material needed for question #7.

(B)	Do not count the quiz, but give additional assignments on the material for question #7.

(C)	Give the entire class credit for question #7 and do not spend any more time to explain the material in this question.

(D)	Count the quiz grades and spend more time explaining the material in question #7.

8. Which one of the following types of lessons would be MOST beneficial for a student who is a kinesthetic learner?

   (A) Watching a video on the applications of mathematics to the medical field

   (B) Using algebra tiles for algebraic factoring

   (C) Listening to the teacher's lecture on solving linear equations in one variable

   (D) Reading a set of instructions on how to solve a word problem on rate, time, and distance

9. A student claims that between any two numbers that are multiples of 10, there exist at least three primes. What would be the BEST response on the part of the teacher?

   (A) Agree with the student without any further discussion.

   (B) Agree with the student and ask the class to write a formal proof.

   (C) Show the class that although this claim is true in some cases, it is possible to find an example for which this claim is not true.

   (D) Disagree with the student and require the class to provide a counterexample.

10. Which of the following is the MOST important element in instruction?

   (A) Focusing on the learner

   (B) Concentrating on the curriculum

   (C) Teaching to the high-level achiever

   (D) Completing the topics in the prepared lesson

Solutions

1. **(C)**

   If $x = 3$, then the denominator of $x - 3$ has a value of zero.

2. **(B)**

   The student must first find the radius, given the circumference. Then, the area of the circle must be determined. Finally, a proportion must be used that includes the area of the circle, the central angle, and 360°. A scoring rubric can be used for each of these steps. For answer choices (A), and (C), only one arithmetic step is needed. For answer choice (D), substitution into an algebraic formula will yield the correct answer.

3. (A)

In small group arrangements, students can share their ideas more freely than when the teacher is presenting a lesson to the entire class. With a small group, students may communicate their thoughts with less fear of a possible negative reaction from the other classmates.

4. (C)

Auditory learners tend to better understand material by listening to discussions and dialogues.

5. (A)

The teacher should respond directly to the question because there may be other students who would benefit from the explanation. Since the topic was covered in a previous lesson, a lengthy explanation need not be given. Answer choice (B) is not the best option because it is demeaning to the student.

6. (D)

The errors include (a) multiplying the 8's where there is an addition symbol, and (b) adding exponents where the bases are connected by addition, not by multiplication. The correct way to find this sum is to calculate 8^4 and 8^5 separately, then add the results. (The correct answer is 36,864. The value of 64^{20} is approximately 1.33×10^{36}.) Each of answer choices (A), (B), and (C) shows a single error.

7. (D)

Since the class scores were fairly good, the teacher should count the quiz grades. Based on the fact that the majority of the class missed question #7, the teacher should spend additional time explaining the material contained in this question.

8. (B)

Kinesthetic learners (also referred to as tactile learners) tend to learn best through a hands-on approach, such as the use of algebra tiles.

9. (C)

The teacher should acknowledge that the student's claim is correct in some instances, but there are examples for which the claim is not true. An example where the claim is false occurs in the interval of integers between 60 and 70. Only the integers 61 and 67 are prime. Answer choice (D) would create a more hostile setting for the student and for the class.

10. (A)

The single most important element of instruction is to focus on the learner. Other elements are important, such as covering the curriculum requirements and teaching the topics in a given lesson. However, these elements are secondary. Teaching that is directed toward the high-level achiever will exclude the majority of students.

Practice Test 1

TExES Mathematics 115

This test is also on CD-ROM in our interactive TestWare® for this TExES Mathematics Assessment. We strongly recommend that you first take this exam on computer. You will then have the benefits of enforced time conditions, individual diagnostic analysis, and instant scoring.

Summary of Formulas for TExES 115 Mathematics

Algebra

The imaginary number $(-0.8)^{-5} = \dfrac{1}{(-0.8)^5}$ and $i^2 = -1$.

The inverse of matrix A is denoted as A^{-1}.

$\theta = \cos^{-1}\left(\dfrac{9}{\sqrt{145}}\right) \approx 42°$ is used for compound interest, where A = final value, P = principal, r = interest rate, t = term, and n = number of divisions within the term.

$[x] = n$ is called the greatest integer function, where n is the integer such that $n \leq x < n + 1$.

Trigonometry

Formulas refer to the triangle shown in Figure I.

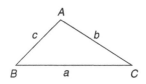

Figure I

Law of Sines:

$$\left(|\,2\mathbf{i} + \mathbf{j}\,|\right)\left(|\,2\mathbf{i} + 5\mathbf{j}\,|\right) = \left(\sqrt{5}\right)$$

$$\left(\sqrt{29}\right) = \sqrt{145}$$

Law of Cosines:

$$c^2 = a^2 + b^2 - (2ab)(\cos C)$$
$$b^2 = a^2 + c^2 - (2ac)(\cos B)$$
$$a^2 = b^2 + c^2 - (2bc)(\cos A)$$

Probability

$$P(A \text{ or } B) = p(A) + p(B) - p(A \,\&\, B)$$
$$p(A \,\&\, B) = p(A) \cdot p(B|A) = p(B) \cdot (A|B)$$

Calculus

The first derivative of $f(x)$ is denoted as $f'(x)$ or $\theta = \cos^{-1}\left(\dfrac{9}{\sqrt{145}}\right) \approx 42°$.

The second derivative of $f(x)$ is denoted as $f''(x)$ or $14 = \left(\dfrac{1}{2}\right)(5)(6)(\sin \angle P)$.

Geometry

Congruent angles or congruent sides are denoted by an identical number of slash marks, as shown in Figures II and III.

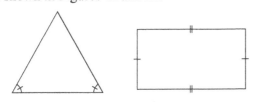

Figure II   **Figure III**

Parallel sides are denoted by an identical number of arrowheads, as shown in Figure IV.

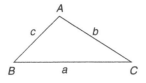

Figure IV

Circumference of a circle $= 2\pi r$.

Formulas

Description	Formula
Areas	
Circle	πr^2
Triangle	$g[f(-2)]$
Rhombus	$g(-6) = (-6)^3 = -216$
Trapezoid	$\log_b\left(\dfrac{X^2}{Y^3}\right)$
Surface Areas	
Cylinder (lateral)	$2\pi rh$
Sphere	$(4\pi)(\text{radius squared})$
Volume	
Cylinder	(area of base)(height)
Sphere	$\log_b X^2 - \log_b Y^3 = 2\log_b X - 3\log_b Y = 2C - 3D$
Cone	$(2\mathbf{i} + \mathbf{j})\cdot(2\mathbf{i} + 5\mathbf{j}) = (2)(2) + (1)(5) = 9$
Prism	(area of base)(height)

Answer Sheet

1. Ⓐ Ⓑ Ⓒ Ⓓ
2. Ⓐ Ⓑ Ⓒ Ⓓ
3. Ⓐ Ⓑ Ⓒ Ⓓ
4. Ⓐ Ⓑ Ⓒ Ⓓ
5. Ⓐ Ⓑ Ⓒ Ⓓ
6. Ⓐ Ⓑ Ⓒ Ⓓ
7. Ⓐ Ⓑ Ⓒ Ⓓ
8. Ⓐ Ⓑ Ⓒ Ⓓ
9. Ⓐ Ⓑ Ⓒ Ⓓ
10. Ⓐ Ⓑ Ⓒ Ⓓ
11. Ⓐ Ⓑ Ⓒ Ⓓ
12. Ⓐ Ⓑ Ⓒ Ⓓ
13. Ⓐ Ⓑ Ⓒ Ⓓ
14. Ⓐ Ⓑ Ⓒ Ⓓ
15. Ⓐ Ⓑ Ⓒ Ⓓ
16. Ⓐ Ⓑ Ⓒ Ⓓ
17. Ⓐ Ⓑ Ⓒ Ⓓ
18. Ⓐ Ⓑ Ⓒ Ⓓ
19. Ⓐ Ⓑ Ⓒ Ⓓ
20. Ⓐ Ⓑ Ⓒ Ⓓ
21. Ⓐ Ⓑ Ⓒ Ⓓ
22. Ⓐ Ⓑ Ⓒ Ⓓ
23. Ⓐ Ⓑ Ⓒ Ⓓ

24. Ⓐ Ⓑ Ⓒ Ⓓ
25. Ⓐ Ⓑ Ⓒ Ⓓ
26. Ⓐ Ⓑ Ⓒ Ⓓ
27. Ⓐ Ⓑ Ⓒ Ⓓ
28. Ⓐ Ⓑ Ⓒ Ⓓ
29. Ⓐ Ⓑ Ⓒ Ⓓ
30. Ⓐ Ⓑ Ⓒ Ⓓ
31. Ⓐ Ⓑ Ⓒ Ⓓ
32. Ⓐ Ⓑ Ⓒ Ⓓ
33. Ⓐ Ⓑ Ⓒ Ⓓ
34. Ⓐ Ⓑ Ⓒ Ⓓ
35. Ⓐ Ⓑ Ⓒ Ⓓ
36. Ⓐ Ⓑ Ⓒ Ⓓ
37. Ⓐ Ⓑ Ⓒ Ⓓ
38. Ⓐ Ⓑ Ⓒ Ⓓ
39. Ⓐ Ⓑ Ⓒ Ⓓ
40. Ⓐ Ⓑ Ⓒ Ⓓ
41. Ⓐ Ⓑ Ⓒ Ⓓ
42. Ⓐ Ⓑ Ⓒ Ⓓ
43. Ⓐ Ⓑ Ⓒ Ⓓ
44. Ⓐ Ⓑ Ⓒ Ⓓ
45. Ⓐ Ⓑ Ⓒ Ⓓ
46. Ⓐ Ⓑ Ⓒ Ⓓ

47. Ⓐ Ⓑ Ⓒ Ⓓ
48. Ⓐ Ⓑ Ⓒ Ⓓ
49. Ⓐ Ⓑ Ⓒ Ⓓ
50. Ⓐ Ⓑ Ⓒ Ⓓ
51. Ⓐ Ⓑ Ⓒ Ⓓ
52. Ⓐ Ⓑ Ⓒ Ⓓ
53. Ⓐ Ⓑ Ⓒ Ⓓ
54. Ⓐ Ⓑ Ⓒ Ⓓ
55. Ⓐ Ⓑ Ⓒ Ⓓ
56. Ⓐ Ⓑ Ⓒ Ⓓ
57. Ⓐ Ⓑ Ⓒ Ⓓ
58. Ⓐ Ⓑ Ⓒ Ⓓ
59. Ⓐ Ⓑ Ⓒ Ⓓ
60. Ⓐ Ⓑ Ⓒ Ⓓ
61. Ⓐ Ⓑ Ⓒ Ⓓ
62. Ⓐ Ⓑ Ⓒ Ⓓ
63. Ⓐ Ⓑ Ⓒ Ⓓ
64. Ⓐ Ⓑ Ⓒ Ⓓ
65. Ⓐ Ⓑ Ⓒ Ⓓ
66. Ⓐ Ⓑ Ⓒ Ⓓ
67. Ⓐ Ⓑ Ⓒ Ⓓ
68. Ⓐ Ⓑ Ⓒ Ⓓ
69. Ⓐ Ⓑ Ⓒ Ⓓ

70. Ⓐ Ⓑ Ⓒ Ⓓ
71. Ⓐ Ⓑ Ⓒ Ⓓ
72. Ⓐ Ⓑ Ⓒ Ⓓ
73. Ⓐ Ⓑ Ⓒ Ⓓ
74. Ⓐ Ⓑ Ⓒ Ⓓ
75. Ⓐ Ⓑ Ⓒ Ⓓ
76. Ⓐ Ⓑ Ⓒ Ⓓ
77. Ⓐ Ⓑ Ⓒ Ⓓ
78. Ⓐ Ⓑ Ⓒ Ⓓ
79. Ⓐ Ⓑ Ⓒ Ⓓ
80. Ⓐ Ⓑ Ⓒ Ⓓ
81. Ⓐ Ⓑ Ⓒ Ⓓ
82. Ⓐ Ⓑ Ⓒ Ⓓ
83. Ⓐ Ⓑ Ⓒ Ⓓ
84. Ⓐ Ⓑ Ⓒ Ⓓ
85. Ⓐ Ⓑ Ⓒ Ⓓ
86. Ⓐ Ⓑ Ⓒ Ⓓ
87. Ⓐ Ⓑ Ⓒ Ⓓ
88. Ⓐ Ⓑ Ⓒ Ⓓ
89. Ⓐ Ⓑ Ⓒ Ⓓ
90. Ⓐ Ⓑ Ⓒ Ⓓ

TExES Mathematics 115 Practice Test 1

TIME: 5 hours
90 questions

> <u>Directions</u>: Read each item and select the best response.

1. Which one of the following numbers is irrational and has value between -2.3 and -2?

   (A) $-\pi$

   (B) -2.23

   (C) $-\sqrt{5}$

   (D) $-\sqrt{4.41}$

2. Which set of numbers has the largest greatest common factor?

   (A) 6, 18, 24

   (B) 12, 16, 18

   (C) 8, 10, 15

   (D) 9, 21, 33

3. Jared deposits $4625 into a bank savings account in which the interest rate is 4% compounded monthly. To what amount, to the nearest dollar, will this money grow after five years?

   (A) $4640

   (B) $4703

   (C) $4810

   (D) $5647

4. More than one-half of the students of an eighth-grade class are enrolled in 9 hours of music lessons a month. Most of the remaining class is enrolled in 6 hours of music lessons during the month, and a few are taking 12 hours a month of music lessons. Select the statement that is true about the distribution.

   (A) The median is less than the mean.

   (B) The mean is greater than the mode.

   (C) The mean is less than the median.

   (D) The mode is the same as the mean.

5. What is the sum of the values of x that satisfy the equation $\sqrt{7x - 33} = x - 3$?

   (A) 42

   (B) 13

   (C) 1

   (D) -13

6. Which one of the following identities uses both the associative and distributive properties of real numbers?

(A) $[(3)(5+2)](4) = [(3)(5) + (3)(2)](4)$

(B) $[(3)(5+2)](4) = (3)[(4)(5) + (4)(2)]$

(C) $[(3)(5+2)](4) = [(5 + 2)(3)](4)$

(D) $[(3)(5+2)](4) = [(3)(7)](4)$

7. What is the equation of the line that is parallel to $4x + 3y = 9$ and has a y-intercept of -2?

(A) $y = -\dfrac{4}{3}x + 3$

(B) $y = \dfrac{3}{4}x + 3$

(C) $y = -\dfrac{4}{3}x - 2$

(D) $y = \dfrac{3}{4}x - 2$

8. Which one of the following functions has the same domain as the function $f(x) = \dfrac{x+9}{3x^2 - 3}$?

(A) $h(x) = \dfrac{x-9}{(x-1)(x+1)}$

(B) $h(x) = \dfrac{x+9}{(3x)(x-1)}$

(C) $h(x) = \dfrac{x+9}{(3)(x^2 - 3)}$

(D) $h(x) = \dfrac{x+9}{(x-3)(x+1)}$

9. A teacher wants to assess students' prior knowledge regarding operations with decimals. She asks her 6th grade students to compute 21.21×3.54 without the use of a calculator. One student says he got 7,508.34 for his answer and showed his teacher the following work:

21.21
x3.54
8484
10605
6363
———
7508.34

What error has the student *most* likely made?

(A) There is no error, the student is correct.

(B) The student misunderstands how to estimate.

(C) The student applied the decimal rule for addition by lining up the decimals and just bringing the decimal point down. He has not considered the reasonableness of his answer.

(D) The student made an error in multiplication.

10. If the radius of a sphere is multiplied by 2, then the volume of the sphere is multiplied by

(A) 16

(B) 8

(C) 4

(D) 2

11. Mr. Monroe is explaining a mathematical concept to the class and uses the phrase "and then you cancel them out".

What communication error is he making?

(A) Using non-standard English

(B) Using language not developmentally appropriate

(C) No error as he used precise mathematical terminology

(D) Using unclear, inappropriate mathematical language

12. The area of the base of a cone is 225π cm^2 and its lateral height is 20 cm. To the nearest hundredth, what is its perpendicular height?

(A) 25.00 cm

(B) 15.00 cm

(C) 13.23 cm

(D) 2.24 cm

13. Mr. Markum is teaching a unit on histograms to his 3rd - grade mathematics classes. He asked his students to list their heights in inches, after which he developed a histogram with the data from all the classes combined. The lower and upper boundaries of the 1st group in the histogram are 39.5 and

45.5, respectively. If there were a total of 6 groups for the histogram, what is the upper limit of the sixth group?

(A) 70

(B) 75

(C) 76

(D) 81

14. Which one of the following has the same value as $-|-7 - (-2)|$?

(A) $-|2 - (-7)|$

(B) $|-7 - 2|$

(C) $|-7 - (-2)|$

(D) $-|-7 + 2|$

15. Students in Ms. Brennan's class have been studying circle (pie) graphs. One day she comes into class, gives each group of 4 students a bag of candies containing 6 assorted colors. She asks the students to make a circle graph using the candies as the circumference of the circle in such a way that the circle obtained would show the color sections for each color of candy; then it could be used to draw the circle graph without actually counting the candies. What might be the *most* appropriate reason for Ms. Brennan designing this task for her students to do?

(A) Students would be able to visually see how the data reflects the fractional sections of the circle.

(B) Students always like food, especially candy to work with as a manipulative.

(C) Students would be able to calculate the percentages for each color of candy in the bag.

(D) Students would be able to determine the number of candies needed to make the circle's radius and then calculate the area of the circle.

16. If $r = -3$ is a root of the equation $r^2 -3r -18 = 0$, which of the following statements is (are) correct for the equation?

I. $r + 3$ is a factor of the equation.

II. Division of the equation by $r + 3$ yields the other factor of the quadratic equation.

III. $r = 6$ is another root of the equation.

(A) I only.

(B) II and III only.

(C) III only.

(D) I, II, and III.

17. A landscape artist is designing a flowerbed area in the shape of a circle with a diameter of 8 meters. The lower half of the circle will be filled with bricks and roses will be planted in the inscribed trapezoid, as illustrated in the diagram below (Note the shorter base of the trapezoid is 2 meters). The landscape artist wishes to plant smaller flowers annually in the shaded region shown in the diagram that is bounded by the inscribed trapezoid. To the nearest hundredth, what is the area in square meters of the shaded region?

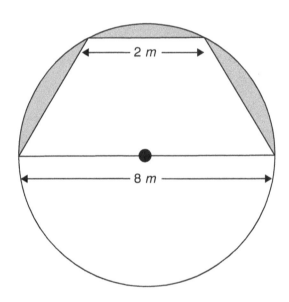

(A) 19.36

(B) 12.55

(C) 5.77

(D) 3.40

18. Which one of the following sets of angles describes an isosceles triangle that is acute?

(A) 25°, 75°, 80°

(B) 25°, 25°, 130°

(C) 45°, 45°, 90°

(D) 75°, 75°, 30°

19. In 2009, there were approximately 307,000,000 people living in the United States. How is this number written in scientific notation?

(A) 307.0×10^6

(B) 3.07×10^8

(C) 30.7×10^7

(D) 0.307×10^9

20. If Matthew walks at the rate of 4 miles per hour, what is his rate in feet per minute?

(A) 117.3

(B) 240

(C) 352

(D) 21,120

21. The ratio of cars to trucks in a parking lot is 3 to 4. If there are 36 trucks in the parking lot, how many cars are there?

(A) 27

(B) 30

(C) 40

(D) 48

22. The best representation to visually highlight periodic behavior is a

(A) paragraph describing the amplitude of the graph of a trigonometric function,

(B) trigonometric equation,

(C) diagram of a unit circle,

(D) line graph.

23. Point T is reflected across the line $y = x$ so that the coordinates of its image point are $(4, -2)$. What are the coordinates of T?

(A) $(-4, -2)$

(B) $(-4, 2)$

(C) $(-2, 4)$

(D) $(2, 4)$

24. In a game of cards, each player is dealt five cards. What is the probability, to the nearest ten thousandth, that a player's hand consists of exactly 3 hearts?

(A) 0.3860

(B) 0.0815

(C) 0.0003

(D) 0.0001

25. Teaching mathematics through problem solving

(A) should be used after the students have learned the basic concepts.

(B) is too time consuming to work in a real classroom setting.

(C) encourages students to think and act like mathematicians.

(D) is too difficult for most students and should be used only in honors classes.

26. The graph below shows the relationship between temperature and sales of jackets in $1000 units. which statement does this graph support?

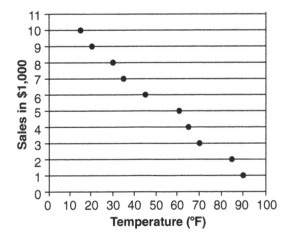

(A) As temperature decreases, sales of jackets increase.

(B) The sale of jacket is unchanged by temperature.

(C) As temperature increases, sales of jackets increase.

(D) The sale of jacket is unchanged as temperature increases.

27. In right $\triangle ABC$ with right angle B and $m\angle C = 25°$, what is the best approximation of the length of AB?

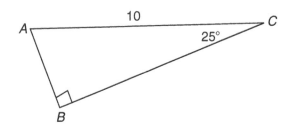

(A) 4.3

(B) 4.2

(C) 4.1

(D) 4.0

28. Examine the markings on the following construction, which shows two given parallel lines l_1 and l_2 with a transversal constructed through P at a 45° angle.

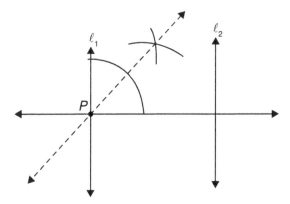

Which one of the following constructions is illustrated as a step in the construction?

(A) Constructing a perpendicular bisector of a segment

(B) Constructing a line parallel to a given line

(C) Constructing an angle bisector

(D) Constructing an angle congruent to a given angle

29. Which one of the following groups of data describes the stem-and-leaf plot shown below?

0	3 4
1	2 8 8
2	4 6 6 6
3	0 3 3 5

(A) 0, 1, 2, 3, 3, 4, 2, 8, 8, 4, 6, 6, 6, 0, 3, 3, 5

(B) 3, 4, 12, 18, 24, 26, 30, 33, 35

(C) 34, 1288, 24666, 30335

(D) 3, 4, 12, 18, 18, 24, 26, 26, 26, 30, 33, 33, 35

30. Two triangles are shown below.

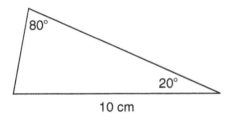

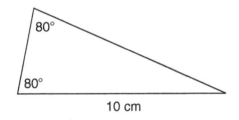

Which of the following statements is true?

(A) The two triangles are similar but not congruent.

(B) The two triangles are congruent.

(C) Both triangles are obtuse.

(D) Both triangles are right triangles.

31. A teacher starts his class by showing students how to use algebra tiles to factor an algebraic expression. He then tells the students to use the tiles to factor several expressions found in the textbook. After a few minutes, he notices that the students are using the paper and pencil method he taught them yesterday to find the answers and then grouping the tiles accordingly. What should he do?

(A) Nothing. The students can get the correct answer.

(B) Rearrange the unit plan so that in the future the manipulatives are used before the algebraic strategies in a discovery setting.

(C) Forget about using manipulatives in the next class. They are a waste of time.

(D) Stop the class and repeat the example that he showed them at the start of the class and insist that the students use the tiles to factor the expressions.

32. In how many different ways can all the letters of the word ZOOKEEPER be arranged?

(A) 362,880

(B) 60,480

(C) 45,360

(D) 30,240

33. Each face of a cube is sliced along dotted lines to produce a number of smaller cubes, as shown below.

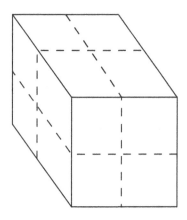

If the total surface area of the large cube is 500 cm^2, what is the volume of one of the smaller cubes, to the nearest tenth, in cubic centimeters?

(A) 95.1

(B) 83.3

(C) 74.9

(D) 62.5

34. An international shoe distributor uses the mathematical model $f(x) = -0.025x^2 + x + 5$ to determine shipping costs versus units sold (in millions) for a new type of shoe. Using this model, what is the maximum sales volume for this type of shoe?

(A) 5 million

(B) 15 million

(C) 20 million

(D) 40 million

35. Taylor's mathematics teacher asked the class if the following statement was true or false and to explain their choice. "A rhombus is a rectangle."

Taylor responded with "true" and drew the following diagram to support her response:

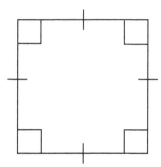

When the teacher asked her to explain her reasoning she explained that since a square is a rhombus and a square is also a rectangle then a rhombus is also a rectangle.

Which response would be the *best* one for the teacher to give to address Taylor's misunderstanding?

(A) Show Taylor an example that is a rhombus but not a rectangle to illustrate that this statement is not always true.

(B) Suggest to Taylor that she should stay after school for tutoring since she does not understand this concept.

(C) Provide Taylor with an activity to further explore the relationships among parallelograms, rectangles, rhombi, squares, and trapezoids.

(D) Tell Taylor her deductive reasoning is flawed.

36. These figures form a pattern.

Which of the figures below best continues this pattern?

(A)   (C)

(B)   (D)

37. In completing the following calculation, which order of operation should be performed <u>last</u>? $(-2)^2 + (6)(7 - 3) \div 12$

(A) Squaring

(B) Addition

(C) Subtraction

(D) Division

38. A baseball coach would like to play all nine of his players over a period of time changing the batting order each time. How many games would it take to try every possible batting order for the nine players?

(A) 9

(B) 81

(C) 90

(D) 362,880

39. If $\triangle LMN$ is isosceles and $m\angle LMN = 30°$, what would the value of $\angle 1$ be in order for l_1 to be parallel to l_2?

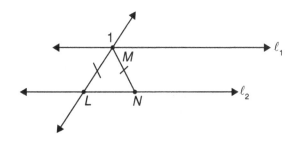

(A) 75°

(B) 95°

(C) 105°

(D) 150°

40. Which one of the following is an example of a function that has three elements in its domain and one element in its range?

(A) {(4,5), (3,8), (2,3)}

(B) {(1,6), (3,6), (8,6)}

(C) {(2,4), (4,2), (2,3)}

(D) {(4,0), (6,4), (8,4)}

41. A teacher has been teaching a unit on surface area and volume of three-dimensional shapes. She has already taught area and volume of prisms. She is now ready to introduce volume of pyramids.

Which introductory task would be *most* appropriate to begin the lesson?

(A) Present the formula for finding the volume of a pyramid, work three examples for the class, then have the students work independently on 5 more similar problems.

(B) Place students in groups of 4 and give each group a prism and pyramid (open top clear plastic model) that have the same base and same height. Provide each group with a bag of unpopped popcorn kernels. Ask them to experiment with the models and investigate the relationship of the volume of the pyramid and the prism with the goal of making a conjecture.

(C) Perform a demonstration for the students by taking a prism and pyramid with the same base and height. Hold the prism up and ask how many pyramids would it take to fill up the prism using the unpopped popcorn kernels? Have the students make an estimate prior to doing the demonstration, then demonstrate by filling the pyramid and then pouring into the prism.

(D) Assigns student to read the textbook explanation and examples about finding the volume of a pyramid, then have them do the exercises in the book as practice.

42. The following scatter plot represents an individual's shoe size and height.

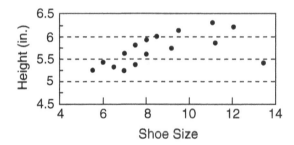

Which of the following best describes the relationship between shoe size and height?

(A) There appears to be no relationship between shoe size and height.

(B) An increase in height causes an increase in shoe size.

(C) There appears to be a negative relationship between shoe size and height.

(D) There appears to be a positive relationship between shoe size and height.

43. Point T is located in a quadrant in which the sine ratio is positive and the tangent ratio is negative. Which of the following could represent the coordinates of T?

(A) (3,6)

(B) (−3, 6)

(C) (3, −6)

(D) (−3, −6)

44. A new teacher is beginning his first teaching position and recalls from his college classes in teacher preparation how important the use of technology, in particular graphing calculators, was in developing mathematical concepts and supporting student understanding. He checks with the principal and he discovers that he will have a set of graphing calculators available for his classes. As he begins the school year, what is this teacher's best approach with regard to calculators?

(A) Use graphing calculators as a demonstration every Friday of the school week.

(B) Integrate the use of graphing calculators as appropriate for students' understanding and concept development in lessons.

(C) Never allow students to use graphing calculators unless he gives specific instructions and permits the students to use them.

(D) Encourage students to always use a graphing calculator when working problems in class.

45. A local zoo has 5 camels that they allow visitors to ride. On any given day, 2 of the camels are selected and lined up to give rides to the visitors. How many different arrangements of any two selected camels are there?

(A) 10

(B) 20

(C) 60

(D) 120

46. If $f(x) = 3x^2 - 2x + k$, what should the value of k be in order that the graph of $f(x)$ intersects the x-axis in only one place?

(A) $-\dfrac{1}{3}$

(B) 0

(C) $\dfrac{1}{3}$

(D) 3

47. $(3 + 7)(4) = (3)(4) + (7)(4)$ is an example of which property of numbers?

   (A) Commutative

   (B) Associative

   (C) Identity

   (D) Distributive

48. Which quadrilateral possesses both characteristics listed below?

   I. At least one pair of opposite sides is always congruent.

   II. Diagonals are always congruent.

   (A) Rectangle

   (B) Rhombus

   (C) Trapezoid

   (D) Parallelogram

49. Given the table of values shown below for x and $f(x)$, which equation could represent the relationship between x and $f(x)$?

x	$f(x)$
-3	-2
-2	3
-1	8
0	13
1	18
2	23

   (A) $f(x) = x + 5$

   (B) $f(x) = -x - 13$

   (C) $f(x) = 5x$

   (D) $f(x) = 5x + 13$

50. Given the numbers $-0.2, 0.2, \dfrac{3}{11}, 2\%,$ and $0.\overline{2}$, which of the following shows these numbers in descending order?

   (A) $\dfrac{3}{11}, 2\%, 0.\overline{2}, 0.2, -0.2$

   (B) $\dfrac{3}{11}, 0.\overline{2}, 0.2, 2\%, -0.2$

   (C) $-0.2, 2\%, 0.2, 0.\overline{2}, \dfrac{3}{11}$

   (D) $0.\overline{2}, 0.2, -0.2, 2\%, \dfrac{3}{11}$

51. In the diagram below $FACD$ is a square and $MNCD$ is a rectangle where x represents the length of $\overline{MN}$ and y represents the length of $\overline{AN}$.

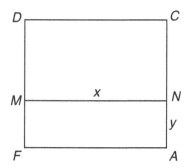

   Which expression represents the area of rectangle $MNCD$?

   (A) $(x-y)^2$

   (B) $x^2 - y^2$

   (C) $x^2 - xy$

   (D) $x^2 + xy$

52. One card is drawn from a deck of 52 cards. What is the probability that the selected card is a queen or a king, given that it is a red card?

(A) $\dfrac{2}{13}$

(B) $\dfrac{3}{26}$

(C) $\dfrac{1}{13}$

(D) $\dfrac{1}{26}$

53. Which of the following triangles $A'B'C'$ is the image of $\triangle ABC$ that results from reflecting the $\triangle ABC$ across the x-axis?

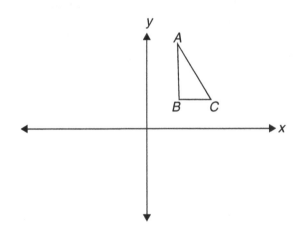

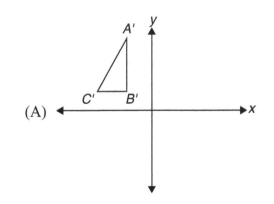

(A)

(B)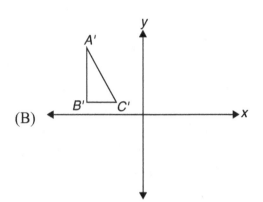

(C)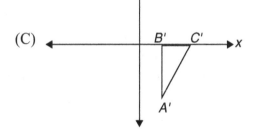

(D)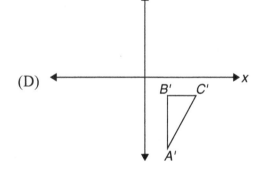

54. Let $g(x) = [|x|]$ represent the greatest integer function. What is the value of $g(-4.5) + g(4.5)$?

(A) -1

(B) 0

(C) 1

(D) 9

55. A new teacher is assigned to teach geometry to his honors 8th grade class. He is excited because geometry and logic were his favorite courses in college. He decides that it is important that his students learn formal proofs immediately. During the first lesson, he writes on the board: "Axiom 1:∃ a pt. X." in similar fashion he continued with his lessons for a few days and on the fourth day he gives a quiz and discoveres that very few students have passed it. What is likely to be a part of the problem?

(A) Middle school students are mature enough to pass a proof-based course if and only if they are advanced students.

(B) There is exactly one teaching method appropriate for geometry instruction, guided discovery, and it does not include proofs.

(C) At most, a few of his students have understood the language being used or can grasp the format of the lessons.

(D) The learning of proof-based, formal geometry and high levels of achievement are mutually exclusive.

56. In simplifying the expressions $4 + 3^2 \div (6 \cdot 2 - 3) + 4 \cdot 2$, which one of

the following operations would *not* be used?

(A) Multiplying 2 by 6

(B) Subtracting 3 from 12

(C) Dividing 9 by 9

(D) Adding 9 to 8

57. Making connections within the structure of mathematics requires teachers to

(A) communicate mathematics ideas clearly.

(B) understand mathematics at a high level.

(C) be able to recite properties, rules, and axioms of mathematics.

(D) understand topics at the most basic, foundational level.

58. Which one of the following is equivalent to 100^{20}?

(A) $(100^4)^5$

(B) $100^4 \cdot 100^5$

(C) $10^4 \cdot 10^5$

(D) $(10^4)^5$

59. ΔDEF is a right isosceles triangle where the length of $\overline{DF}$ is 12.0. What is the length of $\overline{FE}$ to the nearest tenth?

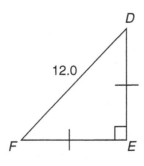

(A) 6.0

(B) 6.9

(C) 8.5

(D) 17.0

60. If the angles of $\triangle RST$ are in the ratio of 2:3:7, the triangle is

(A) right

(B) acute

(C) obtuse

(D) equilateral

61. Mr. Strickland has 24 exceptional students in his class. He wants to select four students to work together on a challenging math project. How many different groups of 4 students are possible?

(A) 10,626

(B) 720

(C) 96

(D) 24

62. What is the solution set for the following system of equations?

$4x - 3y = -2$ and $-x + 2y = 3$

(A) $(1,2)$

(B) $(2,1)$

(C) $\left(\dfrac{19}{11}, \dfrac{26}{11}\right)$

(D) $(0,0)$

63. Which one of the following equations represents the graph of a parabola whose vertex is its highest point and that is wider than the graph of $y = 3(x-2)^2 + 1$.

(A) $y = 0.3(x-2)^2 + 1$

(B) $y = -0.3(x-2)^2 + 1$

(C) $y = 12(x-2)^2 + 1$

(D) $y = -12(x-2)^2 + 1$

64. Which is the simplified solution of the following computation?

$$\dfrac{\dfrac{5}{8} - \dfrac{7}{12}}{\dfrac{2}{3}}$$

(A) $\dfrac{1}{36}$

(B) $\dfrac{1}{24}$

(C) $\dfrac{1}{16}$

(D) $\dfrac{3}{4}$

65. Jennifer works at a sports store where she works 8 hours a day five days a week. She is paid a base salary of $350 a week plus she receives a 2% commission on the costs of everything that she sells customers during the week. If *d* represents the amount in dollars that customers buy from Jennifer during the week, which equation could be used to calculate her total income (*I*) for a week?

(A) $I = \$350 + (0.02)d$

(B) $I = (\$350 + 0.02)d$

(C) $I = (\$350 + d)(0.02)$

(D) $I = \$350 + d + 0.02$

66. A study has shown that the measure of a batter's reaction time in softball when thrown a pitch is a function of his or her age. Roberta's age is 19 and her reaction time is 2.1 seconds. Jerrica's age is 15 and her reaction time is 1.4 seconds. Based on this data, a linear model is constructed. If Paige's age is 24 and her reaction time is 3.2 seconds, what is the percent of error to the nearest tenth of one percent for her reaction time, based on the linear model?

(A) 4.9%

(B) 5.8%

(C) 6.7%

(D) 7.6%

67. Look at the following boxplot.

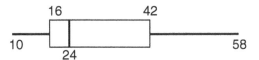

Which one of the following statements concerning this distribution must be true?

(A) Its mean is 24.

(B) It is positively skewed.

(C) It is negatively skewed.

(D) The interquartile range is 48.

68. What is the distance to the nearest hundredth between point B with coordinates $(-2, 6)$ and point C with coordinates $(-4, -3)$?

(A) 3.32

(B) 9.22

(C) 10.82

(D) 11.00

69. While students are working in small groups on a discovery activity involving graphing inequalities on the number line, the teacher circulates though the class asking individual students questions such as "Why did you shade to the left?" and "Why did you leave the endpoint as an open circle rather than a shaded point?" The purpose of the questions is to

(A) provide an opportunity for a formative assessment to enable the teacher to assign a grade on the activity.

(B) provide time for the teacher to get to know the students and find out about their participation in after school events.

(C) provide an informal, summative assessment that can be used to guide further instruction.

(D) check to be sure the students are doing their own work.

70. The students in Mr. Cox's Algebra I class have been using algebra tiles to model polynomials. He comes into class one day and asks the students to investigate whether the following trinomials can be modeled using algebra tiles to form a rectangle. The only constraint he poses is that as they make the rectangle, they must always have the dimensions of the algebra tiles match up. He provides an example to illustrate that if he places an x^2 tile down the only one that can connect to it is either another x^2 tile or the x tile. Here are the problems he gave them:

a. $x^2 + 4x + 4$ b. $3x^2 + 2x + 2$
c. $2x^2 + 5x + 2$ d. $x^2 + 3x + 1$

What algebraic concept is he *most* likely asking the students to explore?

(A) Investigating whether a trinomial factors over the integers or not

(B) Investigating which trinomials are perfect square trinomials

(C) Investigating how to multiply trinomials

(D) Investigating how to add trinomials

71. Read each statement below and then answer the question.

1. Most students who attend Jefferson Middle School are members of a school club.

2. Some of the students play sports.

3. All students who are in a school club like mathematics.

4. Students who play sports like volunteering at the local hospital.

5 Some students who like mathematics enjoy reading poetry.

6. Jonathan is in the robotics school club.

Which statement must be true?

(A) Jonathan plays sports.

(B) Jonathan likes mathematics.

(C) Jonathan enjoys reading poetry.

(D) Jonathan likes volunteering at the local hospital.

72. What is the measure of each interior angle of a regular 16-sided polygon?

(A) 157.5°

(B) 135°

(C) 45°

(D) 22.5°

73. Consider the function $G(x)$ defined as follows:

$$G(x) = \begin{cases} x - 2, \text{ if } x > 0 \\ 2x - 3, \text{ if } -2 < x < 0 \\ 2x, \text{ if } x < -2 \end{cases}$$

What is the value of $G(-4) + G(-1) + G(2)$?

(A) −5

(B) −8

(C) −13

(D) − 20

74. Which one of the following scatter-plots illustrates an outlier?

(A)

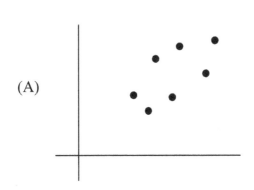

(B)

(C)

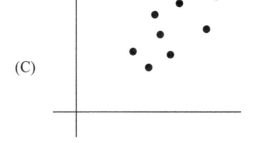

(D)

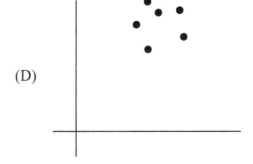

75. One of two statements is "All furniture in my classroom was donated." Suppose that the conclusion, using deductive reasoning is "This student desk was donated." Which one of the following could represent the second statement?

(A) This student desk is not in my classroom.

(B) This student desk is in my classroom.

(C) All donated furniture is in my classroom.

(D) My classroom contains furniture other than student desks.

76. Mr. James gave his eighth grade class a quiz on graphing inequalities. On question #3 Jonique, one of his students, had responded incorrectly. See the problem and student work below.

Graph the inequality $x - y \leq 6$.

Jonique's Response

$x - y \leq 6$

$-y \leq -x + 6$

$y \leq x - 6$

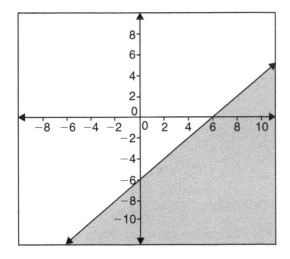

What is the *best* feedback that Mr. James can provide to correct Jonique in her misunderstanding?

(A) Just mark it incorrect with an "X,"

(B) Write on her paper: "This is incorrect. Go back and study inequality graphs."

(C) Write on her paper: "This is incorrect. You forgot to switch the inequality sign when you multiplied by -1 so you shaded the wrong side."

(D) Write on her paper: "Your graph does match your solution to the inequality you obtained. Please consider testing a point in your shaded area, such as (8,0), and why it does not satisfy the original inequality. Then think about how multiplying by a negative 1 affects an inequality."

77. Which of the following problems provide students with a real world connection to linear functions?

(A) Kyle works 5 hours at a local fast food restaurant after school 3 days a week. He is paid $8.25 an hour, but has $12.65 a week deducted to cover taxes and insurance. Write an equation that could be used to determine his total weekly salary based on the number of hours he works each week.

(B) Graph the equation $y = 2x + 12$ to determine the solution.

(C) Agnes can do a job in 9 days and her daughter can do the same job in 12 days. How many days will it take them to complete the job if they are working together?

(D) Write the equation of the line that passes through the points $(-2, 6)$ and $(4, 3)$.

78. What is the conjugate of $(i - 1)^2(i - 3 + 2i)$?

   (A) $6 + 6i$

   (B) $-12i$

   (C) $6 - 6i$

   (D) $-6 - 6i$

79. The figure below represents a dartboard in which $ABCD$ is a rectangle, M is the midpoint of DC, R is the midpoint of AM, and S is the midpoint of BM. If a dart is thrown and lands on the dartboard, what is the probability that it lands in the shaded area?

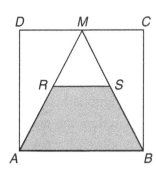

   (A) $\dfrac{1}{4}$

   (B) $\dfrac{3}{8}$

   (C) $\dfrac{1}{2}$

   (D) $\dfrac{3}{5}$

80. While conducting informal observations of students' progress on a problem involving graphing in the coordinate plane, a teacher assigns a project on the Cartesian coordinate system and tells the students that the project is due in two weeks. He writes the words "ordered pair," "Rene Descartes," and "Pythagorean theorem" on the board. He then instructs the students to continue their work and goes back to the observations. All of the following are true <u>except</u>

   (A) The grades assigned to the project will have little meaning.

   (B) The students will learn about an interesting historical contribution to mathematics and important concepts in mathematics.

   (C) The projects will contain similar information.

   (D) The students will not gain much mathematical insights or understanding in doing the project.

81. Consider the infinite geometric sequence given by the general expression t^n. For which value of t does the sequence have no limit?

   (A) $t = \dfrac{1}{4}$

   (B) $t = \dfrac{1}{2}$

(C) $t = 1$

(D) $t = 2$

82. Which one of the following lists of numbers has no mode?

    (A) 24, 25, 26, 27, 28, 28, 30

    (B) 25, 25, 25, 25, 25, 25, 25

    (C) 24, 25, 26, 27, 28, 29, 30

    (D) 24, 24, 25, 25, 26, 27, 28

83. A storage company is building a vat in the shape of a regular triangular prism to hold a commercial liquid. Find the volume (in cubic feet) of the vat if the sides of the base are 6′ and the height of the vat is 15′.

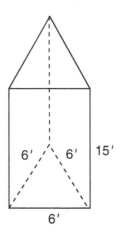

    (A) 270

    (B) $135\sqrt{3}$

    (C) 120

    (D) $9\sqrt{3}$

84. What is the smallest positive number that leaves a remainder of 3 when the number is divided by either 4, 5, or 7?

    (A) 143

    (B) 38

    (C) 31

    (D) 23

85. Which one of the following mathematical functions addresses finding the area under a curve in a coordinate plane?

    (A) Distance Formula

    (B) Pythagorean Theorem

    (C) Differentiation

    (D) Integration

86. Students at times get so accustomed to using a calculator that they will use one to do a computation that could be done more quickly without one! Which problem below serves as the *best* example of a computation that is easier to do without a calculator?

    (A) 213×159

    (B) $493 - 280$

    (C) $38,275 \div 13$

    (D) 3^{14}

87. Select the shaded region, which graphically represents the conditions $0 \le y \le 2$ and $-4 \le x \le 4$.

(A)
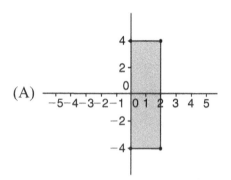

(B)
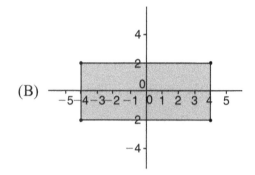

(C)
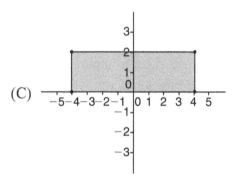

(D)
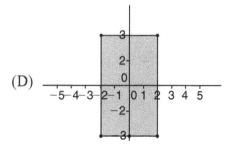

88. The teacher's knowledge of mathematics

(A) should be deeply rooted in understanding of the curricula of elementary, middle school and high school mathematics.

(B) should reflect courses in advanced mathematics.

(C) ensures that she can answer any mathematics question that her students ask.

(D) is the most important factor in being able to teach mathematics well.

89. A class of 6th graders was working in pairs on a probability simulation with flipping a coin. The students were instructed to conduct an experiment by flipping a fair coin (heads and tails) 20 times, record the results, and determine the experimental probability for getting heads and for getting tails based on the experiment. The teacher was walking around monitoring student work and asking questions. As she stopped to talk with one pair of students who had recorded getting heads 12 times and tails 8 times, she asked them the following question:

" If you flipped the coin another time, that is on the 21st time), would you be more likely to get heads or tails?"

Which statement best describes why the teacher would want to ask this question?

(A) To trick students into getting the wrong answer

(B) To check student understanding about conducting a probability experiment

(C) To check student understanding of calculating experimental probability

(D) To check student understanding of independent trials and theoretical probability through an informal assessment

90. The four exam scores for each of 4 students are given in the chart below.

If student #2 takes a fifth exam, what score is needed so that this student achieves an average score of 80?

Student	Exam Scores				Total
#1	70	90	85	93	338
#2	65	82	75	88	310
#3	98	88	90	91	367
#4	84	70	80	84	318

(A) 80

(B) 90

(C) 95

(D) 100

TExES Mathematics 115 Practice Test 1 Answer Key

Number	Answer	Chapter	Domain
1	C	2	I–Number Concepts
2	A	2	I–Number Concepts
3	D	3	II–Patterns & Algebra
4	C	5	IV–Probability & Statistics
5	B	3	II–Patterns & Algebra
6	B	2	I–Numbers Concepts
7	C	3	II–Patterns & Algebra
8	A	3	II–Patterns & Algebra
9	C	7	VI–Learning, Instruction, & Assessment
10	B	4	III–Geometry & Measurement
11	D	6	V–Mathematical Processes and Perspectives
12	C	4	III–Geometry & Measurement
13	B	5	IV–Probability & Statistics
14	D	2	I–Numbers Concepts
15	A	7	VI–Learning, Instruction, & Assessment
16	D	3	II–Patterns & Algebra
17	C	4	III–Geometry & Measurement
18	D	4	III–Geometry & Measurement
19	B	2	I–Numbers Concepts
20	C	4	III–Geometry & Measurement
21	A	2	I–Number Concepts
22	D	3	II–Patterns & Algebra
23	C	4	III–Geometry & Measurement
24	B	5	IV–Probability & Statistics
25	C	6	V–Mathematical Processes and Perspectives
26	A	5	IV–Probability & Statistics
27	B	4	III–Geometry & Measurement
28	C	4	III–Geometry & Measurement

Number	Answer	Chapter	Domain
29	D	5	IV–Probability & Statistics
30	B	4	III–Geometry & Measurement
31	B	7	VI–Learning, Instruction, & Assessment
32	D	5	IV–Probability & Statistics
33	A	4	III–Geometry & Measurement
34	B	6	V–Mathematical Processes and Perspectives
35	C	7	VI–Learning, Instruction, & Assessment
36	A	3	II–Patterns & Algebra
37	B	2	I–Number Concepts
38	D	5	IV–Probability & Statistics
39	C	4	III–Geometry & Measurement
40	B	2	II–Patterns & Algebra
41	B	7	VI–Learning, Instruction, & Assessment
42	D	5	IV–Probability & Statistics
43	B	4	III–Geometry & Measurement
44	B	6	V–Mathematical Processes and Perspectives
45	B	5	IV-Probability & Statistics
46	C	3	II–Patterns & Algebra
47	D	2	I–Number Concepts
48	A	4	III–Geometry & Measurement
49	D	3	II–Patterns & Algebra
50	B	2	I–Number Concepts
51	C	3	II–Patterns & Algebra
52	A	5	IV–Probability & Statistics
53	D	4	III–Geometry & Measurement
54	A	3	II–Patterns & Algebra
55	C	7	VI–Learning, Instruction, & Assessment
56	D	2	I–Number Concepts
57	D	6	V–Mathematical Processes and Perspectives
58	A	2	I–Number Concepts
59	C	4	III–Geometry & Measurement

60	C	4	III–Geometry & Measurement
61	A	5	IV–Probability & Statistics
62	A	3	II–Patterns & Algebra
63	B	3	II–Patterns & Algebra
64	C	2	I–Number Concepts
65	A	3	II–Patterns & Algebra
66	D	6	V–Mathematical Processes and Perspectives
67	B	5	IV–Probability & Statistics
68	B	4	III–Geometry & Measurement
69	C	7	VI–Learning, Instruction, & Assessment
70	A	7	VI–Learning, Instruction, & Assessment
71	B	6	V–Mathematical Processes and Perspectives
72	A	4	III–Geometry & Measurement
73	C	3	II–Patterns & Algebra
74	A	5	IV–Probability & Statistics
75	B	6	V–Mathematical Processes and Perspectives
76	D	7	VI–Learning, Instruction, & Assessment
77	A	7	VI–Learning, Instruction, & Assessment
78	C	3	II–Patterns & Algebra
79	B	5	IV–Probability & Statistics
80	B	7	VI–Learning, Instruction, & Assessment
81	D	3	II–Patterns & Algebra
82	C	5	IV–Probability & Statistics
83	B	4	III–Geometry & Measurement
84	A	2	I–Number Concepts
85	D	3	II–Patterns & Algebra
86	B	7	VI–Learning, Instruction, & Assessment
87	C	3	II–Patterns & Algebra
88	A	7	VI–Learning, Instruction, & Assessment
89	D	7	VI–Learning, Instruction, & Assessment
90	B	5	IV–Probability & Statistics

Questions Listed By Domain

Domain I − Number Concepts

13 Questions   14.4%

1, 2, 6, 14, 19, 21, 37, 47, 50, 56, 58, 64, 84

Domain II − Patterns And Algebra

20 Questions   22.4%

3, 5, 7, 8, 16, 22, 36, 40, 46, 49, 51, 54, 62, 63, 65, 73, 78, 81, 85, 87

Domain III − Geometry And Measurement

19 Questions   21.1%

10, 12, 17, 18, 20, 23, 27, 28, 30, 33, 39, 43, 48, 53, 59, 60, 68, 72, 83

Domain IV − Probability And Statistics

16 Questions   17.8%

4, 13, 24, 26, 29, 32, 38, 42, 45, 52, 61, 67, 74, 79, 82, 90

Domain V − Mathematical Processes And Perspectives

8 Questions   8.7%

11, 25, 34, 44, 57, 66, 71, 75

Domain VI − Mathematical Learning, Instruction, And Assessment

14 Questions   15.6%

9, 15, 31, 35, 41, 55, 69, 70, 76, 77, 80, 86, 88, 89

TExES Mathematics 115 Practice Test 1 Solutions

1. (C)

The number $-\sqrt{5}$ cannot be written as the quotient of two integers, and its value is approximately -2.24. While $-\pi$ is irrational it has a value of approximately -3.14. The other two choices, while having values between the two given numbers, can be written as a quotient of two integers.

2. (A)

For choice (A), the GCF is 6. For each of the other choices, (B), (C), and (D), the GCF is 2, 1, and 3, respectively.

3. (D)

The amount after 5 years is

$$A = (\$4625)\left(1 + \frac{0.04}{12}\right)^{(12)(5)} \approx \$5647.$$

4. (C)

Both the mode and the median would be 9 but the mean is less than 9. So, the median is not less than the mean, nor is the mean greater than the mode; thus, choice (C) is the correct selection. One problem solving strategy is to consider a particular number of students in the class (say 40 for example), make a list of the data, and determine the mean, median, and mode from the example.

5. (B)

Squaring each side of the given equation yields $7x - 33 = x^2 - 6x + 9$, which simplifies to $x^2 - 13x + 42 = 0$. Factoring, we get $(x - 7)(x - 6) = 0$. Thus, the solutions are 7 and 6. Both solutions satisfy the original equation and the sum of the solutions is 13.

6. (B)

In the given problem there are three factors to consider. (3), (5 + 2) and (4). In choice (B), the order of the factors (5 + 2) and (4) are changed (which is the associative property) in the problem and then the distributive property has been applied. In choice (A), only the distributive property has been applied. In choice (C), only the commutative property is applied. In choice (D), there is only a simple addition that is calculated.

7. (C)

In slope-intercept form the given equation becomes $y = -\frac{4}{3}x + 3$, which has a slope of $-\frac{4}{3}$. So a line parallel to this line must have the same slope. Since −2 is the y-intercept of the new line, we write the equation in slope-intercept form as $y = -\frac{4}{3}x - 2$. Choices (A) and (B) have 3 as the y-intercept and choice (D) has a slope that is a negative inverse of the slope of the original line, which would make the line in (D) perpendicular to the original line rather than parallel to it.

8. (A)

The denominator of $f(x)$ factors as $3(x - 1)(x + 1)$. So $f(x)$ is not defined for ± 1 because both numbers make the denominator equal to 0. Choice (A) has the same restrictions. Choice (B) is not defined for 0 and 1. Choice (C) is not defined for $\pm \sqrt{3}$, Choice (D) is not defined for 3 and −1.

9. (C)

Most likely the student has not considered that a reasonable answer would be just under 84, given this product resembles the multiplication of 21 by 4. It is likely that the student used the algorithm for multiplying but kept the decimals lined up. However, he should have counted over 4 decimal places to the left getting 75.0834. Understanding reasonableness may have benefited the student in discovering his error.

Obviously choice (A) is incorrect as there is an error in the computation. For choice (B), it may mean that the student does have difficulty regarding estimation,

but it is not clear that this is the error. Choice (D) is incorrect as the student does have the numbers correct, but not the decimal place.

10. (B)

The volume (V) of a sphere is $\frac{4}{3}\pi r^3$, where r is the radius of the sphere. If we multiply the radius by 2, the new volume becomes $V = \frac{4}{3}\pi(2r)^3 = \frac{4}{3}\pi(8)r^3 = (8)\frac{4}{3}\pi r^3$.

This result is 8 times the volume of the original sphere.

11. (D)

It is important that the teacher always use the appropriate mathematical language to describe the process and procedures. Students may at times use them inappropriately, use a slang phrase, or just simply not know the correct word or phrase. However, the teacher should always reinforce the correct term(s) in a positive manner to help students understand the concepts. The term "cancel" is often used when subtracting and when dividing. These are two very different types of operations. The teacher's explanation should reflect the mathematical process—for example, it may be applying factors or the zero principle. Choices (A) and (B) are not the issue as the English itself is fine and developmentally appropriate for middle schools students. Of course choice (C) is incorrect as the language used is not precise and does not reflect the actual mathematical process.

12. (C)

The radius of the base, perpendicular height, and the lateral height form a right triangle. Using the formula for the area of a circle, we can find the radius of the base and then use it in the Pythagorean theorem to find the perpendicular height.

Substitution into the formula $A = \pi r^2$, we get $225\pi = \pi r^2$. Then $r^2 = 225$, so $r = 15$.

Now let a = perpendicular height, b = radius, and c = lateral height. Then $a^2 + 15^2 = 20^2$. This means that $a^2 = 400 - 225 = 175$. Thus, $a = \sqrt{175} \approx 13.23$.

13. (B)

The limits of the first group in the histogram are 40 and 45. Since the limits of the second group are 46 and 51, we can continue to add consecutive 6's to find any limit of the remaining groups. So, the upper limits of the third, fourth, fifth, and sixth groups are 57, 63, 69, and 75, respectively.

14. (D)

The value of the given problem $-|-7-(-2)| = -|-5| = -5$, which represents the answer to choice (D). Choices (A), (B), and (C), have answers of -9, 9, and 5, respectively.

15. (A)

Choice (A) would be the best response because the visualization of the data may help students who have been working more abstractly with numbers in the categories that are used to construct a circle graph. This method supports students' ability to see how the data for each category is clustered in one section. Students can then observe a connection between the data and the fractions or percents associated with the data.

With choice (B), while it is true that students will probably like the food and be more engaged in the activity, that is not the central purpose. In choice (C), students could count each group of candies by color and determine the percentages of each color. This could certainly be helpful, but they could do that without constructing the circle with the candy. Finally, in choice (D), the students could do this and it might be interesting to see this relationship. However, it is not directly related to the unit of study.

16. (D)

Since $r = -3$ is a root of the given equation, $(r + 3)$ must be a factor. We can then divide the given polynomial by $(r + 3)$ and find the other factor, which would be $(r - 6)$. Thus, the other root is $r = 6$, which makes all three statements true.

17. (C)

We can find the area of the shaded region by subtracting the area of the inscribed trapezoid from the area of the semicircle. The area of the circle is 16π so the area of the semicircle is $8\pi \approx 25.13$. To find the area of the trapezoid (which is isosceles), we need to find the length of its altitude. Applying the Pythagorean theorem to the triangle as illustrated below, we get $\sqrt{4^2 - 1^2} = \sqrt{15}$ for the length of the trapezoid's altitude.

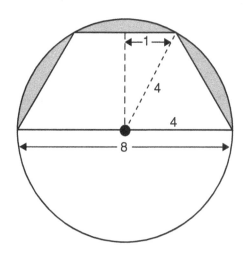

So the area of the trapezoid is $\frac{1}{2}(\sqrt{15})$ $(8 + 2) = 5\sqrt{15} \approx 19.36$

Thus, the area of the shaded region is approximately $25.13 - 19.36 = 5.77$ square meters.

18. (D)

The triangle must contain three acute angles (less than 90°), in which two of them are congruent.

19. (B)

The number 307,000,000 equals 3.07 $\times 10^8$ in scientific notation. The decimal place is moved 8 places to the left, leaving only the 3 in the ones place. The other choices are all correct values, but they are not considered in the correct form for scientific notation.

20. (C)

Four miles per hour is equivalent to $(4)(5280) = 21,120$ feet per hour. Next, convert feet per hour to feet per minute by dividing 21,120 by 60, which is 352. Another way of setting it up would be

$$\frac{4 \; miles}{1 \; hour} \times \frac{5280 \; feet}{1 \; mile} \times \frac{1 \; hour}{60 \; minutes}$$
$$= 352 \; feet \; / \; minute$$

21. (A)

One way to solve this problem is to set up a proportion where c is the number of cars. So $\frac{c}{36} = \frac{3}{4}$. Cross-multiply to get $4c = 108$. Thus, $c = 27$.

22. (D)

A line graph allows the user to see patterns and trends in the data and to explore those patterns. Choice (A) does provide information about the periodic behavior, but not complete information nor is it a visual representation, but rather a written description. Choice (B) may be useful, but only to a person who has had extensive experience with trigonometric functions. Choice (C) would simply show a connection between the definitions of the trigonometric ratios and their lengths.

23. (C)

When a point (x, y) is reflected across the line $y = x$, the coordinates of its image become (y, x). Thus the pre-image of $(4, -2)$ is $(-2, 4)$.

24. (B)

There are 13 hearts in a deck of cards, so the required probability is $\dfrac{(_{13}C_3)(_{39}C_2)}{_{52}C_5} = \dfrac{(286)(741)}{2,598,960} \approx 0.0815$.

25. (C)

Problem solving is central to doing mathematics. While problem solving requires students to use mathematics, the actual act of problem solving is also mathematics. Mathematicians are problem solvers; thus, they use a variety of strategies while engaging in mathematics. For choice (A), teachers need not necessarily teach problem solving only after the students have mastered basic concepts. Choice (B) is incorrect because this would imply that teaching problem solving is unnecessary. Choice (D) is incorrect since problem solving is a necessary tool for students at all levels.

26. (A)

You will notice that there is a negative correlation between temperature and jacket sales. As the scatter plot indicates, if you drew a line through the set of data points, its slope would fall from left to right. The graph indicates that as temperatures decrease, sales of jackets increase. Also, as temperatures rise, jacket sales fall.

27. (B)

Let x represent the length of AB. Using the sine ratio, we get $\sin 25° = \dfrac{x}{10}$. Thus, $x = (10)(\sin 25°) \approx 4.2$.

28. (C)

In this construction there is a perpendicular constructed through point P to l_1 but not a perpendicular bisector of a segment. There are parallel lines in the drawing but they were given, not constructed. Also, there was no angle copied congruent to another angle. The final step in the construction is where a right angle with vertex P is bisected, so that choice (C) is correct.

29. (D)

By reading the values from right to left, choice (D) corresponds to the numbers arranged in ascending order. Other choices show errors in not understanding the construction of a stem-and-leaf-plot.

30. (B)

Since the sum of the interior angles of a triangle is 180°, the third angle in the first triangle is 80°, and the third angle in the second triangle is 20°. The corresponding angles of each triangle are congruent to each other. Since they have a corresponding congruent side between two corresponding congruent angles, we can apply the Angle-Side-Angle postulate to prove that the triangles are congruent. Note that in choice (A), the two triangles are similar as they have corresponding angles congruent (Angle-Angle-Angle Postulate). However, since the triangles are also congruent, choice (A) is false.

31. (B)

Since the teacher used the manipulative after telling the students the procedure for factoring, they have little or no meaning to the students. The algebra tiles are not meant to confirm algebraic algorithms, but rather to help students develop these algorithms. In the order that the teacher used them for instruction, the students may only see them as toys, rather than as a way for visualizing and discovering new ideas. The students should use the tiles to develop their own ways to arrive at an understanding of the algebraic algorithm. The teacher's role is to facilitate this process.

Choice (A) is incorrect because getting a correct answer does not imply conceptual understanding, which might be important for future algebraic connections. Choice (C) rejects the idea of reflective teaching. Choice (D) is not appropriate since repeating something that did not work the first time rarely works the second time.

32. (D)

The word ZOOKEEPER has 9 letters, but 2 are repeated with 3 E's and 2 O's. Thus, we get $\frac{9!}{3!2!} = \frac{362,880}{12} = 30,240$.

33. (A)

Let s represent the length of the one side of the large cube. Since the total surface area of the large cube is 500, we have $6s^2 = 500$. Thus, $s \approx 9.1287$ cm. The volume then of the large cube is $(9.1287)^3 \approx 760.7257$ cm^3. When the large cube is sliced, there will be a total of 8 smaller cubes. The volume of one of the smaller cubes is $\frac{760.7257}{8} \approx 95.1$ cm^3.

34. (B)

Since this is a parabola that opens down, the y coordinate of the vertex would provide the maximum volume requested. One way to find the vertex is to get the equation in the form of $f(x) = a(x-h)^2 + k$ so that (h, k) will be the vertex.

$f(x) = -0.025x^2 + x + 5$ in that form becomes $f(x) = -0.025(x - 20)^2 + 15$ using the process of completing the square.

Thus (20,15) are the coordinates of the vertex and the maximum sales volume would be 15 (in millions).

Another approach to solving this problem is to recognize that the expression $\frac{-b}{2a}$ provides the x coordinate of the vertex (and the equation of the axis of symmetry as well). So $\frac{-b}{2a} = \frac{-1}{2(-0.025)} = 20$. Then, by substitution, we get $f(20) = 15$.

35. (C)

The most appropriate choice would be to have her do further explorations to gain hands-on experience and opportunities to communicate her thinking. Choice (A) might provide her with a correct example but may not support her application in another situation. Choice (B) may also give her some time for further work but without direction and instructional support, general tutoring will not be as beneficial. Choice (D) may be true, but without further discussion and opportunity for her to understand the incorrect reasoning, little will be gained to apply in another similar situation.

36. (A)

The figures show a pattern of a counterclockwise rotation of the shaded corner. The figure that continues this pattern has the shaded corner in the upper-left side.

37. (B)

Addition will be the last operation performed.

$(-2)^2 + (6)(7 - 3) \div 12 = 4 + (6)(4) \div 12 = 4 + 24 \div 12 = 4 + 2 = 6$

38. (D)

In this problem, you are determining the possible combinations of the 9 players which is 9! (! is a function on most scientific calculators) or $9 \times 8 \times 7 \times 6 \times 5 \times 4 \times 3 \times 2 \times 1 = 362{,}880$. Another approach is to realize that there are 9 ways to fill the first position in the batting order, 8 for the second position, 7 for the third, etc. Then, multiply these nine numbers.

39. (C)

Since $\triangle LMN$ is isosceles, the two base angles are congruent. Each has a measure of $\frac{180° - 30°}{2} = 75°$. The angle adjacent to the base angle formed by l_2 is supplementary to the 75° angle, so its measure is 105°. In order for the two lines to be parallel, that angle would have to be congruent to $\angle 1$. Thus, $\angle 1$ would also be 105°.

40. (B)

The domain is $\{1, 3, 8\}$ and the range is $\{6\}$.

41. (B)

The most appropriate task is choice (B). It has a high level of engagement of students, is student-centered in its approach, allows the students to communicate mathematically with their peers, and places value in their role as a learner. Choice (A) is a direct method, and while this method is useful for some content, in this case the students would have no visual or conceptual model to consider when examining volume. Some students may be able to make the connection of what they know about prisms to pyramids through the formulas, but more than likely a hands-on approach that facilitates conjecturing will be helpful.

Choice (C) does provided a strong visual model, but is less engaging as the teacher is demonstrating rather than the students experimenting. Choice (D) would probably be the least beneficial to most middle school students. Some students are able to learn and make connections through reading the material and studying the examples. (And reading mathematics is very important!) Most middle school students are less likely to develop conceptual understanding with this process, particularly as an introduction.

42. (D)

We can see from the graph that as shoe size increases so does height, so there is a positive relationship, which eliminates choices (A) and (C) . Choice (B) is problematic because neither variable causes a change in the other variable.

43. (B)

In quadrant II, the sine ratio is positive and the tangent ratio is negative. Of the points given in the answer choices, only the point $(-3,6)$ lies in the second quadrant.

44. (B)

It is important for students to learn to use appropriate technology, but in ways that facilitate learning and support development of concepts and problem solving. Choice (B) reflects this approach. Choice (A) just provides a superficial view of the use of a graphing calculator, as it is not integral to the teaching and learning process. Choice (C) focuses on the word "never," which is not correct. Choice (D), by using the word "always," does not support students in learning when technology is beneficial and supportive.

45. (B)

Five camels are available to be selected for the first position, leaving 4 that can be selected for the second position. Using the Fundamental Counting Principle we get $5 \times 4 = 20$.

46. (C)

The function given is represented graphically as a parabola. A parabola will intersect the x-axis in only one place if both roots are equal, which means the discriminant $= 0$. Recall that the discriminant ($b^2 - 4ac$) is the radical portion of the quadratic formula. In this problem, $a = 3$, $b = -2$, and $c = k$. Thus we have $(-2)^2 - 4(3)(k) = 0$. This equation simplifies to $4 = 12k$. Thus, $k = \dfrac{1}{3}$.

47. (D)

The number 4 is distributed multiplicatively over the sum of $(3+7)$. The distributive property states that $(a + b)(c) = (a)(c) + (b)(c)$. In this case $a = 3$, $b = 7$, and $c = 4$.

48. (A)

A rectangle has at least one pair of opposite sides congruent (both pairs of opposite sides are actually congruent), and the diagonals are also always congruent. Choices (B) and (D) satisfy I but not II. Choice (C) satisfies neither I nor II.

49. (D)

One way to determine the correct equation is to take any one of the ordered pairs in the table and substitute into each equation. This will result in incorrect answers for choices (A), (B), and (C), but will be correct for choice (D). In fact, each ordered pair satisfies the equation in choice (D). An alternative approach is to observe that there is a constant difference of 5 between each $f(x)$ value for each one unit difference between each x value. This constant arithmetic difference means that the relationship is linear, and that the slope of the associated line is 5. The only possible answer choices are (C) and (D). By substituting the point $(2, 23)$, we find that $f(x) = 5x + 13$.

50. (B)

Change each to a number with two decimal places. $\dfrac{3}{11} \approx 0.27$, $2\% = 0.02$, $0.2 = 0.20$, $-0.2 = -0.20$, $0.\overline{2} \approx 0.22$.

Then the original numbers appear as $-0.20, 0.20, 0.27, 0.02,$ and 0.22. Thus $0.27 > 0.22 > 0.20 > 0.02 > -0.20$. So the correct order is $\dfrac{3}{11}, 0.\overline{2}, 0.2, 2\%, -0.2$.

51. (C)

Since $MN = x$ and $MNCD$ is a rectangle, $CD = x$. Since $FACD$ is a square, $CA = x$. Thus $CN = x - y$. The area of $MNCD$ is $x(x - y) = x^2 - xy$.

52. (A)

There are 26 red cards in the deck, including two red queens and two red kings. Thus, the required probability is $\dfrac{4}{26} = \dfrac{2}{13}$.

53. (D)

The reflection of ΔABC across the x-axis will be a triangle that is congruent to the original, where the side of the triangle parallel to the x-axis is on the opposite side of the x-axis but the same distance from this axis as the original triangle. The x-axis will be the perpendicular bisector of each of $\overline{AA'}$, $\overline{BB'}$, and $\overline{CC'}$.

54. (A)

$g(-4.5) = -5$ and $g(4.5) = 4$, thus $g(-4.5) + g(4.5) = -5 + 4 = -1$. The other choices relate to common errors with the greatest integer function.

55. (C)

In order to teach middle school students, the teacher needs to understand their developmental level, present information using appropriate mathematical language and symbolism, and organize information in a manner that addresses potential misunderstandings of students. While proof is an important topic in geometry, there are multiple ways of teaching it that can guide students and provide a foundation for advanced studies such as those that the teacher experienced in college. Choice (A) is incorrect in that conceptual understanding is attainable by students whether they have been identified as gifted or not. Choice (B) assumes there is only one way to teach while there are many ways of successfully teaching proofs. Choice (D) claims that proof-based, formal geometry and high achievement can never occur simultaneously, which is not true.

56. (D)

In $4 + 3^2 \div (6 \cdot 2 - 3) + 4 \cdot 2$, first multiply 6 and 2 and subtract 3. Next compute 3 squared. Then multiply 2 times 4. At this point we have $4 + 9 \div 9 + 8$, so we divide 9 by 9 to get 1. Finally we have $4 + 1 + 8 = 13$. Below is another look at the order of operations. At no point did we add 9 to 8.

$$4 + 3^2 \div (6 \cdot 2 - 3) + 4 \cdot 2 = 4 + 9 \div (12 - 3) + 8 = 4 + 9 \div 9 + 8 = 4 + 1 + 8 = 13.$$

57. (D)

Choice (D) supports the concept that teachers must deeply understand foundational mathematics in order to make connections within the structure of mathematics. They need to understand the how and why of each idea or concept within a topic. Although communication is an invaluable tool, the question asks what is needed by the teacher in order to make connections within mathematics, - not necessarily to communicate the connections to her students. So choice (A) is incorrect. Choice (B) is incorrect because although the understanding has to be deep, the mathematics does not have to be necessarily at a high level. The connections being made can be about basic operations such as addition and multiplication. Choice (C) is incorrect because the ability to recite rules and axioms says little about understanding.

58. (A)

When an expression involving a base and an exponent is raised to an exponent, the base remains unchanged and the exponents are multiplied. Therefore $(100^4)^5 = 100^{20}$

59. (C)

Since this is a right isosceles triangle, the two acute angles are congruent. So, it is a 45°-45°-90° triangle, where the hypotenuse is $\sqrt{2}$ times the length of the leg. Thus, we can take the length of the hypotenuse, 12, and divide it by $\sqrt{2}$ to find the length of $\overline{FE}$ to be approximately 8.5. We could also use the Pythagorean theorem and let x represent the length of $\overline{FE}$. We would then have $x^2 + x^2 = 12^2$. Then $2x^2 = 144$ and $x \approx 8.5$.

60. (C)

The sum of the angles can be written as $2x + 3x + 7x = 180$ so that $x = 15$. Thus, the three angles are 30°, 45°, and 105°. Since one of the angles is greater than 90°, it is an obtuse triangle.

61. (A)

We want the number of combinations of 24 students taken 4 at a time, so

$$_{24}C_4 = \frac{24!}{20!4!} = \frac{24 \times 23 \times 22 \times 21 \times 20!}{20!(4 \times 3 \times 2 \times 1)}$$

$$= \frac{24 \times 23 \times 22 \times 21 \times 20!}{20!(24)}$$

$$= 23 \times 22 \times 21 = 10,626$$

You can also just put $_{24}C_4$ in your scientific calculator and it will do the calculation for you! The other choices are related to common calculation errors.

62. (A)

There are several methods that can be used, one of which is elimination (also called the addition method).

$$4x - 3y = -2$$
$$-x + 2y = 3$$

Multiplying the second equation by 4 and then adding will eliminate x.

$$4x - 3y = -2$$
$$\underline{-4x + 8y = 12}$$
$$5y = 10, \text{ thus } y = 2$$

By substituting $y = 2$ into either equation, we can solve for x.

$4x - 3(2) = -2$. Then $4x = 4$, so $x = 1$. Thus, the ordered pair (1,2) is the solution for the system of equations.

63. (B)

In the form $y = a(x - h)^2 + k$, the coefficient a determines the width (how fast the parabola rises or falls) and whether it opens up or down. For the vertex to be the highest point, the parabola must open down, which eliminates choices (A) and (C). Since the value of a in choice (B) is smaller than the value of a in the given equation, the graph for choice (B) must be wider than the graph for the original equation.

64. (C)

We first need to get a common denominator (and in this case the least common denominator (LCD) for $\frac{5}{8} - \frac{7}{12}$ which is 24. After completing the subtraction portion of the problem, we then must divide the two fractions.

$$\frac{\frac{5}{8} - \frac{7}{12}}{\frac{2}{3}} = \frac{\frac{15}{24} - \frac{14}{24}}{\frac{2}{3}} = \frac{\frac{1}{24}}{\frac{2}{3}} = \frac{1}{24} \div \frac{2}{3}$$

$$= \frac{1}{24} \times \frac{3}{2} = \frac{1}{16}.$$

The other choices provided reflect various calculation errors that one might make.

65. (A)

$I = \$350 + (0.02)d$ is the correct choice as it represents the initial $350 that Jennifer is paid each week, plus the 2% commission that is added to her base salary.

66. (D)

Let x represent age (in years) and y represent reaction time (in seconds). The two given points are (19, 2.1) and (15, 1.4). The slope of the linear model is $\frac{1.4 - 2.1}{15 - 19} = \frac{-.07}{-4} = \frac{7}{40} = 0.175$. Substituting (19, 2.1) into $y = 0.175x + b$, we get $b = -1.225$. Thus, the linear model is $y = 0.175x - 1.225$. Since Paige's age is 24 we can use the linear model to predict her reaction time. Then $(0.175)(24) - 1.225 = 2.975$ seconds. Since her actual reaction time is 3.2 seconds, the error is

$$\frac{3.2 - 2.975}{2.975} \times 100\% \approx 7.6\%.$$

67. (B)

When the right tail of the boxplot is longer than its left tail, the distribution is positively skewed. Note that choice (A) is incorrect because 24 represents the value of the median. Choice (D) is incorrect because the interquartile range is $42 - 16 = 26$, not 48.

68. (B)

Using the distance formula, we get

$$d = \sqrt{(x_2 - x_1)^2 + (y_2 - y_1)^2}$$
$$d = \sqrt{(-4 - (-2))^2 + (-3 - 6)^2}$$
$$d = \sqrt{4 + 81}$$
$$d = \sqrt{85} \approx 9.22$$

69. (C)

Because no grades are being assigned, the purpose of the question is to determine depth of understanding so that the teacher can make adjustments for future instruction, ask follow-up questions, or provide extensions which are all characteristic of summative assessments rather than formative assessment. So, we can eliminate choice (A). While the question does provide time to have conversations with the students, it is not the purpose. We can eliminate choice (B). Choice (D) may be important just to ensure individual student understanding, but this is not the purpose of the teacher's question.

70. (A)

As students work to form rectangles, they should discover that (a) and (c) will each form a rectangle, demonstrating that they can be factored over the integers In fact, (a) forms a square showing a perfect square trinomial. However (b) and (d) do not form rectangles, which shows that they cannot be factored. So the focus is on the factoring concept. The point of the activity would be an introduction to the concept that some trinomials form rectangles and others do not. Furthermore, this exercise might lead to exploring why this occurs and how it can be used.

As an example, here is how the tiles could appear for $2x^2 + 5x + 2$.

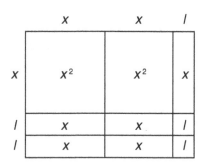

71. (B)

Using deductive reasoning, statement #6 states that Jonathan is in the robotics school club and statement #3 says that all student who are in a school club like mathematics. Thus, Jonathan must like mathematics.

Choice (A) is incorrect as statement #2 indicates some play sports. But this may not include Jonathan. Choice (C) is incorrect because statement #5 only assures us that some students who like mathematics also enjoy reading poetry. Therefore, some students who like mathematics may not enjoy reading poetry. Choice (D) is incorrect because there is no logical connection between students who like mathematics and those who volunteer at the local hospital.

72. (A)

The number of degrees in each interior angle of a regular n-sided figure is $\dfrac{(180)(n-2)}{n}$. Thus, for $n = 16$, each interior angle is $\dfrac{(180)(16-2)}{16} = 157.5°$.

73. (C)

$G(-4) = 2(-4) = -8$, $G(-1) = 2(-1) - 3 = -5$, and $G(2) = 2 - 2 = 0$. Thus $G(-4) + G(-1) + G(2) = -8 + -5 + 0 = -13$.

74. (A)

Choice (A) shows a positive correlation that appears to be a linear relationship. However, there is one point that is far away from the trend line, indicating that it is an outlier. In choice (B) there is a point that is situated away from the other points, but it is in line with the trend line (or regression line). So, it is not an outlier. Choice (C) demonstrates the same positive correlation as choice (A), but all points are clustered about the trend line. Choice (D) simply shows a cluster of points without a mathematical relationship among them.

75. (B)

The second statement must be "This student desk is in my classroom." Then the two given statements are:

1. All furniture in my classroom was donated.

2. This student desk is in my classroom.

Then, by deductive reasoning, we can conclude that this student desk was donated.

76. (D)

Choice (D) provides the most support and detail related to assessing the student's misunderstanding and providing instruction. It provides a positive, specific comment about what she does understand. It also gives a suggestion on how she might go back and think about why her response was incorrect and where the error might have occurred. Providing detailed, specific feedback (indicative of a formative assessment) gives students an opportunity to continue to learn and then be more successful on a future summative assessment. Choice (A) provides no useful feedback. Choice (B) indicates she should just figure out her mistake on her own. Choice (C) does identify the specific error she made, but does not give any useful direction on how to correct it or to understand where she made the error.

77. (A)

The linear function is $T(w) = \$8.25(w) - \$12.65$, where T is the total weekly salary and w is the number of hours worked each week. Thus choice (A) provides a real world context for students with linear functions. Choices (B) and (D) are linear functions but without a real world context. Choice (C) provides a real world context but is not a linear function.

78. (C)

$(i-1)^2(i-3+2i) = (i^2-2i+1)$ $(-3+3i) = (-2i)(-3+3i) = 6i-6i^2$ $= 6i+6$ or $6+6i$. Thus, the conjugate is $6-6i$.

79. (B)

Triangle ABM and rectangle $ABCD$ share the same base and have the same height. This means that the area of $\triangle ABM$ is one-half the area of rectangle $ABCD$. Furthermore, since $\overline{RS}$ is parallel to $\overline{AB}$ and $\triangle ABM$ is isosceles, $\angle MRS \cong \angle MSR \cong \angle MAB \cong \angle MBA$. Triangles MRS and ABM are similar and the ratio of their corresponding sides is 1:2. Then the area of $\triangle MRS$ is $\left(\dfrac{1}{2}\right)^2 = \dfrac{1}{4}$ the area of $\triangle ABM$. Consequently, the area of trapezoid $ABSR$ is $1-\dfrac{1}{4} = \dfrac{3}{4}$ the area of $\triangle ABM$.

The required probability is the ratio of the area of trapezoid $ABSR$ to rectangle $ABCD$, which is $\dfrac{3}{4} \times \dfrac{1}{2} = \dfrac{3}{8}$.

80. (B)

Students will learn little if anything that can be assessed, as assessment was not planned with any clear objective in mind and the students have no rubric to describe expectations. The grades will have little meaning because the students do not know the criteria on which they are being graded. This means that choice (A) is incorrect.

Choice (C) is incorrect because students have only been asked to do a project. This will most likely result in general reports on the topic with students using similar resources getting similar results. Choice (D) is incorrect because the students have not been asked to do anything that would require them to understand the mathematics related to the Cartesian coordinate system.

81. (D)

For $t = 2$, the geometric sequence t^n increases in value without bound. You can see this by substituting in values for n beginning with $n = 1$. We get 2, 4, 8, 16, 32, 64, ... For $t = \dfrac{1}{4}$ and $t = \dfrac{1}{2}$ in choices (A) and (B), respectively, the values get increasingly smaller and actually approach zero. For choice (C), the number 1 raised to any power is 1, so its limit is 1.

82. (C)

If no number appears more than once in a list of numbers, there is no mode.

83. (B)

The volume of a regular prism is found by finding the area of the base and multiplying it by its height ($V=Bh$). The height of an equilateral triangle is given by the expression $\dfrac{s\sqrt{3}}{2}$, where s is the length of each side. Since $s = 6$, the height is $3\sqrt{3}$. Then using the area formula for a triangle, we get $(\frac{1}{2})(6)(3\sqrt{3}) = 9\sqrt{3}$ square feet. Thus $V = (9\sqrt{3})(15) = 135\sqrt{3}$ cubic feet.

84. (A)

The least common multiple (LCM) of these numbers is $(4)(5)(7) = 140$. This is the smallest number that can be divided by 4, 5, and 7 and leave no remainder. Thus, 143 would leave a remainder of 3 when divided by 4, 5, or 7.

85. (D)

Integration is used to find the sum of the rectangular regions that are subdivided under a given curve, which is equivalent to finding the area under a curve. Choice (A) is used to find the distance between two points. Choice (B) addresses the relationship of the sides of a right triangle. Choice (C) is related to rates of change, not area.

86. (B)

The subtraction of 280 from 493 can be quickly computed by first subtracting 280 from 500 (instead of 493) to get 220. Then subtract the difference of 500 and 493 (7) from 220 to get the final answer of 213. While the other computations can be done with paper and pencil methods using traditional algorithms, they are more quickly done with a calculator, especially if they are part of a larger problem or application where the computation is not the focus. Students need to be able to make decisions about appropriate applications of mental mathematical strategies versus using a calculator.

87. (C)

The vertical lines that pass through -4 and 4 on the x- axis bound the region $-4 \le x \le 4$. The horizontal lines that pass through 0 and 2 (which is the x −axis) bound the region $0 \le y \le 2$.

88. (A)

In order to effectively plan, assess, and instruct middle school mathematics, teachers need an understanding of the mathematics curriculum prior to the curriculum expectations at the middle grades, a deep understanding at the middle grade level they are teaching, and ability to connect to the mathematics the students will be studying in high school. While advanced courses (choice (B)) may be helpful, they do not necessarily provide the connections needed. For choice (C), it is not realistic that a teacher will be able to answer all students' questions. For choice (D), knowledge of mathematics is a key factor in teaching, but it is not necessarily the most important factor. Equally important is knowledge of mathematical pedagogy.

89. (D)

Choice (D) is the best choice, as it demonstrates an example of informal assessment and is related to a common misunderstanding about the relationship between experimental and theoretical probability. Even though the experiment demonstrated more heads than tails, on the next flip the probability of either a heads or tails is still 0.50, as the next trial is independent of the previous trials. The intent of an assessment should never be to trick a student, which eliminates choice (A). Regarding choices (B) and (C), these are topics that the teacher could have informally assessed. However, her question is not directed toward these topics.

90. (B)

According to the table, the total score for the four exams for Student #2 is 310. Let x be the score for the fifth exam. In order for this student's average to be 80, he needs a total of $(5)(80) = 400$ points. Then $65 + 82 + 75 + 88 + x = 400$. Thus, $x = 90$.

Practice Test 2

TExES Mathematics 115

This test is also on CD-ROM in our interactive TestWare® for this TExES Mathematics Assessment. We strongly recommend that you first take this exam on computer. You will then have the benefits of enforced time conditions, individual diagnostic analysis, and instant scoring.

Answer Sheet

1. Ⓐ Ⓑ Ⓒ Ⓓ	24. Ⓐ Ⓑ Ⓒ Ⓓ	47. Ⓐ Ⓑ Ⓒ Ⓓ	70. Ⓐ Ⓑ Ⓒ Ⓓ
2. Ⓐ Ⓑ Ⓒ Ⓓ	25. Ⓐ Ⓑ Ⓒ Ⓓ	48. Ⓐ Ⓑ Ⓒ Ⓓ	71. Ⓐ Ⓑ Ⓒ Ⓓ
3. Ⓐ Ⓑ Ⓒ Ⓓ	26. Ⓐ Ⓑ Ⓒ Ⓓ	49. Ⓐ Ⓑ Ⓒ Ⓓ	72. Ⓐ Ⓑ Ⓒ Ⓓ
4. Ⓐ Ⓑ Ⓒ Ⓓ	27. Ⓐ Ⓑ Ⓒ Ⓓ	50. Ⓐ Ⓑ Ⓒ Ⓓ	73. Ⓐ Ⓑ Ⓒ Ⓓ
5. Ⓐ Ⓑ Ⓒ Ⓓ	28. Ⓐ Ⓑ Ⓒ Ⓓ	51. Ⓐ Ⓑ Ⓒ Ⓓ	74. Ⓐ Ⓑ Ⓒ Ⓓ
6. Ⓐ Ⓑ Ⓒ Ⓓ	29. Ⓐ Ⓑ Ⓒ Ⓓ	52. Ⓐ Ⓑ Ⓒ Ⓓ	75. Ⓐ Ⓑ Ⓒ Ⓓ
7. Ⓐ Ⓑ Ⓒ Ⓓ	30. Ⓐ Ⓑ Ⓒ Ⓓ	53. Ⓐ Ⓑ Ⓒ Ⓓ	76. Ⓐ Ⓑ Ⓒ Ⓓ
8. Ⓐ Ⓑ Ⓒ Ⓓ	31. Ⓐ Ⓑ Ⓒ Ⓓ	54. Ⓐ Ⓑ Ⓒ Ⓓ	77. Ⓐ Ⓑ Ⓒ Ⓓ
9. Ⓐ Ⓑ Ⓒ Ⓓ	32. Ⓐ Ⓑ Ⓒ Ⓓ	55. Ⓐ Ⓑ Ⓒ Ⓓ	78. Ⓐ Ⓑ Ⓒ Ⓓ
10. Ⓐ Ⓑ Ⓒ Ⓓ	33. Ⓐ Ⓑ Ⓒ Ⓓ	56. Ⓐ Ⓑ Ⓒ Ⓓ	79. Ⓐ Ⓑ Ⓒ Ⓓ
11. Ⓐ Ⓑ Ⓒ Ⓓ	34. Ⓐ Ⓑ Ⓒ Ⓓ	57. Ⓐ Ⓑ Ⓒ Ⓓ	80. Ⓐ Ⓑ Ⓒ Ⓓ
12. Ⓐ Ⓑ Ⓒ Ⓓ	35. Ⓐ Ⓑ Ⓒ Ⓓ	58. Ⓐ Ⓑ Ⓒ Ⓓ	81. Ⓐ Ⓑ Ⓒ Ⓓ
13. Ⓐ Ⓑ Ⓒ Ⓓ	36. Ⓐ Ⓑ Ⓒ Ⓓ	59. Ⓐ Ⓑ Ⓒ Ⓓ	82. Ⓐ Ⓑ Ⓒ Ⓓ
14. Ⓐ Ⓑ Ⓒ Ⓓ	37. Ⓐ Ⓑ Ⓒ Ⓓ	60. Ⓐ Ⓑ Ⓒ Ⓓ	83. Ⓐ Ⓑ Ⓒ Ⓓ
15. Ⓐ Ⓑ Ⓒ Ⓓ	38. Ⓐ Ⓑ Ⓒ Ⓓ	61. Ⓐ Ⓑ Ⓒ Ⓓ	84. Ⓐ Ⓑ Ⓒ Ⓓ
16. Ⓐ Ⓑ Ⓒ Ⓓ	39. Ⓐ Ⓑ Ⓒ Ⓓ	62. Ⓐ Ⓑ Ⓒ Ⓓ	85. Ⓐ Ⓑ Ⓒ Ⓓ
17. Ⓐ Ⓑ Ⓒ Ⓓ	40. Ⓐ Ⓑ Ⓒ Ⓓ	63. Ⓐ Ⓑ Ⓒ Ⓓ	86. Ⓐ Ⓑ Ⓒ Ⓓ
18. Ⓐ Ⓑ Ⓒ Ⓓ	41. Ⓐ Ⓑ Ⓒ Ⓓ	64. Ⓐ Ⓑ Ⓒ Ⓓ	87. Ⓐ Ⓑ Ⓒ Ⓓ
19. Ⓐ Ⓑ Ⓒ Ⓓ	42. Ⓐ Ⓑ Ⓒ Ⓓ	65. Ⓐ Ⓑ Ⓒ Ⓓ	88. Ⓐ Ⓑ Ⓒ Ⓓ
20. Ⓐ Ⓑ Ⓒ Ⓓ	43. Ⓐ Ⓑ Ⓒ Ⓓ	66. Ⓐ Ⓑ Ⓒ Ⓓ	89. Ⓐ Ⓑ Ⓒ Ⓓ
21. Ⓐ Ⓑ Ⓒ Ⓓ	44. Ⓐ Ⓑ Ⓒ Ⓓ	67. Ⓐ Ⓑ Ⓒ Ⓓ	90. Ⓐ Ⓑ Ⓒ Ⓓ
22. Ⓐ Ⓑ Ⓒ Ⓓ	45. Ⓐ Ⓑ Ⓒ Ⓓ	68. Ⓐ Ⓑ Ⓒ Ⓓ	
23. Ⓐ Ⓑ Ⓒ Ⓓ	46. Ⓐ Ⓑ Ⓒ Ⓓ	69. Ⓐ Ⓑ Ⓒ Ⓓ	

TExES Mathematics 115 Practice Test 2

TIME: 5 hours
90 questions

> **Directions**: Read each item and select the best response.

1. Which one of the following describes a distribution of data that is positively skewed, and has a mode of 50?

   (A) mean = 40 and median = 55

   (B) mean = 30 and median = 35

   (C) mean = 60 and median = 45

   (D) mean = 85 and median = 70

2. What is the simplified expression for $(2a + b)(a^2 - 5b)$?

   (A) $2a^3 + a^2b - 10ab - 5b^2$

   (B) $2a^3 - a^2b - 7ab - 5b^2$

   (C) $2a^3 - 9a^2b - 5b^2$

   (D) $2a^3 + 9a^2b - 5b^2$

3. Look at the following stem−and−leaf plot

Stem	Leaf
1	0 0 3 8
2	1 5 5 7 8
3	3 4 6 6 6 6 9
4	0 4
5	2 7

   What is the value of the median?

   (A) 31

   (B) 33.5

   (C) 36

   (D) 39.5

4. Which of the following is equivalent to 150^{60}?

   (A) $(150^{50})^{10}$

   (B) $(100^{60})(50^{60})$

   (C) $(150^{40})(150^{20})$

   (D) $(15^{30})(10^{30})$

5. What is the conjugate of $\dfrac{1+i}{2i}$?

   (A) $-\dfrac{1}{2}i - \dfrac{1}{2}$

   (B) $-\dfrac{1}{2}i + \dfrac{1}{2}$

   (C) $\dfrac{1}{2}i - \dfrac{1}{2}$

   (D) $\dfrac{1}{2}i + \dfrac{1}{2}$

6. An 8–sided die contains the numbers 1 through 8. This die will be tossed until the number 8 appears. To the nearest thousandth, what is the probability that the first time that the number 8 appears is on the fifth toss?

(A) 0.003

(B) 0.035

(C) 0.073

(D) 0.125

7. Mr. Factorstein teaches an algebra class. He wants to show a numerical example that illustrates the identity $a^2 - b^2 = (a - b)(a + b)$. Which of the following would be the best example to use?

(A) Divide 500 by 100.

(B) Multiply 103 by 97

(C) Add 250 to 350.

(D) Subtract 30 from 300

8. Annette's copier can make ten copies of a booklet in three minutes. How many minutes will it take for the copier to make 55 copies?

(A) 14.5

(B) 15.5

(C) 16.5

(D) 17.5

9.

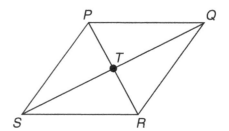

In the figure above, which of the following provides sufficient information to classify $PQRS$ as a rhombus?

(A) $\overline{PQ} \cong \overline{QR}$ and $\overline{RS} \cong \overline{SP}$.

(B) $\overline{SP}$ is parallel to $\overline{QR}$ and $\overline{PQ}$ is parallel to $\overline{RS}$.

(C) $\overline{PR}$ and $\overline{QS}$ are perpendicular bisectors of each other.

(D) $\angle QPS \cong \angle QRS$ and $\angle PSR \cong \angle PQR$.

10. A student is given the following problem:
There are 4 white shirts and 6 blue shirts in a dark closet. If you choose one shirt at random, what is the probability that it is white?
If the student's answer is 2.5, what type of error did he make?

(A) He found the probability of choosing a blue shirt.

(B) He found the odds of choosing a white shirt instead of the probability.

(C) He found the reciprocal of the probability of choosing a white shirt.

(D) He found the incorrect value for the number of shirts.

11. Look at the following arrangement of Algebra Tiles.

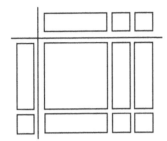

Which algebraic expression do these tiles represent?

(A) $(x + 2)(x + 1)$

(B) $(x + 2)(x - 1)$

(C) $(x + 2)(x + 3)$

(D) $(x + 2)(x - 3)$

12. In $\triangle DEF$, $DE = EF$ and the measure of $\angle D$ is 54°. What is the measure of $\angle E$?

(A) 50°

(B) 54°

(C) 72°

(D) 90°

13. Rhonda is baking a cake. The recipe calls for $1\frac{1}{2}$ teaspoons of salt for every 2 cups of flour. If she plans to use 5 cups of flour, what procedure should she use in order to determine how many teaspoons of salt are needed?

(A) Multiply 5 by $1\frac{1}{2}$, then divide by 2.

(B) Multiply 2 by 5, then divide by $1\frac{1}{2}$.

(C) Multiply all three numbers.

(D) Add $1\frac{1}{2}$ to 2, then divide by 5.

14. Which one of the following relations has a domain consisting of three elements and a range consisting of two elements?

(A) $\{(4, 1), (3, 1), (2, 1)\}$

(B) $\{(0, 5), (1, 3), (0, 3), (1, 5), (2, 5)\}$

(C) $\{(9, 2), (8, 1), (9, 3), (8, 3)\}$

(D) $\{(3, 2), (2, 3), (2, 2), (3, 3)\}$

15. The area of a trapezoid is 180 square inches and the height is 20 inches. The length of one base is twice as large as the length of the other base. Which of the following represents the length of one of the bases?

(A) 4 inches

(B) 10 inches

(C) 12 inches

(D) 16 inches

16. A group of data has no mode. Which of the following is a valid conclusion?

(A) The mean and median have the same value.

(B) The range is larger than the mean.

(C) Each different value occurs only once.

(D) The interquartile range is greater than the median.

17. Which of the following is an example of inappropriate mathematical language?

(A) To solve the equation $2x - 7 = 9$, the first step should be to move the 7 over to the other side.

(B) Check your solution to an equation by substituting your answer into the original equation.

(C) When solving the equation $\frac{63}{y} = \frac{5}{7}$, use the cross–multiplication principle.

(D) Let the variable x represent the unknown value when solving an application problem.

18. Ms. Teller is discussing solving literal equations with her class. She is working with the formula for changing degrees Fahrenheit to degrees Celsius. The question is to solve the formula $C = \frac{5}{9}(F - 32)$ for F. She asks the students which step they would perform first. Tom wants to multiply both sides of the equation by $\frac{9}{5}$. Joan wants to distribute $\frac{5}{9}$. What is Ms. Teller's best response?

(A) Tom is correct.

(B) Everyone in the class should solve the problem the same way

(C) Tom's approach is the easiest.

(D) Both Tom and Joan are correct. There is more than one way to solve the problem.

19. Doreen will randomly select two cards from a deck of 52 cards, one at a time, with replacement of the first card before selecting the second card. What is the probability that at least one of her selections will be a club?

(A) $\frac{9}{16}$

(B) $\frac{7}{16}$

(C) $\frac{5}{16}$

(D) $\frac{1}{16}$

20. A rectangular piece of cloth has an area of 24 square inches and a perimeter of 22 inches. What are the cloth's length and width dimensions?

(A) 6 inches by 4 inches

(B) 8 inches by 3 inches

(C) 24 inches by 1 inch

(D) 12 inches by 2 inches

21. For a quadratic function $f(x)$, the axis of symmetry is $x = -2$. If $f(-5) = 2$, which of the following points must lie on the graph of $f(x)$?

(A) $(-5, 0)$

(B) $(1, 2)$

(C) $(0, -2)$

(D) $(1, -5)$

22. Consider the following three statements.

I. The greatest common factor of 8 and 9 is 1.

II. The greatest common factor of 84 and 85 is 1.

III. The greatest common factor of 151 and 152 is 1.

Based on inductive reasoning, which of the following statements would be the <u>best</u> conclusion?

(A) The greatest common factor of any two integers is 1.

(B) The greatest common factor of 1 and any other integer is 1.

(C) The greatest common factor of two consecutive integers is 1.

(D) The greatest common factor of two consecutive even integers is 1.

23. What is the simplified form for $2i^3 - 3i^8 + (5 + i)(2 - i)$?

(A) $6 - 3i$

(B) $2 + 5i$

(C) $10 + 3i$

(D) $8 - 5i$

24. In the figure below, the two horizontal lines are parallel.

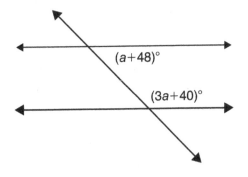

What is the value of a?

(A) 20

(B) 23

(C) 25

(D) 28

25. Suppose that W varies inversely as T. When $T = 5$, $W = 21$. If the value of T is tripled, how is the value of W changed?

(A) It is increased by 10.

(B) It is increased by 42.

(C) It is decreased by 10.

(D) It is decreased by 14.

26. In the figure below, which transformation will map $\triangle ABC$ onto $\triangle DEF$?

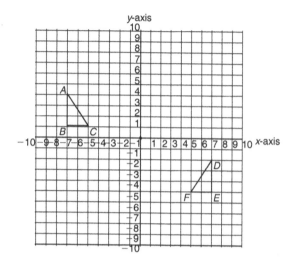

(A) Reflect $\triangle ABC$ over the y−axis and slide up 6 spaces.

(B) Reflect $\triangle ABC$ over the x−axis and slide up 6 spaces.

(C) Reflect $\triangle ABC$ over the y−axis and slide down 6 spaces.

(D) Reflect $\triangle ABC$ over the x−axis and slide down 6 spaces.

27. The use of a grading rubric for a problem is effective when credit can be assigned for the work shown, not just for an answer. For which of the following problems would a grading rubric be most appropriate?

(A) Find the volume of a cube whose length is 12 inches.

(B) Find the perimeter of a triangle with sides of 3 feet, 6 feet, and 8 feet.

(D) Find the area of a parallelogram with a height of 4 meters and a base of 8 meters.

(D) In a circle whose diameter is 6 inches, find the area of a sector whose central angle is 90°.

28. In evaluating the expression $60 \div (10 - 6) \times (2 + 6 \div 2)$, which of the following steps would not be used?

(A) Adding 2 to 3

(B) Subtracting 6 from 10

(C) Dividing 60 by 4

(D) Adding 2 to 6

29. Which function represents a shift of 4 units to the left for the graph of the parent function $f(x) = x^3$?

(A) $f(x) = (x - 4)^3$

(B) $f(x) = (x + 4)^3$

(C) $f(x) = x^3 - 4$

(D) $f(x) = x^3 + 4$

30. Which of the following identities uses both the distributive and commutative properties of numbers?

(A) $(8)(6 + 5) = (6)(8) + (5)(8)$

(B) $(4)(3 + 2) = (4)(3) + (4)(2)$

(C) $(5)(6 + 4) = (6 + 4)(5)$

(D) $7 \times (2)(5) = (7)(2) \times 5$

31. In which one of the following tables does y vary inversely as x?

(A)

x	2	3	15
y	30	20	4

(B)

x	2	5	9
y	8	20	36

(C)

x	2	6	10
y	10	14	18

(D)

x	2	7	12
y	18	13	8

32. Look at the following completed construction.

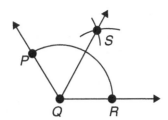

Which construction does this represent?

(A) Copying an angle

(B) Creating alternate interior angles

(C) Creating corresponding angles

(D) Bisecting an angle

33. There are seven women and five men in a room. The average weight of all these people is 149 pounds. The average weight for the men is 184 pounds.

What is the average weight, in pounds, for the women?

(A) 129

(B) 124

(C) 119

(D) 114

34. A bacterium is about 2.8×10^{-3} millimeters in length. How is this number written in standard notation?

(A) 0.00028

(B) 0.0028

(C) 2800

(D) 28,000

35. The manager of Joe's Ice Cream Shop orders waffle cones that are 14 cm. tall and have a diameter of 6 cm. To the nearest cubic cm, what is the volume of these cones?

(A) 305

(B) 150

(C) 132

(D) 124

36. Which of the following provides hands−on activities that would be useful in expanding students' learning from concrete to abstract ideas?

(A) Discussions

(B) Projects

(C) Manipulatives

(D) Working in groups

37. What part of $\frac{4}{5}$ is $\frac{1}{3}$?

(A) $\frac{4}{15}$

(B) $\frac{5}{12}$

(C) $\frac{17}{15}$

(D) $\frac{12}{5}$

38. Consider the following net of a three-dimensional figure.

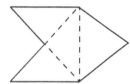

Which one of the following represents the corresponding three-imensional figure when the net is folded up along the dotted lines?

(A)   (C)

(B) 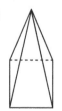   (D)

39. A student claims that $8x^3$ is the lowest common denominator for the two fractions $\frac{1}{2x}$ and $\frac{3}{4x^2}$. Based on this error, what algebraic concept does this student not understand?

(A) Complex fractions

(B) The greatest common factor

(C) Reciprocals of fractions

(D) The least common multiple

40. A survey asked a group of children to name their favorite flavor of ice cream. The results from this survey are shown in the following chart.

Favorite Ice Cream	
Ice Cream	**Number of Children**
Chocolate	18
Mint Chocolate Chip	7
Rocky Road	12
Strawberry	20
Vanilla	23

If one child were randomly selected from this survey, what is the probability that the child's favorite flavor of ice cream is rocky road?

(A) 5%

(B) 10%

(C) 15%

(D) 25%

41. Given a sample mean value $\bar{x}$, the critical z values for the 98% confidence interval of the population mean (μ) is ± 2.33. Sixty four people were asked how long they take in filling out a job application. The results showed a mean of 35 minutes, with a standard deviation of 4.5 minutes. What is the 98% confidence interval for the value of μ?

(A) $33.69 < \mu < 36.31$

(B) $34.09 < \mu < 35.91$

(C) $34.53 < \mu < 35.47$

(D) $34.93 < \mu < 35.07$

42. Which of the following numbers is not between 0.25 and 0.26?

(A) $0.2\overline{51}$

(B) $0.2\overline{59}$

(C) 0.259

(D) 0.261

43. Ten people are to be seated in a row with 10 seats in a movie theater. Two of the people do not want to sit in either of the two end seats in this row. In how many accommodating ways can all ten people be seated?

(A)   20,120

(B)   40,320

(C)   2,257,920

(D)   3,628,800

44. In right triangle BCD, $\angle C$ is a right angle. If $\sin \angle B = \dfrac{8}{17}$, what is the value of $\cos \angle B$?

(A) $\dfrac{17}{8}$

(B) $\dfrac{15}{8}$

(C) $\dfrac{15}{17}$

(D) $\dfrac{8}{15}$

45. Which of the following statements is true?

(A) All fractions are terminating decimals.

(B) All whole numbers are natural numbers.

(C) All integers are rational numbers.

(D) All decimals are irrational numbers.

46. What knowledge must a student have in order to determine the surface area of a three-dimensional geometric figure?

(A) How to find the volume of three-dimensional figures

(B) How to find the area of two-dimensional figures

(C) How to find the perimeters of two-dimensional figures

(D) How to find the nets of three-dimensional figures

47. The cost of a phone call is $4.00 for the first three minutes, plus $0.50 for each additional minute. If y represents the total cost of a phone call and x represents the total number of minutes, which of the following equations can be used to determine the total cost for x minutes?

(A) $y = \$4.00 + (\$0.50)(x - 3)$

(B) $y = (\$4.50)(x + 3)$

(C) $y = (\$4.00)(3) + \$0.50x$

(D) $y = (\$4.50)(x - 3)$

48. Which of the following is an example of a summative assessment?

(A) A series of oral questions to different groups working on a class project

(B) A 10−question written quiz on permutations and combinations

(C) A cumulative test on an entire chapter that deals with consumer math

(D) A worksheet that deals with changing fractions to their decimal equivalents

49. What is the most effective way to assess whether your students understand the concept of slope?

(A) Ask them to find the slope of the line through the points (1, 3) and (6, −2).

(B) Ask them to find the slope of a line from a graph.

(C) Ask them for the slope of a horizontal line.

(D) Ask them to explain how the grade of a highway corresponds to the slope concept.

50.

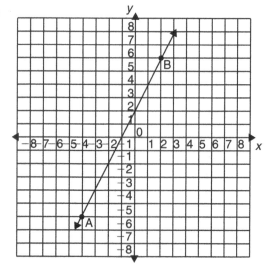

What is the slope of the line shown above?

(A) −2

(B) $-\dfrac{1}{2}$

(C) $\dfrac{1}{2}$

(D) 2

51. Amy, Beth, Craig, and Dave go to a restaurant. Normally each person pays the amount that corresponds to his/her bill. Their bills total $10, $12, $15, and $18, respectively. Since Beth is celebrating a birthday, the other three people decide to split Beth's amount ($12) evenly among them. Which of the following represents the amount that Craig should pay?

(A) $\dfrac{\$15+\$12}{3}$

(B) $\$15+\dfrac{\$12}{3}$

(C) $\dfrac{\$15+\$12}{4}$

(D) $\$15+\dfrac{\$12}{4}$

52. 6% of 360 is equivalent to what percent of 14.4?

(A) $166\dfrac{2}{3}$

(B) 150

(C) $66\dfrac{2}{3}$

(D) 50

53. Assume that the following three statements are true.

I. All people who enjoy doing exercises have blue eyes.

II. Some people with blue eyes enjoy playing golf.

III. No one who enjoys golf enjoys doing exercises.

Which of the following <u>must be false</u>?

(A) Some people who enjoy playing golf have blue eyes.

(B) All people with blue eyes enjoy playing golf.

(C) No one who enjoys playing golf has brown eyes.

(D) Some people with blue eyes do not enjoy doing exercises.

54. To the nearest hundredth, what is the distance between the points whose coordinates are $(2, -4)$ and $(8, 5)$?

(A) 10.8

(B) 11.3

(C) 11.8

(D) 12.3

55. What is the simplified form for $\dfrac{6b^3}{5c^5d^4} \div \dfrac{1}{15c^3d}$?

(A) $\dfrac{2b^3}{c^2d^3}$

(B) $\dfrac{12b^3c^2}{d^3}$

(C) $\dfrac{18b^3d^3}{c^2}$

(D) $\dfrac{18b^3}{c^2d^3}$

56.

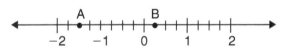

Using the number line above, what is the product of the values corresponding to points A and B?

(A) $-\dfrac{3}{8}$

ing expressions such as $(2^3)^4$. Which of the following would be a good approach to assist students in overcoming this difficulty?

(A) Rewrite the original problem as 8^4, multiply 8 by itself four times to get 4096, then show that this is equivalent to 2^{12}

(B) Demonstrate that $2^{3 \times 4}$ is greater than 2^{3+4}

(C) Switch the exponents and show that $(2^3)^4$ has the same value as $(2^4)^3$

(D) Use an example such as $(2^2)^2$ and show that 2^{2+2} is equivalent to $2^{2 \times 2}$

68. Using the pie chart below, if there are a total of 282 people in Smallville who are under 11 years old or over 40 years old, how many people are between the ages of 11 and 30, inclusive?

Age Distribution of People Living in Smallville

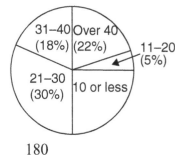

(A)   180

(B) 210

(C) 330

(D) 460

69.

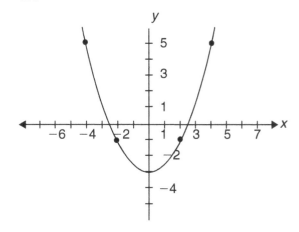

Which equation represents the above graph?

(A) $y = \dfrac{1}{2}x^2 + 3$

(B) $y = -\dfrac{1}{2}x^2 - 3$

(C) $y = \dfrac{1}{2}x^2 - 3$

(D) $y = -\dfrac{1}{2}x^2 + 3$

70. A number line is shown below, with a solution to a linear inequality.

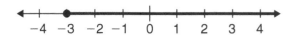

Which statement describes this inequality?

(A) All numbers greater than or equal to -3.

(B) All numbers less than or equal to -3.

(C) All numbers less than -3.

(D) All numbers greater than -3.

71. A cat is sitting on a limb of a tree. A fireman places a 26-foot ladder against the tree. The top of the ladder is on the limb and the bottom of the ladder is 24 feet from the bottom of the tree. What is the distance from the bottom of the tree to the limb on which the cat is sitting?

(A) 10 feet

(B) 12 feet

(C) 14 feet

(D) 16 feet

72. What is the quotient for $(m^2 + m - 14) \div (m + 4)$?

(A) $m + 3 + \dfrac{-4}{m + 4}$

(B) $m - 3 + \dfrac{-2}{m + 4}$

(C) $m - 2 + \dfrac{-6}{m + 4}$

(D) $m + 2 + \dfrac{-8}{m + 4}$

73. The graph below shows the frequency of test scores on a history exam.

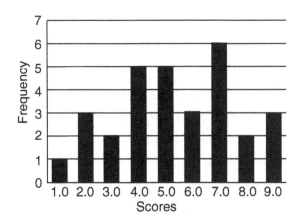

To the nearest hundredth, what is the difference in values between the mode and the mean?

(A) 0.63

(B) 1.63

(C) 2.63

(D) 3.63

74. The sum of the multiplicative inverses of 3 and 5 is equal to the multiplicative inverse of what number?

(A) $\dfrac{8}{15}$

(B) $\dfrac{3}{5}$

(C) $\dfrac{5}{3}$

(D) $\dfrac{15}{8}$

75. In Mr. Radical's class, students are not allowed to use a calculator. The students are assigned the task of estimating the value of $\sqrt{165}$ to the nearest integer. Which of the following is the best approach?

(A) Divide 165 by 2 to get 82.5. Then select any integer less than 82.

(B) Divide 165 by 5 to get 33. Then select any number between 5 and 33.

(C) $10^2 = 100$, $20^2 = 400$, and 165 is closer to 100 than to 400. Select a number between 10 and 20, but closer to 10.

(D) $10^2 = 100, 20^2 = 400$, Since 165 > 100, select any number between 10 and 20, but closer to 20.

76. In how many different ways can all the letters of the word MATTRESSES be arranged?

(A) 3,628,880

(B) 1,209,600

(C) 453,600

(D) 151,200

77. A student in Ms. Linear's class claims that the sum of three different proper fractions is always at least 1. Which of the following examples could Ms. Linear use to show the student that his claim is incorrect?

(A) $\frac{3}{7}, \frac{1}{2}, \frac{1}{5}$

(B) $\frac{1}{8}, \frac{1}{2}, \frac{1}{10}$

(C) $\frac{1}{3}, \frac{1}{2}, \frac{1}{6}$

(D) $\frac{1}{2}, \frac{1}{4}, \frac{2}{5}$

78.

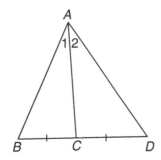

In the figure shown above, $BC = CD$. Which additional information would **not** be sufficient to conclude that $\overline{AC}$ is perpendicular to $\overline{BD}$?

(A) $\angle B \cong \angle D$

(B) $\triangle ABC$ is equilateral

(C) $AB = AD$

(D) $\angle 1 \cong \angle 2$

79. In the figure shown below, $\triangle ABC$ is a right triangle.

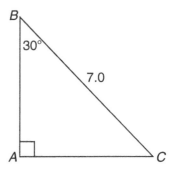

What are the lengths of $\overline{AC}$ and $\overline{AB}$? Round off your answers to the nearest tenth.

(A) 4.9, 4.9

(B) 2.0, 6.1

(C) 3.5, 4.9

(D) 3.5, 6.1

80. In a new lottery game, the upper section of a ticket consists of the numbers 1 through 30. The bottom section of the ticket has the five vowels of the alphabet.

A player must select four numbers and two vowels. How many different lottery tickets are possible?

(A) 274,050

(B) 1,623,160

(C) 6,577,200

(D) 1,168,675,200

81. What is the equation of the line that is parallel to the graph of $6x + 3y = 4$ and has a y-intercept of -6?

(A) $2x - y = 6$

(B) $6x - 3y = -4$

(C) $6x + 3y = -4$

(D) $2x + y = -6$

82. Allison wanted to find out what the students at her school believe about the new homework policy. Which of the following samples is most appropriate for surveying?

(A) The first 46 students exiting the school

(B) The girls in her math club

(C) 25 students in Mrs. Jackson's English class

(D) 6 students on her bus

83. If the area of a circle is 196π, what is the circumference?

(A) 56π

(B) 28π

(C) 14π

(D) 7π

84. The students in Mr. Rhombi's class are having great difficulty in reducing fractions to their lowest terms. Mr. Rhombi decides to create a worksheet to be completed during class. Which of the following would be an objective that would best assist students in overcoming their difficulty?

(A) To convert fractions to their decimal equivalents

(B) To identify proper and improper fractions

(C) To determine a list of factors for numerators and denominators of each fraction

(D) To multiply and divide both proper and improper fractions

85. Which of the following systems of equations has no solution?

(A) $\begin{array}{l} 2x - 3y = 10 \\ 2x + 3y = 10 \end{array}$

(B)
$$2x - y = 10$$
$$4x - 2y = 20$$

(C)
$$3x + 4y = 5$$
$$4x + 3y = -5$$

(D)
$$3x + y = 4$$
$$9x + 3y = 8$$

86. You roll a pair of dice. If the first die shows a 6, what is the probability that the sum of the dice is greater than 9?

(A) $\dfrac{1}{6}$

(B) $\dfrac{1}{3}$

(C) $\dfrac{1}{2}$

(D) $\dfrac{2}{3}$

87. In a specific word problem on coins, the variable x represents a number of dimes.

One student wrote the associated equation for this word problem as $3x + 19 = 30$. Which of the following is the <u>best</u> reason for stating that this equation is incorrect?

(A) The numbers on the left side do not add up to 30.

(B) A dime cannot be worth 19 cents.

(C) The value of a dime is not divisible by 3.

(D) The solution for x is a non-integer.

88. Miss Angleson teaches a geometry class. One of the homework questions was stated as follows: "In a certain triangle, the measure of the second angle is twice the measure of the first angle. Using the variable x, write the algebraic expression for the third angle." Miss Angleson wrote the expression $180° - \dfrac{3}{2}x$, whereas most students wrote the expression $180° - 3x$. What error did Miss Angleson make?

(A) She made no error. Both equations are correct.

(B) She used the incorrect expression for the second angle

(C) She used the incorrect expression for the first angle.

(D) An angle cannot have a fractional coefficient.

89. What are the values of x in the equation $2x^2 - 1 = 3x$?

(A) $\dfrac{3 \pm \sqrt{17}}{2}$

(B) $1, -\dfrac{1}{2}$

(C) $\dfrac{3 \pm \sqrt{17}}{4}$

(D) $-1, \dfrac{1}{2}$

90.

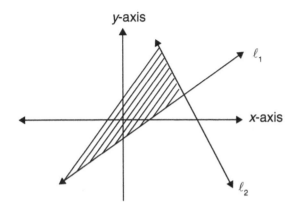

In the above graph, line l_1 represents the equation $y = x - 1$ and line l_2 represents the equation $y = -2x + 8$. Which of the following systems of inequalities does the shaded region represent?

(A) $y \geq x - 1$
$y \geq -2x + 8$

(B) $y \leq x - 1$
$y \geq -2x + 8$

(C) $y \leq x - 1$
$y \leq -2x + 8$

(D) $y \geq x - 1$
$y \leq -2x + 8$

TExES Mathematics 115 Practice Test 2 Answer Key

Number	Answer	Chapter	Domain
1	D	5	IV – Probability and Statistics
2	A	3	II – Patterns and Algebra
3	B	5	IV – Probability and Statistics
4	C	2	I – Number Concepts
5	D	2	I – Number Concepts
6	C	5	IV – Probability and Statistics
7	B	6	V – Mathematical Processes and Perspectives
8	C	3	II – Patterns and Algebra
9	C	4	III – Geometry and Measurement
10	C	7	VI – Math Learning, Instruction, and Assessment
11	A	3	II – Patterns and Algebra
12	C	4	III – Geometry and Measurement
13	A	6	V – Mathematical Processes and Perspectives
14	B	3	II – Patterns and Algebra
15	C	4	III – Geometry and Measurement
16	C	5	IV – Probability and Statistics
17	A	7	VI – Math Learning, Instruction, and Assessment
18	D	7	VI – Math Learning, Instruction, and Assessment
19	B	5	IV – Probability and Statistics
20	B	4	III – Geometry and Measurement
21	B	3	II – Patterns and Algebra
22	C	6	V – Mathematical Processes and Perspectives
23	D	2	I – Number Concepts
24	B	4	III – Geometry and Measurement
25	D	3	II – Patterns and Algebra
26	C	4	III – Geometry and Measurement
27	D	7	VI – Math Learning, Instruction, and Assessment
28	D	6	V – Mathematical Processes and Perspectives

Number	Answer	Chapter	Domain
29	B	3	II – Patterns and Algebra
30	A	2	I – Number Concepts
31	A	4	III – Geometry and Measurement
32	D	4	III – Geometry and Measurement
33	B	5	IV – Probability and Statistics
34	B	2	I – Number Concepts
35	C	4	III – Geometry and Measurement
36	C	7	VI – Math Learning, Instruction, and Assessment
37	B	2	I – Number Concepts
38	A	4	III – Geometry and Measurement
39	D	7	VI – Math Learning, Instruction, and Assessment
40	C	5	IV – Probability and Statistics
41	A	5	IV – Probability and Statistics
42	A	2	I – Number Concepts
43	C	5	IV – Probability and Statistics
44	C	4	III – Geometry and Measurement
45	C	2	I – Number Concepts
46	B	7	VI – Math Learning, Instruction, and Assessment
47	A	3	II – Patterns and Algebra
48	C	7	VI – Math Learning, Instruction, and Assessment
49	D	7	VI – Math Learning, Instruction, and Assessment
50	D	3	II – Patterns and Algebra
51	B	6	V – Mathematical Processes and Perspectives
52	B	2	I – Number Concepts
53	B	6	V – Mathematical Processes and Perspectives
54	A	4	III – Geometry and Measurement
55	D	3	II – Patterns and Algebra
56	A	2	I – Number Concepts
57	D	4	III – Geometry and Measurement
58	C	2	I – Number Concepts
59	C	4	III – Geometry and Measurement

60	D	7	VI – Math Learning, Instruction, and Assessment
61	B	6	V – Mathematical Processes and Perspectives
62	B	4	III – Geometry and Measurement
63	A	3	II – Patterns and Algebra
64	B	3	II – Patterns and Algebra
65	D	2	I – Number Concepts
66	A	2	I – Number Concepts
67	A	7	VI – Math Learning, Instruction, and Assessment
68	B	5	IV – Probability and Statistics
69	C	3	II – Patterns and Algebra
70	A	3	II – Patterns and Algebra
71	A	4	III – Geometry and Measurement
72	B	3	II – Patterns and Algebra
73	B	5	IV – Probability and Statistics
74	D	2	I – Number Concepts
75	C	7	VI – Math Learning, Instruction, and Assessment
76	D	5	IV – Probability and Statistics
77	B	7	VI – Math Learning, Instruction, and Assessment
78	D	4	III – Geometry and Measurement
79	D	4	III – Geometry and Measurement
80	A	5	IV – Probability and Statistics
81	D	3	II – Patterns and Algebra
82	A	5	IV – Probability and Statistics
83	B	4	III – Geometry and Measurement
84	C	7	VI – Math Learning, Instruction, and Assessment
85	D	3	II – Patterns and Algebra
86	C	5	IV – Probability and Statistics
87	D	6	V – Mathematical Processes and Perspectives
88	A	6	V – Mathematical Processes and Perspectives
89	C	3	II – Patterns and Algebra
90	D	3	II – Patterns and Algebra

Questions Listed By Domain

Domain I – Numbers And Concepts

14 questions   15.6%

4, 5, 23, 30, 34, 37, 42, 45, 52, 56, 58, 65, 66, 74

Domain II – Patterns And Algebra

19 questions   21.1%

2, 8, 11, 14, 21, 25, 29, 47, 50, 55, 63, 64, 69, 70, 72, 81, 85, 89, 90

Domain III – Geometry And Measurement

19 questions   21.1%

9, 12, 15, 20, 24, 26, 31, 32, 35, 38, 44, 54, 57, 59, 62, 71, 78, 79, 83

Domain IV – Probability And Statistics

15 questions   16.6%

1, 3, 6, 16, 19, 33, 40, 41, 43, 68, 73, 76, 80, 82, 86

Domain V – Mathematical Processes And Perspectives

9 questions   10%

7, 13, 22, 28, 51, 53, 61, 87, 88

Domain VI – Math Learning, Instruction, And Assessment

14 questions   15.6%

10, 17, 18. 27, 36, 39, 46, 48, 49, 60, 67, 75, 77, 84

TExES Mathematics 115 Practice Test 2 Solutions

1. (D)

For a positively skewed distribution of data, the mode must be less than the median, which in turn must be less than the mean. In this case, $50 < 70 < 85$.

2. (A)

The answer is the result of taking all possible products of terms in the first parentheses and those in the second parentheses. Then $(2a)(a^2) + (b)(a^2) + (2a)(-5b) + (b)(-5b) = 2a^3 + a^2b - 10ab - 5b^2$.

3. (B)

The median of this group of 20 numbers lies midway between the tenth and eleventh numbers. Thus, the median equals $\frac{33 + 34}{2} = 33.5$.

4. (C)

For any real numbers x, m, and n, $(x^m)(x^n) = x^{m+n}$. In answer choice (C), $x = 150$, $m = 40$, and $n = 20$. Answer choice (A) has the same value as 150^{500}. Answer choice (B) has the same value as 5000^{60}. Answer choice (D) has the same value as 150^{30}.

5. (D)

Rewrite the given division as $\frac{1+i}{2i}$ $\times \frac{i}{i} = \frac{i + i^2}{2i^2} = \frac{i-1}{-2} = \frac{1}{2} - \frac{1}{2}i$. The conjugate of $a + bi$ is $a - bi$. Thus, the required conjugate is $\frac{1}{2} + \frac{1}{2}i$.

6. (C)

This is a geometric distribution for which the probability for "success" is 0.125. Therefore, the probability that the first time a "success" occurs is on the fifth toss is $(0.125)(0.875)^4 \approx 0.073$.

7. (B)

Let $a = 100$ and let $b = 3$. Then $a - b = 97$ and $a + b = 103$. Then the product of 103 and 97 can be calculated as $100^2 - 3^2 = 10,000 - 9 = 9991$.

8. (C)

We'll set up a direct proportion, with number of copies in the numerators and number of minutes in the denominators. Let x represent the required number of minutes. Then $\frac{10}{3} = \frac{55}{x}$, which becomes $10x = 165$ upon cross-multiplication. Thus, $x = 16.5$.

9. (C)

If the diagonals of a quadrilateral bisect each other, then the figure must be a rhombus. Answer choice (A) would be sufficient information for a kite. Each of answer choices (B) and (D) would be sufficient for any parallelogram.

10. (C)

Instead of finding the correct probability of $\frac{4}{10}$, the student used its reciprocal, which is $\frac{10}{4}$, then wrote the decimal equivalent. Students must be aware that probability values must lie between 0 and 1, inclusive.

11. (A)

For each rectangle, the length is represented by x and 1 represents the width. For each small square, 1 represents a side. For the large square, x represents a side.

12. (C)

Because $DE = EF$, this figure is an isosceles triangle. Therefore, the measure of each of $\angle D$ and $\angle F$ is 54°. Since the sum of all three angles of a triangle is 180°, the measure of $\angle E = 180° - 54° - 54° = 72°$.

13. (A)

Let x represent the number of teaspoons of salt that is needed. Then the proportion $\frac{1\frac{1}{2}}{2} = \frac{x}{5}$ can be used to solve for x. The solution is found by multiplying 5 by $1\frac{1}{2}$, then dividing by 2.

14. (B)

The domain is $\{0, 1, 2\}$ and the range is $\{3, 5\}$. Thus, the domain consists of three elements and the range consists of two elements.

15. (C)

Let x and $2x$ represent the lengths of the two bases. Then $180 = \left(\frac{1}{2}\right)(20)(x + 2x)$. This equation simplifies to $180 = 30x$. Thus, $x = 6$ and $2x = 12$. The lengths of the bases are 6 and 12.

16. (C)

If a group of data has no mode, then each different value must occur only once.

17. (A)

Instead of using the statement "move the 7 over to the other side," it is more appropriate to use the statement "add 7 to both sides of the equation."

18. (D)

Although choices (A) and (D) are true, Ms. Teller's best response is to emphasize that there is more than one correct way to solve many problems.

19. (B)

The probability of selecting a club on any one draw is $\frac{13}{52} = \frac{1}{4}$. Then the probability of selecting at least one club in two draws is $\frac{1}{4} + \frac{1}{4} - \left(\frac{1}{4}\right)\left(\frac{1}{4}\right) = \frac{7}{16}$.

20. (B)

For each answer choice, the area is 24 square inches. Only answer choice (B) has a perimeter of 22 inches, since $(2)(8) + (2)(3) = 22$. Answer choice (A) has a perimeter of 20 inches, answer choice (C) has a perimeter of 50 inches, and answer choice (D) has a perimeter of 28 inches.

21. (B)

The function $f(x)$ is a parabola and its axis of symmetry is $x = -2$. For any point that lies on its graph, its reflection across the line $x = -2$ must also lie on its graph. The reflection of the point $(-5, 2)$ across $x = -2$ is the point $(1, 2)$.

22. (C)

Each of the three examples gives two consecutive integers. In each case, the greatest common factor is 1. Thus, by inductive reasoning, the greatest common factor of any two consecutive integers is 1. Answer choices (A) and (D) are false. Answer choice (B) is true, but this conclusion is not based on the three examples that are given.

23. (D)

We have $i^3 = -i$ and $i^8 = 1$. Then $2i^3 - 3i^8 + (5 + i)(2 - i) = -2i - 3 + 10 - 3i - i^2$. The term $i^2 = -1$, so the simplified form is $8 - 5i$.

24. (B)

If two parallel lines are intersected by a transversal, the interior angles on the same side of the transversal are supplementary. Therefore, $(a + 48) + (3a + 40) = 180$.

This equation simplifies to $4a = 92$, which means that $a = 23$.

25. (D)

When two variables vary inversely, as one of them increases, the other decreases proportionally. So, if T is tripled, the new value of W becomes one−third of its original value. Then the new value of W is $\left(\dfrac{1}{3}\right)(21) = 7$. Thus, W has changed from 21 to 7, which is a decrease of 14.

26. (C)

Reflecting triangle ABC over the y−axis moves it to Quadrant 1. To move it to the position of triangle DEF, slide the triangle down six spaces.

27. (D)

In order to find the area of this sector, the student must determine the radius, find the area of the circle, then multiply this answer by $\dfrac{1}{4}$. (This is the ratio of 90° to 360°.) A grading rubric can be assigned for each of these calculations.

28. (D)

The solution is found by using the following steps: (a) subtract 6 from 10, (b) divide 6 by 2, (c) add 2 to 3, (d) divide 60 by 4, and (e) multiply 15 by 5. There is no step in which 2 is added to 6.

29. (B)

When the graph of a function is shifted four units to the left, the variable x is replaced by $x + 4$. Thus, $f(x) = x^3$ changes to $f(x) = (x + 4)^3$.

30. (A)

The distributive law is $(a)(b + c) = ab + ac$ and the commutative law (of multiplication) is $ab = ba$. In answer choice (A), $a = 8$, $b = 6$, and $c = 5$. In fact, the commutative law is used twice in this answer choice. Answer choice (B) uses only the distributive property. Answer choice (C) uses only the commutative property. Answer choice (D) uses the associative property of multiplication.

31. (A)

If y varies inversely as x, then the product of their corresponding paired values must be a constant. In answer choice (A), this constant is 60.

32. (D)

The construction shows the bisection of $\angle PQR$ into two congruent angles, namely $\angle PQS$ and $\angle SQR$.

33. (B)

The total weight for all 12 people is $(12)(149) = 1788$ pounds. The total weight for the men is $(5)(184) = 920$ pounds. So, the total weight for the women must be $1788 - 920 = 868$ pounds. Thus, the average weight for the women is $\frac{868}{7} = 124$ pounds.

34. (B)

The number $10^{-3} = 0.001$. When a number is multiplied by 0.001, the decimal point moves three places to the left and zeros are added as needed. Thus, $2.8 \times 10^{-3} = 0.0028$.

35. (C)

The radius is 3 cm, so the area of the circular base is $(\pi)(3^2) = 9\pi$ sq. cm. Thus, the volume becomes $\left(\frac{1}{3}\right)(9\pi)(14) = 42\pi \approx 132$ cu. cm.

36. (C)

The use of manipulatives is an effective hands-on method to assist students to understand abstract ideas. Some examples of manipulatives are (a) base ten blocks for arithmetic, (b) geoboards for geometry, and (c) algebra tiles for algebra.

37. (B)

$$\frac{1}{3} \div \frac{4}{5} = \left(\frac{1}{3}\right)\left(\frac{5}{4}\right) = \frac{5}{12}$$

38. (A)

By folding the net along the dotted lines, we would get a three-dimensional figure that has triangles for all four of its sides.

39. (D)

The lowest common denominator for these two fractions is $4x^2$. This concept is equivalent to the least common multiple.

40. (C)

There are a total of 80 children who were surveyed. Since there were 12 children who chose rocky road as their favorite flavor, the required probability is $\frac{12}{80} = 15\%$.

41. (A)

The 98% confidence interval is $35 \pm (2.33) \left(\dfrac{4.5}{\sqrt{64}} \right) \approx 35 \pm 1.31$. Since 35 ± 1.31 is equivalent to the two numbers 33.69 and 36.31, the confidence interval becomes $33.69 < \mu < 36.31$.

42. (A)

$0.\overline{25} = .252525\dots, 0.\overline{26} = 0.262626\dots,$ and $0.\overline{251} = .251251251\dots$ Since $0.\overline{251}$ is actually less than $0.\overline{25}$, it cannot lie between $0.\overline{25}$ and $0.\overline{26}$.

43. (C)

The number of ways to assign the left-most seat is 8, since two people cannot be seated there. The number of remaining ways to assign the right-most seat is 7, since one person has already been assigned to the left-most seat. Remember that there are an additional two people who cannot be assigned to either end seat. Since there are no restrictions on the assignment of the remaining 8 seats, they can be assigned in $8! = (8)(7)(6)(\dots)(1) = 40{,}320$ ways. Thus, the number of ways to seat all ten people is $(8)(8!)(7) = 2{,}257{,}920$.

44. (C)

Since the side opposite $\angle B$ is 8 and the hypotenuse is 17, the side adjacent to $\angle B$ is $\sqrt{17^2 - 8^2} = \sqrt{225} = 15$. Then, by definition, $\cos \angle B = \dfrac{15}{17}$.

45. (C)

A rational number can be written in the form $\dfrac{p}{q}$, where $q \neq 0$. This definition includes all integers because an integer can be written as itself over 1. Answer choice (A) is wrong; as an example $\dfrac{1}{3} = 0.3333\dots = 0.\overline{3}$. Answer choice (B) is wrong because zero is a whole number, but is not a natural number. Answer choice (D) is wrong because any repeating or terminating decimals are rational numbers.

46. (B)

In order to determine the surface area of a three−dimensional figure, the student must be able to determine the areas of the corresponding surfaces of this figure. As an example, a pyramid consists of a polygonal base and triangular sides. The student needs to be able to find the area of the polygon (usually a square or a rectangle) that forms the base, as well as the area of each triangle that forms a side.

47. (A)

For the first three minutes, the cost is $4.00. If a call lasts x minutes, the number of additional minutes (beyond the first three minutes) is $x - 3$. For each one of these

$x - 3$ minutes, the cost is $0.50. This means that the cost for these additional minutes is ($0.50)($x - 3$).

48. (C)

A summative assessment is an evaluation of students' progress at the end of a formal learning experience. Examples of this type of assessment would be chapter exams and final exams.

49. (D)

The students must be able to conceptualize the idea that the steepness of a road is a measure of its slope. If a road is uphill, the slope is positive; if a road is downhill, the slope is negative. Each of choices (A), (B), and (C) requires only a calculation.

50. (D)

Choose any two points on the graph, for example $(-1, 0)$ and $(0, 2)$. The slope is equal to the change in y values divided by the change in x values, which is $\dfrac{2-0}{0-(-1)} = 2$.

51. (B)

Craig should pay his $15 bill, plus one-third the amount of Beth's bill. This is represented by the expression $\$15 + \dfrac{\$12}{3}$.

52. (B)

6% of 360 = (0.06)(360) = 21.6. Now the question reduces to "21.6 is what percent of 14.4?" The answer is found by dividing 21.6 by 14.4, then multiplying by 100. Thus, the required percent is $\left(\dfrac{21.6}{14.4}\right)(100) = 150.$

53. (B)

This statement must be false. We already know that the people who enjoy golf and the people who enjoy doing exercises are mutually exclusive. Since all the people who enjoy doing exercises have blue eyes, this implies that some people with blue eyes do not enjoy playing golf. Here are two possible Venn diagrams to illustrate statements I, II, and III.

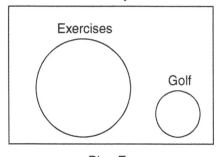

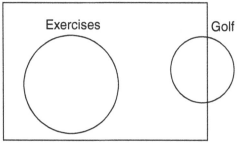

54. (A)

The required distance is

$$\sqrt{(8-2)^2 + (5-[-4])^2}$$
$$= \sqrt{36+81} = \sqrt{117} \approx 10.8.$$

55. (D)

In a division problem, we multiply by the reciprocal of the second quantity. Also, the exponents of common bases are subtracted. Thus, the solution becomes $\frac{6b^3}{5c^5d^4} \times \frac{15c^3d}{1} = \frac{90b^3c^3d}{5c^5d^4} = \frac{18b^3}{c^2d^3}.$

56. (A)

Point A corresponds to $-\frac{3}{2}$ and point B corresponds to to $\frac{1}{4}$. Then $\left(-\frac{3}{2}\right)\left(\frac{1}{4}\right)$ $= -\frac{3}{8}.$

57. (D)

The difference in their weights is 56 pounds. Thus, their weight difference in kilograms is $\frac{56}{2.2} \approx 25.5$ kilograms.

58. (C)

If $|a + b| \neq |a| + |b|$, then a and b have opposite signs. Using the values of answer choice (C), $|a + b| = 2$, whereas $|a| + |b| = 8$. In each of the other answer choices, $|a + b| = |a| + |b|$.

59. (C)

To find the amount of gift paper needed to cover the box, find the surface area. This prism has two rectangular faces that measure 8 inches by 4 inches, two rectangular bases that measure 8 inches by 3 inches, and two rectangular bases that measure 4 inches by 3 inches. Therefore, the surface area is (2)(8)(4) + (2)(8)(3) + (2)(4)(3) = 64 + 48 + 24 = 136 square inches.

60. (D)

The topic of music would be more appealing to middle school students than the topics of post offices, nuclear waste, or skin cancer.

61. (B)

$(-2) + (-7) = -9$. Then $(-9) - (-20) = (-9) + (+20) = +11.$

62. (B)

The third angle must be $180° - 35° - 55° = 90°$. This means that we have a right triangle. Since no two angles have the same measure, this triangle is also scalene. Answer choice (C) represents an isosceles right triangle. Neither answer choice (A) nor (D) represents a right triangle because $9^2 + 12^2 \neq 16^2$ and $8^2 + 10^2 \neq 14^2$.

63. (A)

Using the ordered pair (0, 2), each of the answer choices (B), (C), and (D) can be shown to be wrong. However, each of the ordered pairs satisfies the equation in answer choice (A).

64. (B)

Looking at all the odd-positioned numbers, we have the pattern 7, 9, 11, x, and 15. There is a constant difference of 2, so that $x = 11 + 2 = 13$. Looking at all the even-positioned numbers, we have the pattern 10, 12, 14, 16, and y. Since the common difference is 2, $y = 16 + 2 = 18$. Thus, the sum of x and y is 31.

65. (D)

First, calculate $7 \times 2 - 2 = 14 - 2 = 12$. Second, calculate $6^2 = 36$. Third, divide 36 by 12 to get 3. Fourth, multiply 3 by 4 to get 12. Finally, add 3 to 12 to get 15. In none of these steps is 3 added to 36.

66. (A)

An irrational number is one that cannot be written as a quotient of two integers. The number to $\sqrt{7}$ is one such number. Answer choice (B) is wrong because to $\sqrt{9} = 3$, which can be written as to $\frac{3}{1}$. Answer choice (C) is wrong because any fraction is already expressed as a quotient of two inte-

gers. Answer choice (D) is wrong because to $0.\overline{57}$ is equivalent to to $\frac{19}{33}$.

67. (A)

Most likely, the students mistakenly believe that $(2^3)^4$ could be equivalent to 2^7. Using the approach in choice (A) should enable the students to realize the reason that these exponents are multiplied.

68. (B)

The percent of people age 10 or less is $(100 - 5 - 22 - 18 - 30)\% = 25\%$. Thus, $25\% + 22\% = 47\%$ of the people are either under 11 years old or over 40 years old. Let x represent the total population of Smallville. Then $0.47x = 282$, which means that $x = 600$. Since $5\% + 30\% = 35\%$ of the population is between the ages of 11 and 30 inclusive, the number of people in this age bracket is $(0.35)(600) = 210$.

69. (C)

This parabola faces upward, so the coefficient of the x^2 term must be positive. In addition, the graph passes through the point $(0, -3)$. Only answer choice (C) satisfies both of these conditions. As a check, note that the points $(2, -1)$ and $(-2, -1)$ lie on this graph. Both points satisfy the equation to $y = \frac{1}{2}x^2 - 3$.

70. (A)

Since the arrow includes a dot on -3, this number must be included in the solution. Also, the arrow points to the right. This means that all numbers greater than -3 must be included in the solution.

$$\frac{(1.0)(1)+(2.0)(3)+(3.0)(2)+(4.0)(5)+}{(5.0)(5)+(6.0)(3)+(7.0)(6)+(8.0)(2)+}{(9.0)(3)}$$
$$\frac{}{1+3+2+5+5+3+6+2+3}$$

$$=\frac{161}{30}\approx 5.37. \text{ Finally, } 7.0-5.37=1.63.$$

71. (A)

The ladder represents the hypotenuse of a right triangle, in which the other two distances represent the legs. Let x represent the distance from the bottom of the tree to the limb where the cat is sitting. Then $x^2 + 24^2 = 26^2$. This equation simplifies to $x^2 = 100$, so $x = 10$ feet.

74. (D)

The multiplicative inverses of 3 and 5 are $\frac{1}{3}$ and $\frac{1}{5}$, respectively. Their sum is $\frac{5}{15}+\frac{3}{15}=\frac{8}{15}$. The number $\frac{8}{15}$ is the multiplicative inverse of $\frac{15}{8}$.

75. (C)

Since 165 lies closer to 100 than to 400, our best guess is to use a number that lies closer to 10 than to 20. If, for example, the number 14 is selected, then 14^2 is computed as 196. Since $165 < 196$, the student should then select either 13 or 12. The correct estimate will be 13, because $13^2 = 169$ (which is very close to 165).

72. (B)

$(m^2 + m - 14) \div (m + 4)$

$$\begin{array}{r} m \quad\quad -3 \\ m+4\overline{)m^2 + m - 14} \\ \underline{-(m^2 + 4m)} \\ -3m - 14 \\ \underline{-(-3m-12)} \\ -2 \end{array}$$

The answer is $m - 3 + \dfrac{-2}{m+4}$

73. (B)

The mode is 7.0, since this value occurs most frequently. The value of the mean is to

76. (D)

There are a total of ten letters, including two T's, two E's, and three S's. Thus, the number of arrangements is $\dfrac{10!}{(2!)(2!)(3!)} = \dfrac{3,628,800}{24} = 151,200.$

77. (B)

The sum of $\dfrac{1}{8}$, $\dfrac{1}{2}$, and $\dfrac{1}{10}$ is $\dfrac{29}{40}$, which is less than 1. For each of choices (A) and (D), the sum of the fractions is greater than 1. For choice (C), the sum of the fractions is exactly 1.

78. (D)

If $\angle 1 \cong \angle 2$, then triangles ABC and ACD would have two pairs of congruent sides and a pair of non-inclusive congruent angles. This would be insufficient to prove that the triangles are congruent This means that we cannot conclude that $\angle ACB \cong \angle ACD$, which further implies that we cannot conclude that $\overline{AC}$ is perpendicular to $\overline{BD}$.

Answer choice (A) would imply that $\triangle ABC \cong \triangle ADC$ by side-angle-side, so $\angle ACB \cong \angle ACD$ by corresponding parts. This would imply that $\overline{AC}$ is perpendicular to $\overline{BD}$.

Answer choice (B) would already establish that since $\angle B \cong \angle D$, $\angle ACB \cong \angle ACD$. Thus, we would conclude that $\overline{AC}$ is perpendicular to $\overline{BD}$.

Answer choice (C) would imply that $\triangle ACB \cong \triangle ACD$ by side-side-side, so $\angle ACB \cong \angle ACD$ by corresponding parts. This would imply that $\overline{AC}$ is perpendicular to $\overline{BD}$.

79. (D)

This is a 30°-60°-90° right triangle. The hypotenuse $(\overline{BC})$ is twice the length of the shorter leg $(\overline{AC})$. So, $AC = \dfrac{BC}{2} = 3.5$. The length of the longer leg $(\overline{AB})$ is the product of the length of the shorter leg and $(\sqrt{3})$. Thus, $AB = (3.5)(\sqrt{3}) \approx 6.1$.

80. (A)

The number of groups of four numbers is $_{30}C_4 = 27{,}405$ and the number of groups of two vowels is $_5C_2 = 10$. Then the number of possible lottery tickets is $(27{,}405)(10) = 274{,}050$.

81. (D)

Write $6x + 3y = 4$ in the slope−intercept form by first subtracting $6x$ from each side to get $3y = -6x + 4$. Dividing by 3, the equation becomes $y = -2x + \dfrac{4}{3}$. Since parallel lines must have the same slope, we are looking for an equation whose slope is -2. Also, the y−intercept must be -6. Thus, the required equation is $y = -2x - 6$, which is equivalent to answer choice (D).

82. (A)

The first 46 students exiting the building would provide the most random representative sample, because there would most likely be a mix of genders and grade levels. In choice (B), Allison would only ask girls, which is not a representative sample of the population of the school (assuming it is not a girls−only school). In choice (C), the 25 students in Mrs. Jackson's English class are not a representative sample, because they all come from one class. In choice (D), the six students on the bus might be somewhat representative, but six students is not an adequate sample size.

83. (B)

Since $196\pi = \pi r^2$, we know that the radius $r = \sqrt{196} = 14$. Thus, the circumference must be $(2\pi)(14) = 28\pi$.

84. (C)

When students experience difficulty in reducing fractions to their lowest terms, a very useful exercise is to determine factors of both numerator and denominator. of each fraction. In this way, students will be able to divide out common factors until a given fraction is reduced to lowest terms.

85. (D)

Equations that have no solution represent parallel lines, which means that their slopes are equal. In answer choice (D), the slope of each line is -3.

86. (C)

If the first die shows a 6, you need to determine how many possibilities on the second die would result in a sum greater than 9. In this case, you would need to roll a 4, 5, or 6. This represents three of the six possible numbers that you could roll. Therefore, the required probability is $\frac{3}{6} = \frac{1}{2}$.

87. (D)

Each of the answer choices is true. However, the equation cannot be correct because when it is simplified, we have $3x = 11$. The answer of $\frac{11}{3}$ is impossible since x represents the number of dimes.

88. (A)

She did not make an error. The students used x to represent the measure of the first angle and $2x$ to represent the measure of the second angle. Then the measure of the third angle becomes $180° - x - 2x = 180° - 3x$. Miss Angleson used x to represent the measure of the second angle and $\frac{1}{2}x$ to represent the measure of the first angle. Then the measure of the third angle becomes $180° - x - \frac{1}{2}x = 180° - \frac{3}{2}x$.

89. (C)

Rewrite the equation in the form $2x^2 - 3x - 1 = 0$. Then, apply the quadratic formula to get $x = \dfrac{-(-3) \pm \sqrt{(-3)^2 - (4)(2)(-1)}}{(2)(2)} = \dfrac{3 \pm \sqrt{17}}{4}$.

90. (D)

The shaded region lies above line l_1, which implies that $y \geq x - 1$. But the shaded region also lies below line l_2. This implies that $y \leq -2x + 8$. Only answer choice (D) contains both inequalities.

Index

Cubes, 155–156
Cylinders, 151–153

D

Data. *See* Statistics
Decagons, 103
Decimals, 21–23, 24
Deductive reasoning, 105, 224–225
Defined terms, 95–98
Dependent equations, 62
Dependent events, 193–194
Dependent variables, 46, 187
Derivatives, 83
Diameter, 130–132
Dilations, 147–149
Direct variation, 70–71
Discriminant of quadratic equation, 59–60
Dispersion, 181–187
Distance formula, 135–137
Distributive property of multiplication over addition, 16
Division
  decimals, 23
  polynomials, 42–44
Dodecagons, 103
Domain, 46

E

Elimination method, 62
English Language Learners (ELL), 222
Equiangular triangles, 99
Equilateral triangles, 99
Euclidean geometry, 103–104. *See also* Geometry and measurement
Events, 191
Experimental probability, 190
Exponentiation, 25
Exponents, 25–27

F

Factorials, 197–199
Factoring method, 56
Formal assessments, 236
Formative assessments, 236–238

Fractions, 18–21, 24
Functions
  defined, 46
  graphs, 47–48
  linear functions, 48–51
  quadratic functions, 55–61
  transformations, 51–55
Fundamental Counting Principle, 196
Fundamental Theorem of Calculus, 84

G

Geometric distributions, 202–203
Geometry and measurement, 93–165
  introduction, 93
  measurement precision, 159–160
  terms, 93–98
  trigonometry, 138–143
  See also Three-dimensional shapes; Two-dimensional shapes
Graphing method for linear equations, 62–63
Graphs and graphing, 167–180
  bar graphs, 169
  box-and-whiskers plots, 173
  choice of, 178
  circle graphs, 168
  drawing tools, 178
  of functions, 47–48
  histograms, 175–176
  of inequalities, 73
  of linear equations, 62–63
  of linear inequalities, 74–77
  line graphs, 169–171
  pie charts, 168
  of quadratic functions, 60–61
  of quadratic inequalities, 77–81
  of relations, 47–48
  scatter plots, 176–177
  stem-and-leaf plots, 174–175
Greatest possible error, 160

H

Height, of pyramids, 156
Hendecagons, 103
Heptagons, 103
Hexagons, 103

Histograms, 175–176
Hyperbolic geometry, 103

I

Identity element of addition, 16
Identity element of multiplication, 16
Improper fractions, 18
Inconsistent systems, 62
Independent events, 193
Independent variables, 46, 187
Inductive reasoning, 35–37, 105
Inequalities
  graphing on number line, 73
  linear inequalities, 74–77
  quadratic inequalities, 77–81
Inferential statistics, 207–208
Informal assessments, 236
Instruction and assessment, 231–244
  assessment methods, 235–239
  content vs. pedagogical knowledge, 232–235
  introduction, 231
  learner-focused instruction, 231–232
Integers, 14
Integration, 83–84
Interquartile range, 174
Inverse variation, 71–73
Irrational numbers, 14, 1154
Isosceles trapezoids, 126
Isosceles triangles, 99

K

Kites, 127

L

Lateral surface area, of cylinders, 152
Learning styles, 234
Least common denominator (LCD), 20–21
Left half-plane, 74
Legs, 126
Like terms, 40
Limits, 81–82
Linear functions

Unit of measure, 159–160
Upper boundary, 176
Upper limit, 176

V

Variables, 37, 46
Variance, 185–187
Vertical angles, 97
Vertical line test, 47–48
Vertices
angles, 96
polygons, 102

pyramids, 156
Volume
cones, 154
cylinders, 152
defined, 151
prisms, 156
pyramids, 157
spheres, 158

W

Whole numbers, 14

X

X-intercept, 50

Y

Y-intercept, 50

Z

Zero, 14